The Basel Capital Accords in Developing Countries

The Basel Capital Accords in Developing Countries

Challenges for Development Finance

Edited by

Ricardo Gottschalk

palgrave
macmillan

First published 2010 by
PALGRAVE MACMILLAN

Palgrave Macmillan in the UK is an imprint of Macmillan Publishers Limited,
registered in England, company number 785998, of Houndmills, Basingstoke,
Hampshire RG21 6XS.

Palgrave Macmillan in the US is a division of St Martin's Press LLC,
175 Fifth Avenue, New York, NY 10010.

Palgrave Macmillan is the global academic imprint of the above companies
and has companies and representatives throughout the world.

Palgrave® and Macmillan® are registered trademarks in the United States,
the United Kingdom, Europe and other countries

ISBN 978-0-230-22224-3 hardback

This book is printed on paper suitable for recycling and made from fully
managed and sustained forest sources. Logging, pulping and manufacturing
processes are expected to conform to the environmental regulations of the
country of origin.

A catalogue record for this book is available from the British Library.

A catalog record for this book is available from the Library of Congress.

10 9 8 7 6 5 4 3 2 1
19 18 17 16 15 14 13 12 11 10

Printed and bound in Great Britain by
CPI Antony Rowe, Chippenham and Eastbourne

Contents

Illustrations

Box

Preface

The main aim of this book is to discuss possible impacts of the Basel Capital Accords on development finance. To fulfil this task, the book brings together contributions from a number of researchers and academics who, in the past, have done research on the Basel Capital Accords with the primary concern about their possible developmental impacts in developing countries. In most cases, their research on Basel was conducted under research projects led by Professor Stephany Griffith-Jones and Dr. Ricardo Gottschalk, when both researchers were based in the Institute of Development Studies at the University of Sussex. These research projects had a strong empirical focus. A considerable part of it drew on interviews with developing country based stakeholders to gather their views and concerns on the Basel Accords.

The contributors have strong expertise in a wide range of areas that are important for grasping the multiple dimensions that the Basel Capital Accords involves. Professor Stephany Griffith-Jones, long-standing academic based in the UK and more recently at Columbia University in the US, is a leading world expert on international finance, having worked on a wide range of aspects of international finance and on Basel related issues in particular. Her main contribution in the book is her focus on the impacts of Basel on international bank lending to developing countries, and on the strong pro-cyclical bias in the new Basel rules. Professor Sunanda Sen, based in India, is an international expert on financial systems, having written and published extensively on the subject. Together with Soumya Ghosh, her main contribution is on her analysis on the impacts of the Basel rules on credit to the SMEs and the poor. Soumya Ghosh, also an India based researcher, enriches the analysis with his private sector experience. Ray Barrell and Sylvia Gottschalk, building on their macro-economic modelling experience at the UK based National Institute of Economic and Social Research (NIESR), take a broader, macroeconomic perspective to examine the macroeconomic impacts of the Basel Capital Accord in Brazil and Mexico. Ricardo Gottschalk and Cecilia Sodre draws on their long-term research and professional experience in Brazil to discuss impacts of Basel in the country, with Sodre drawing in particular on her financial sector expertise to bring to the discussion a careful examination of the differentiated impacts within the Brazilian banking system. Finally

Pietro Calice builds on both his professional experience with international rating agencies and as official from the African Development Bank to discuss the potential role of public credit-guarantee schemes in facilitating lending to the SMEs under Basel II. Thus, the book benefits from field research in developing countries and developing country based expertise, which enables it to bring a developing country perspective and thereby to fill an important gap in the debate on possible Basel impacts on development finance, an issue that to date has been little explored. The book in particular discusses the views of Sub-Saharan countries on Basel II implementation in their own countries, thereby contributing to our understanding of Basel impacts in the region, which to date has virtually been left outside the radar of Basel discussions. Going forward, the Editor believes the book is a contribution to the thinking on the role financial regulation can play to ensure domestic financial systems support the goals of growth and sustainable development.

Acknowledgements

A number of people have contributed to this book. I would like to thank in particular the book contributors for their time and dedication in preparing and revising the chapters, Gerson Romantini and Sylvia Gottschalk for reading and commenting on several parts of the book, and two anonymous reviewers for helpful comments and suggestions for improvement. The editor is also thankful to Taiba Batool from Palgrave Macmillan for her early encouragement and support, and also Gemma Papageorgiou and Vidhya Jayaprakash and her team at Newgen Imaging Systems for their editorial assistance and work during the production process. Several of the book chapters are the outcome of research projects funded by the UK Department of International Development, and South Africa based FinMark Trust. Their financial support is greatly acknowledged. Finally, I am grateful to the Middlesex University Business School where I am currently based for the time provided so that I could finalise the book during summer 2009.

Contributors

Ricardo Gottschalk is an economist with long-term experience in applied quantitative work, international and development finance, banking regulation and macroeconomic policy analysis. He has worked as consultant to the UK Department for International Development, European Commission, G-24, UNCTAD, UNDP, UNRISD and the governments of various sub-Saharan African countries, including the government of Ethiopia, to which he has provided technical assistance on macro-econometric modelling and forecasting. He has co-edited the books *International Capital Flows in Calm and Turbulent Times: The Need for New International Architecture* (2003) and *Inequality in Latin America: Issues and Challenges for the 21st Century* (2006). He was a Research Fellow at the Institute of Development Studies, UK, between February 1999 and April 2009, period during which he did research, published extensively in edited volumes and journals, and was the director of the MPhil Programme in Development Studies (2001–2004) and Convenor of the MA in Globalisation and Development (2008–2009). Currently he holds a Senior Lecturer position at the Middlesex University Business School.

Ray Barrell is Senior Research Fellow at the National Institute of Economic and Social Research since 1990, where he is Director of Macroeconomic research and Forecasting for the UK and World Economies. He was a university lecturer in economics from 1976 to 1984, teaching at Sussex, Southampton, Stirling and Brunel and specialising in monetary economics and econometrics. He then moved to be an Economic Advisor at HM Treasury from 1984 to 1987 before arriving at the Institute in 1988. He was a visiting Professor of Economics, Imperial College, London from 1996 to 2004, and was a part-time professor at the European University Institute, Florence, 1998–1999. He is on the editorial boards of Economic Modelling and was on the board of the Journal of Common Market Studies until 2007.

Pietro Calice is Senior Investment Officer, Private Sector Operations, at the African Development Bank, where he covers the financial sector. Prior to that, he spent several years working as a financial institutions credit analyst at a derivatives house and at rating agencies. Pietro holds a BA in Economics from Rome University "La Sapienza", an MSc in

Finance from CUOA, and an MPhil in Development Studies from the Institute of Development Studies, Sussex University.

Soumya Ghosh is an economist and has worked with rating agencies and reputed MNCs. He has over 15 years of experience in risk management, economic and econometric analysis, developing macro-econometric models, working on Indian economy, tracking financial markets and specific Indian industries. He has done consultancy work on banking regulation issues including for the Institute of Development Studies. He holds a PhD from the Jawaharlal Nehru University, Delhi.

Sylvia Gottschalk joined the National Institute of Economic and Social Research (NIESR) in 2001, where she stayed until 2008. She has worked on a wide range of topics in applied economics, such as international trade, macroeconomic and credit risk modelling. She has done extensive research on international trade and economic geography, with emphasis on regional integration and the location of manufacturing industries. She has undertaken research projects for the UK Department for International Development and the BBVA Foundation, on the impacts of the Basel Capital Accord in emerging markets and on the development of macroeconomic measures of credit risk. She has contributed to papers on fiscal and monetary policy, FDI and exchange rate uncertainty and published in the *International Journal of Finance and Economics, Economic Modelling, Journal of Trade and Economic Development* and *Journal of Economic Integration*.

Stephany Griffith-Jones is an economist researching and providing policy advice on capital flows in developing and transition countries and reform of international financial architecture. She led several major international research projects on international financial and macroeconomic issues with networks of senior academics, policy-makers and bankers from developed and developing countries. She has published widely, having written or edited 18 books and numerous journal and other articles. She has advised many international organisations (the European Commission, the World Bank, various UN agencies, IADB and several governments and Central Banks, including the UK, Chilean, Swedish, Tanzanian, Brazilian and Czech. Until early 2008, she was a Research Fellow of the Institute of Development Studies. She has been the Executive Director of the Initiative for Policy Dialogue (IPD) at Columbia University and then Research Director of IPD.

Sunanda Sen had been a Professor at the Jawaharlal Nehru University, New Delhi, and of late a Visiting Professor as well as a Consultant at various national and international organisations. Her published work includes six books – *Colonies and Empire* (1992), *Financial Fragility, Debt and Economic Reforms* (ed., 1996), *Finance and Development* (1998), *Trade and Dependence* (2000), *Global Finance at Risk* (2003) and *Unfreedom and Waged Work: Labour in India's Manufacturing Industry* (2009), as well as a number of articles in edited volumes and journals.

Cecilia Azevedo Sodré is Economic Consultant. She has worked as Special Adviser to the Government of Espírito Santo, Brazil, with a focus on poverty assessment and project planning at the state level. More recently, she has been involved in capacity building for achievement of MDGs in the North Pacific. Her research work focuses on capital flows to developing countries, financial crises in emerging market economies, money, credit and banking. Other areas of special interest include poverty reduction, inequality and growth, and MDG planning, implementing and monitoring.

1
Introduction: Why Basel Matters

Ricardo Gottschalk

1.1 Introduction

The primary aim of banking regulation is to improve the stability of the financial system. In a strict sense, banking regulation is not neutral, since it constrains the space within which banks operate and has the potential to influence their operational and strategic decisions. In the process, bank performance is affected. Banking regulation may be focused solely on the banking system, or it can take a macro-prudential perspective, for example, by focusing on the interactions between macroeconomic events and bank balance sheets. By recognising the interaction between the macroeconomic and banking sector dimensions, it can act to minimise possible negative effects deriving from it. Furthermore, banking regulation may influence the macro-economy directly, for example, when it takes the forms of liquidity regulation and capital regulation. The latter function may reinforce the pro-cyclicality of bank credit and therefore affect the economy as a whole.

This book is about the portion of the banking regulation package that takes the form of capital rules. These rules, designed by the Basel Committee on Banking Supervision (BCBS), are known as the Basel Capital Accords. The book's central concern is with possible impacts the Basel Accords may have on development finance. Broadly, the latter may be understood as the use or channelling of official and private financial resources to support economic growth and poverty reduction. The goals of development finance can be pursued, for example, by supporting long-term projects undertaken by governments or the private sector which have a positive economic and social impact. Development finance can also be used for private sector development, which helps accelerate growth. Development finance also aims at protecting the

1

poor and the most vulnerable, especially from external shocks. This book focuses in particular on two aspects of development finance: credit to the small- and medium-sized enterprises (SMEs), which arguably are the portion of the private sector with the highest capacity for job creation, and the existence of national financial systems that can support growth and poverty reduction.[1]

A main premise in this book is that the Basel capital rules are not neutral – not just in the strictest sense of banking regulation, but also in the broader sense of the banking system as a whole. That is, the book puts forward the view that the rules can affect not only bank performance or the macro-economy of a country, but also the structure of the banking system and its credit patterns, with potential negative implications for development finance. The book further stresses the point that this can happen even when such rules are designed solely with the aim of ensuring the strength and stability of the financial system.

The first Basel Capital Accord was created in 1988, and is known as Basel I. Later in 2004, a new Basel Capital Accord was reached, which came to be known as Basel II. Basel I, although initially intended for internationally active banks from developed countries, has been widely adopted around the world. Basel I adoption, starting in the late 1980s and early 1990s, coincided with major financial liberalisation, initially in developed countries from the early 1980s onward, then followed by liberalisation in developing countries, primarily in the 1990s. Following this dual process of financial liberalisation and Basel I adoption, it is possible to detect significant changes in banking systems: in a number of countries there were distinct trends in banking: toward higher banking concentration; more distinct division of labour between larger and smaller banks (and between foreign and domestic banks); and changes in banks' portfolios away from credit to the private sector and toward government securities. In addition, a trend away from corporate credit and toward consumer credit has been noted.

Basel II, approved in June of 2004, raised a number of concerns, including:

- Basel II as currently designed has the potential to contribute to banking concentration, and to bias credit away from small borrowers and toward larger ones; and away from development finance and toward safer forms of lending.
- Basel II as it currently stand, can inhibit financial innovation for financial inclusion.
- Basel II is highly pro-cyclical.

- Basel II implies massive implementation challenges to developing countries.

It is not possible to anticipate all of these impacts, but it is important to remain alert for possible, unintended consequences, even if these do not materialise in the end.

The 2007–09 global financial crisis has further exposed deficiencies and limitations inherent in the new Basel Capital Accord, particularly its over-reliance on the banks' own risk assessment models to determine capital charges, and its pro-cyclical bias. The crisis has also shown that trends in the banking systems are heading toward the wrong direction, with emphasis on consumer credit and too little credit available to productive activities.

Many developing countries have – in the past 20 years or so – introduced comprehensive market reforms into their banking systems. As a consequence, countries that have privatised their whole banking systems no longer have the financial policy tools to promote development; countries that have placed their entire banking systems in the hands of foreign banks have lost influence on how domestic funds are mobilised. These events are somewhat independent of implementation of the Basel Capital rules, but the latter may contribute to the expansion of banking privatisation and internationalisation.

Not all developing countries have pursued market-oriented financial reforms. Some developing countries have limited the presence of foreign banks, thus ensuring a significant space for domestic national banks, while others have maintained public banks. A banking system where foreign banks co-exist side by side with national, private, and public-owned banks may be perfectly compatible with the Basel rules, provided each different player, with its specific features and purposes, is recognised within the system.

This book reports that this is not the case at present. In developing countries, Basel rules have – to some extent – been adapted to national realities, but not to the degree needed to allow different banks the space they require to survive and to fulfil their specific mandates, especially those with mandates of social orientation. Since Basel II was proposed early in this century, and approved in 2004, the critiques have focused on its strong pro-cyclical bias – a serious issue which this book discusses at length. However, there are also other problems associated with Basel II, such as possible banking concentration, less credit to SMEs, and restriction of financial innovation for development, which have received far less attention. Basel capital rules are needed that are less pro-cyclical, do not have features that bias bank credit away from SMEs and the poor, and that encourage diversity of banks in terms of ownership, role, and size. This requires that the new Basel Capital Accord, or Basel II, whose implementation has already begun, be reformed in order to become compatible with higher financial and economic stability, and development finance. A reformed Basel Capital Accord must also be less complicated and less demanding of technical and high-skill resources. It has to reflect the interests and needs of a broader constituency of countries and banks, rather than the western-based internationally active banks.

This introductory chapter has two main objectives: first, to explain why the Basel Capital Accords matter to developing countries, despite the fact that they have been developed for adoption by the internationally active banks based in developed countries. Second, this chapter will also explain the purposes and organisation of the book, and the gaps in the literature it aims to fill. Following this introduction, Section 1.2 explains why the Basel Capital Accords matter to developing countries. To situate the reader in the Basel discussions, Section 1.3 succinctly describes Basel I and Basel II, and Section 1.4 provides an overview of the debate that has emerged since Basel II approval in 2004. Section 1.5 explains how the book is organised and what issues each chapter addresses.

1.2   Why the Basel capital accords matter to developing countries

The Basel rules matter to developing countries because most such countries around the world have adopted Basel I and most of them also intend to adopt Basel II at some point between 2007 and 2015. However, given such widespread intent, if the latter materialises, the new Basel rules may harm development finance in developing countries, as the rules have not been designed to address and reflect the concerns and needs of individual countries.

This book identifies as a major concern not only the potentially negative development finance impacts in developing countries, but also the fact that there seems to be a lack of debate about these impacts in these countries. The book suggests that this may be partly explained by the fact that the Basel rules, especially Basel II, are so complex that they have absorbed most of the resources and efforts of the developing countries, leaving little energy and capacity left to address broader, development-related issues.

The complexity of the capital rules, particularly those embedded in Basel II, takes us to the second reason as to why Basel matters to developing countries. Although the majority of such countries intend to implement the new rules, both their regulators and banks face massive implementation challenges. These include the need to build a large and reliable data base to run sophisticated risk assessment models, and to build supervisors' capacities to assess, validate and monitor the use of such models. The book also makes the point that Basel II matters even for countries that do not intend to adopt the new regulatory framework. When the foreign banks operating within their jurisdictions are willing to adopt Basel II, these countries will need to deal with Basel II, irrespective of the country's intentions on the matter.

1.3 Basel I and main changes in Basel II

To support our understanding of the issues and impacts, a brief overview of Basel I and Basel II is provided.

Basel I is an agreed regulatory framework for capital adequacy that the Basel Committee on Banking Supervision recommended for implementation in 1988, with the aim of improving the soundness and stability of national banking systems and of the international financial system. Under Basel I, internationally active banks (and increasingly other banks as well) were expected to meet a total capital requirement of at least 8 per cent in relation to their risk-weighted assets. The risk weights, suggested by the Basel Committee, ranged from 0 per cent to 100 per cent. National regulators had the discretion to adapt these to their circumstances and needs (Basel, 1998).

The framework was initially designed to address credit risk. In the subsequent 10 years, it was amended to include other types of risk, including market risk and concentration risk. The risk weights for different categories of assets are displayed in Table 1.1.

The main change in Basel II in relation to Basel I is the fact that internationally active banks are able to adopt their own models to determine risk for capital requirements. The new framework was finally approved in June 2004, after several rounds of consultations and debates that involved numerous stakeholders such as financial market participants, senior policy makers (national, international), national regulators and academics.

The new framework has three mutually reinforcing pillars: 1. The minimum capital requirement; 2. The supervisory review; and 3. Market discipline. The rules for minimum capital adequacy level are set under

Table 1.1   Risk weights for different types of assets as defined by Basel I

Weight (%)	Loans to/Investment in
0	• OECD central governments • Central governments that borrow in the national currency • Borrowers with OECD central governments' collaterals or guarantees
From 0 to 50 (at the discretion of national regulators)	• Domestic public sector entities outside the central government; borrowers with such entities' collaterals or guarantees
20	• Multilateral development banks (MDBs); borrowers with MDBs collaterals or guarantees • OECD banks and securities firms; borrowers with OECD banks and securities firms' collaterals or guarantees • Non-OECD banks with maturity of up to one year; borrowers with non-OECD banks' collaterals or guarantees, with maturity up to one year. • Non-domestic OECD public sector entities outside the central government; borrowers with such entities' collaterals or guarantees
50	• Mortgage borrowers who inhabit the residential property or rent it.
100	• Private sector • Non-OECD Banks with maturity of over one year. • Non-OECD central governments (unless they borrow in the national currency). • Real estate • Capital instruments issued by other banks.

Source: Basel (1998).

Pillar 1 of the new regulatory framework. The minimum capital level recommended by Basel I has been maintained at 8 per cent, but there is an increased differentiation of risk with the recommendation of three alternative approaches for determining risk for different types of assets: the standardised approach, the foundation internal ratings based (F-IRB) approach and the advanced IRB (A-IRB) approach. Under the standardised approach, different risk levels can be assigned to different categories of assets, and the approach allows for external rating agencies to determine risk levels. The basic and advanced IRB approaches differ from the standardised approach in that they require the use of internal modelling techniques to measure risk. The difference between the latter two approaches is that, under the foundation IRB approach, banks can use their own models to determine default risk, but the parameters for loss given default are furnished by the regulatory authorities. In the case of the advanced IRB approach, banks are allowed to determine both default risk and loss given default through their modelling techniques and database.

Pillars 2 and 3 relate closely to the Basel Committee's Core Principles for Effective Banking Supervision (BCP), but in this new context – in which new risk management systems are encouraged for adoption – emphasis is put on supervising the quality of the banks' new systems for risk assessment, and on disclosure of information on risk management practices and different types of risk exposures, along with disclosure of other types of information, such as the banks' financial performance and financial position (Basel, 2004).

In addition, the new accord requires the allocation of capital for operational risk (in addition to credit, market risks, international exposure and other risks), and proposes three methods for measuring this type of risk: the basic indicator method (BIM), the standard indicator method (SIM) and the advanced measurement method (AMM).

The main purpose of the New Basel Capital Accord is to further strengthen the soundness and stability of the international banking system, by encouraging banks to improve their risk management practices. To the extent that various internationally active banks have been adopting internal models to assess different types of risks, the new accord's intent is to align the rules that determine capital allocation with practices already in place in the markets.

The new framework has been designed for adoption by the G-10. At the same time, the Basel Committee recognises that many non-G-10 countries worldwide may wish to adapt the new framework to their own national realities and circumstances, and to have their own timetable for adopting the new rules.[2] The Committee goes further to say that national regulators should aim to ensure that the regulatory systems in their countries meet certain pre-conditions before attempting to implement the new framework in its entirety. This suggested approach reflects a main concern that many countries face limited resource capacity (human, financial) to implement Basel II, and efforts toward this goal may have the undesirable effect of diverting resources needed to ensure a satisfactory level of compliance with the BCP, many elements of which are embodied in the Pillars 2 and 3. Figure 1.1 below summarizes the main pillars and approaches under Basel II.

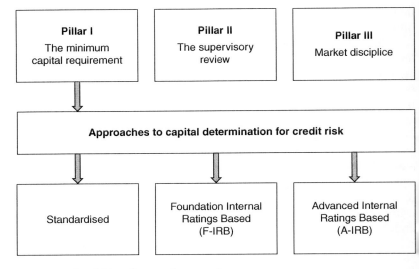

Figure 1.1   Basel II – pillars and approaches
Source: Author's elaboration.

1.4   An overview of the current debate

Issues arising from Basel II implementation are relevant both for developed and developing countries. Among developed countries, concerns with inequity and pro-cyclicality are so prevalent that developments on the ground are somewhat different from what the Basel Committee had expected.

Banking regulators in the U.S. decided to delay adoption of Basel II at least until January 2009. At the same time, they proposed the adoption of two different approaches for the U.S. banks. In September 2006, the four American regulators proposed that the IRB approach should apply to the largest and most internationally active banks only (26 in total). For the remaining banks, the U.S. regulators proposed a revised version of the existing capital rules known as Basel IA.

Moreover, whichever options proposed by the U.S. regulators were eventually to be adopted, banks were asked to observe a three per cent 'tier 1 leverage ratio' (core capital as a percentage of non-risk weighted assets) as a supplementary safety measure, a leverage ratio that has been in place since 1992 following the housing-loan crisis in 1991. The purpose was to establish a floor for capital requirements to avoid the possibility that in some cases, the internal risk models (under Basel II) might result in the banks allocating too little capital. Furthermore, there was pressure from the smaller U.S. banks for a more even playing-level field, given that they were not expected to adopt the IRB approach and would therefore not have major savings of capital. It would thus be very difficult to compete with the large banks. All these developments happened even before the 2007–09 global financial crisis. The latter has led to government intentions to use higher capital charges to curb the size of already very large banks, although the central concern is not so much with competitive issues as before the crisis, but with the risk that a very large bank poses to financial stability itself.

Countries from the European Union (EU) were set to comply with the new Basel rules beginning in January 2007,[3] as they are legally bound after the EU passed a Capital Requirements Directive in September 2005. The same deadline applied to other advanced countries in Asia.

But even in Europe, Basel II as proposed by the EU, was being contested. The European Shadow Financial Regulatory Committee (ESFRC), which is formed of finance professors, have strongly supported some sort of U.S.-style leverage ratio to avoid capital falling below a minimum level which could compromise financial stability. Also, European central bankers and regulators have raised related issues of concern. Economists from the Swiss National Bank affirmed that

> risk-measurement and information-asymmetry issues, which are inherent to banking activities, prevent the implementation of first-best capital adequacy rules, i.e., capital requirement that fully and exactly reflects banks' risks'. (Global Risk Regulator, 2006, p. 21)

In addition to safety and equity concerns, the pro-cyclicality of bank credit has been a major concern in developed countries. An adviser to the Bank of England has noted that at least in principle, Basel II might increase pro-cyclicality of credit provisions due to the fact that bank capital tends to fluctuate over the business cycle, along with measures of risk-weighted assets (Global Risk Regulator, 2006, p. 15). This concern is similar to that expressed by well-known academics in the U.K.

Although the new Basel rules cannot be blamed for the international financial crisis that started in August 2007, their implementation may aggravate two of the concerns raised above, concerns that have been intensified in the crisis: risk under-pricing due to the freedom banks enjoy to assess risk – made possible by the use of their own models – and pro-cyclicality of bank lending, due to incentives to hold less capital in boom times and the need to raise it in difficult times. During the crisis, it has become apparent that many large banks were not sufficiently capitalised. As a result, a new consensus has emerged among regulators, not only from the U.S. but from other developed countries as well, around the need to create capital buffers, for example, by instituting a leverage ratio, as has been the case in the U.S. for many years.

The lack of consensus in the developed world and especially in the U.S., and the resulting different paths countries within the G-10 were adopting, were in turn creating tensions amongst the banks themselves, partly because the existence of different rules across jurisdictions raises competitive issues, partly because their subsidiaries in other jurisdictions have to comply with different rules, thus creating challenges in reconciling numbers to be provided to the foreign jurisdiction. All this suggests that Basel II comprises a complex set of rules on which consensus is hard to reach, particularly due to their possible implications for competitiveness and financial stability. This book argues that many of these critical problems – reconciliation of numbers and rules from different jurisdictions, implications for competitiveness and financial stability – are even more so for developing countries, which find themselves in a far weaker position to address them appropriately.

1.5   Organisation of the book

This book has nine chapters, including this introduction. It covers a wide range of issues, from possible impacts of the Basel rules on banking concentration, to bank portfolio concentration, credit bias away from SMEs, constraints to financial innovation for development finance, pro-cyclicality and capacity implementation in developing countries. It brings views and concerns from different developing countries, including emerging market economies such as Brazil and low-income countries such as Ethiopia and Ghana. It shows that whilst there are many common issues, challenges and concerns facing developing countries in regard to Basel, some of these differ somewhat across countries, due to their different banking structures and phases of development.

The book is aimed at a broad audience and thus its chapters are fairly non-technical. Where a more technical presentation is made, this is placed in the appendix. Although each chapter is based on papers and studies initially prepared to be self-contained, the book versions have been modified to reduce the extent of overlaps. As a consequence, a certain progression exists as the reader moves from one chapter to the next. Unless the reader is well versed on Basel issues, it is recommended that s/he starts with the initial chapters, including this one, which explains the basic features of Basel I and Basel II, then proceeds to the subsequent chapters. Each chapter contains information or a dimension of Basel II and its relation to development finance that is found only there and in no other chapter. Therefore, the reading of all chapters is recommended to those who wish a round view of the issues the book addresses. That is not to say that the book covers all possible development finance aspects relating to Basel. For example, whilst the book focuses on Basel and lending to the SMEs or impacts on financial innovation for financial inclusion, it does not discuss the relation between Basel and financing of large-scale projects or of low-carbon growth, which are areas with important developmental dimensions.

Chapter 2, by Ricardo Gottschalk and Sunanda Sen, addresses the central concern of the book: the impacts of Basel norms on development finance. Taking a broader perspective on banking regulation and supervision, it starts with the argument that prudential norms for the financial system may have unintended consequences for development finance in developing countries. Next, focusing on the Basel rules, which is part of the prudential financial norms package, the chapter reviews the literature on impacts of Basel I adoption on the level of bank credit, focusing on the U.S. experience of the early 1990s. The chapter then discusses how Basel I may have affected credit levels in Brazil and India. It shows that for Brazil and India, Basel I rules have affected credit negatively – in the case of India, its introduction has coincided with less credit to the SMEs as well. Specifically in the case of Brazil, the chapter finds that credit as a proportion of the country's GDP declined gradually between 1994 (when Basel I was adopted) and early this century. The chapter also argues that Basel I rules have probably contributed to the decline in the number of banks in Brazil since 1994, and to banking concentration as well. Next, the chapter puts forward the view that Basel II may have three major implications: banking concentration, banking portfolio concentration, and increased bank credit pro-cyclicality. Chapters 3 and 4 discuss in more detail the implementation of Basel I in Brazil and India, and looks at the possible impacts of Basel II on the banking systems of these countries.

Chapter 3, by Ricardo Gottschalk and Cecilia Sodre, discusses the implementation of Basel I in Brazil during the 1990s, and how credit allocation patterns changed between then and the mid-2000s. It argues that, although Basel I affected credit in Brazil (as indicated in chapter 2), there is no clear evidence that credit to the SMEs, to rural producers, or to the urban poor was negatively affected, at least not in a major way. The chapter suggests that a main reason for this outcome is that credit patterns during the ten years after Basel I adoption were influenced by directed credit policy, which in a number of cases was intended to protect the less favoured segments. Between 2004 and 2008, credit in Brazil expanded very rapidly, but due to factors entirely independent of Basel rules. Next, the chapter discusses how Brazil's regulators have planned to implement Basel II. The chapter then presents the views on the Basel capital accords in Brazil, from banking regulators to bankers, financial consultants and academics. Their views are drawn from interviews conducted by the chapter authors in the country in the second half of 2004 and guided by the concerns and issues raised in chapter 2. In relation to Basel II, the chapter summarises their views on possible implementation challenges and possible impacts over different parts of the financial system.

Chapter 4 deals with the impact of the Basel capital adequacy norms on the Indian Banking Industry with special reference to credit flows to the poor and the SMEs. It provides a background to the issue by dwelling on the evolution of these norms and by taking a critical look at their rationale. The chapter finds that, following Basel I implementation, there was a tendency on the part of the Scheduled Commercial banks to follow a risk-averse strategy by investing more in government securities. It also finds that, despite observing a statutory 40 per cent priority credit norm, banks disburse an increasing portion of even the priority credit on less deserving but more profitable channels, which include many forms of consumer credit. It then argues that such tendencies, of moving away altogether from what used to qualify earlier as 'social control of credit', has generated a new pattern of credit disbursement in India. The worrisome result has been that social priorities of credit, which can be justified by the significant contributions of unorganised industries to aggregate employment, domestic output and exports, have been negatively affected. It then argues that compensatory fiscal policy may not be adequate to fill in the shortfall. The chapter discusses the views of various stakeholders in India on challenges and possible impacts of Basel II implementation in the country. As in Chapter 3, these views were obtained during interviews the chapter authors conducted in late 2004, when Indian authorities had already announced plans to implement the new Basel norms in the country.

Chapter 5, by Ricardo Gottschalk and Stephany Griffith-Jones, examines the implementation of Basel II in low-income countries (LICs)

The aims are to assess the low-income countries' views and concerns on Basel II, whether and how they intend to implement the new Basel Capital Accord, and the challenges they may face in doing so. In particular, the chapter discusses the possible implications of Basel II implementation for competitiveness of LIC banking sectors and financial inclusion. Drawing on a survey conducted by the chapter authors at the end of 2006 which covered low-income countries especially in Africa, the chapter finds that, in addition to technical challenges that include the need to build extensive and reliable data bases to run sophisticated risk assessment models, and to build supervisors' capacities to assess, validate and monitor the use of such models, LICs face broader issues related to Basel II implementation, such as competitiveness of national and foreign banks, access to credit by SMEs, potential increased pro-cyclicality of bank lending and their macroeconomic impacts. The chapter then explores possible implications of Basel rules on financial innovation for financial inclusion, with a focus on pro-poor product development by smaller banks geared to the bottom end of the market. The chapter concludes that LIC regulators may not need just technical assistance but also more 'political' support for their negotiations on regulations with international banks to ensure that their regulatory regimes are consistent with national aims for both financial stability and sufficient credit, especially to SMEs.

Chapter 6, by Ray Barrell and Sylvia Gottschalk, investigates the macroeconomic impacts of changes in capital adequacy requirements, as developed in the Basel Capital Accords, on Brazil and Mexico. To this end, it uses a general equilibrium macro-econometric model, which allows the chapter authors to examine indirect transmission channels. The authors first estimate reduced financial blocks for Brazil and Mexico, which are then integrated into the General Equilibrium Model (NiGEM) of the National Institute of Economic and Social Research (NIESR). The authors simulate a shock to domestic and international capital adequacy ratios.

The simulations show that an increase in capital adequacy ratios – either domestic or international – has adverse impacts on Brazilian and Mexican GDPs. A moderate credit crunch occurs in both cases and in both countries, accompanied by a rise in lending rates. However, important differences between the two countries are found. In Brazil, the simulations show that international and domestic banks adjust their portfolios by switching from higher-risk loans (private sector loans) to zero-risk loans (sovereign and public sector), instead of increasing capital provisions. Sovereign lending, and hence government spending, thus rises sharply in Brazil, thereby offsetting the negative impacts of the decline in private investment that follows the credit crunch. The findings of a credit crunch following higher capital adequacy ratios are consistent with those of the literature review in chapter 2 and trends reported in Brazil and discussed in chapters 2 and 3. In Mexico, sovereign lending from domestic banks remains largely unaffected by changes in capital adequacy ratios. Foreign loans to the Mexican public sector decrease.

The chapter also finds that consumption credit both in Brazil and Mexico is not sensitive to changes in capital ratios. However, household consumption declines, due to indirect channels. The transmission mechanism is carried out through household net wealth. Higher capital ratios lead to higher interest rates, which increase net interest payments of households and therefore reduce their financial wealth.

Chapter 7, by Stephany Griffith-Jones, discusses Basel II by taking a broader, international perspective. It first identifies serious regulatory gaps following the global financial crisis of 2007–2009, and proposes capital and liquidity regulation to close these gaps. It then reviews the literature on counter-cyclical regulation proposals which have been made over the past several years, and also since the onset of the global financial crisis. The chapter then moves on to discuss the risk of a decline of international bank lending to developing countries associated with Basel II. It then proposes the incorporation by Basel II of the benefits of portfolio diversification when measuring banks' risks for calculating capital requirements. The chapter argues that incorporation of such benefits would better reflect risks banks face and would contribute to mitigate possible decline in lending to developing countries and pro-cyclicality of bank credit.

Chapter 8, by Pietro Calice, focuses on the problem of access to credit faced by small and medium enterprises (SMEs) in developing countries and puts forward a policy proposal that addresses that issue. It starts by highlighting the fact that SMEs can make an important contribution to economic growth acceleration, job creation and poverty reduction. However, they historically lack access to bank financing. The new Basel Capital Accord is likely to result in more rationed and costly credit for SMEs. However, because Basel II recognises a strengthened role to credit guarantee schemes (CGSs), the chapter puts forward the view that there is a strong case for the introduction of Regional Guarantee Funds (RGFs) to support SME development. It proposes the RGFs to be designed and operated to achieve the highest credit rating so that lenders have incentives to provide credit to SMEs under Basel II.

Chapter 9, by Ricardo Gottschalk, summarises the key concerns and findings of the book, and puts forward a few proposals to make the new capital rules better aligned with the concerns, needs and interests of developing countries. The chapter also proposes the establishment of a properly resourced monitoring system to track selected financial indicators to monitor possible Basel II impacts, from the moment the new accord is implemented. Finally the chapter concludes suggesting that introduction of reforms in the Basel Capital Accord should be accompanied by developing country efforts to have in place a financial system that support social and economic development.

Notes

1. On the role of the financial system in fostering economic growth and poverty reduction, see Spratt (2008).
2. In this regard, the Basel Committee set up a Working Group in 2003 composed of representatives from mainly non-G-10 countries, including Brazil, to assess Basel II and provide recommendations on how supervisors might want to promote changes toward the new framework (Basel, 2004).
3. It should be noted that some time flexibility exists for Basel II adoption, at least until early 2008.

2
Prudential Norms for the Financial Sector: Is Development a Missing Dimension? The Cases of Brazil and India

Ricardo Gottschalk and Sunanda Sen

2.1 Introduction

Since financial liberalisation in the late 1970s and early 1980s, prudential norms for the financial sector have become increasingly important for enhancing financial stability worldwide. Developing countries in particular have in recent years made some efforts to improve their prudential and regulatory frameworks for the financial system, especially at end of the various financial crises in the emerging market economies in the late 1990s.

Prudential norms relating to finance in developing countries have the clear purpose to help strengthening their domestic financial systems. These, however, are not intended to address their development financing needs. This chapter takes the view that certain components within the package of prudential norms can be even inimical to growth and poverty reduction.

The aim of the present chapter is to discuss the possible negative developmental impacts of the Basel Capital Accords (Basel I and II), which constitutes a part of the current package of prudential financial norms. It does so by looking at Brazil and India's experience with the adoption of Basel I in the early and mid-1990s, and these countries' plans to implement the New Basel Accord, known as Basel II. Brazil and India are chosen because information on prudential norms and on credit levels and distribution are available for both countries. Moreover, in both countries one finds concentrated large portions of the world'<

poor, particularly in India, while in both cases their respective governments have pledged to pursue poverty reduction policies.

It will be seen that the introduction of Basel I in Brazil and India over the early to mid-1990s has contributed to banking concentration in Brazil and also to a steady decline in total credit as a proportion of the country's GDP until early 2000s. In India, implementation of Basel I has contributed to a slowdown in credit expansion in the country in these years. What about the possible impacts of the new Basel rules – known as Basel II worldwide – that were approved in June 2004?

A crucial aspect of the new rules is that it encourages internationally active banks to adopt internal models instead of the standard format for measuring different types of credit risk, used for capital allocation. These rules thus imply significant discrepancies vis a vis the standard Basel I rules, in which risk weights are determined not by the banks but by the regulatory authorities. This chapter argues that those changes in determining how risk is determined for capital allocation may have the following outcomes:

- Banking concentration, due to the fact that under Basel II the risk-sensitive internal models will not be universally adopted, but only by the largest (and internationally exposed) banks.
- Loan portfolio concentration away from SMEs and towards the large corporations.
- An increased pro-cyclicality of bank credit.

These possible outcomes, which this chapter will discuss in some detail, have been pointed out by a number of international policy makers and academics, including Borio, Furfine and Lowe (2003) and Griffith-Jones (2003). In the specific case of bank portfolio concentration away from the SMEs, the issue has been acknowledged and to some extent addressed by the Basel Committee, in response to pressures from the German government.

The present chapter is organised in six sections. Following this introduction, Section 2.2 discusses why it is important to address the possible negative developmental impacts of prudential norms. Section 2.3 reviews the empirical literature on the macroeconomic and credit impacts of Basel I. Section 2.4 reports our findings on the impacts of Basel I implementation in Brazil and India. Section 2.5 briefly highlights the key changes in Basel II relative to Basel I and discusses the possible implications of these changes for development finance and macroeconomic stability. We conclude with Section 2.6.

2.2 Why is it important to address the possible negative developmental impacts of prudential norms?

2.2.1 The background

The flurry of financial liberalisation which started with the big bang in the UK and the introduction of universal banking all over the financial markets in advanced countries during the 1980s aimed to achieve stability and efficiency in the functioning of financial markets. Efficiency in the disbursement of credit was also expected to improve the growth performance of the respective economies.

Putting an end to the earlier practice of segregated banking whereby banks were not permitted to operate in the capital (security) market, the new norms of universal banking removed such barriers. However, exposures to new forms of risks by banks due to their operations in the security market (especially in the case of banks with a global presence) demanded new forms of prudential regulations. Norms related to those prudential regulations for banks were considered necessary by the G-7, in a bid to avoid a sudden crisis. Of those, the application of the capital adequacy rules was treated as the most crucial and binding. These rules along with others aimed to provide uniform guidelines at a global level, with a homogeneous balance-sheet and disclosure patterns which could ensure safety of assets held by depositors and shareholders and also achieve transparency.

In retrospection, it appears that while an end to financial repression under financial liberalisation was treated as a first best Pareto optima, a need arose to modify the prescriptions for full autonomy of the financial market. This was done by instituting, as the second best optima, the prudential norms which sought to ward off the consequences of volatile financial markets. But to what extent were those modifications capable of bringing market efficiency?

The events of 2007–2008 have shown us that not only did the modifications fail to reach market efficiency, but also that these failed to avoid a major global banking crisis, with devastating transmission effects across national borders.

2.2.2 Prudential norms, market efficiency and development finance

Financial markets are characterised by market failures and missing markets. In developing countries in particular there is a lack of certain markets – for example, markets for long-term credits. This is partly due to lack of sophisticated instruments, which make it extremely hard for intermediaries to transform short-term liabilities into long-term finance, a crucial ingredient for large development projects. Moreover, in a number of cases private returns differ from social returns. Banks, therefore, may choose not the project that offers the highest total returns, but the one that the bank itself has the highest return (Stiglitz and Weiss, 1981).

In particular financial markets suffer from information asymmetry, which impairs the ability of the banking system to assess risk. The result is that credit is rationed (Stiglitz and Weiss, 1981). Because markets are not cleared, the banking system ends up operating in an inefficient way. More so, the system is inefficient in how it allocates resources. Due to information asymmetry, the system becomes particularly biased towards lending to big companies and against small borrowers.

Thus market failures remain despite financial liberalisation. Their continued presence further justifies institutional action, to ensure that socially efficient projects are financed, and mitigates the inequity arising from the normal operation of the markets. However, developing countries have, in the past twenty years or so, lacked the financial resources to build institutions to support development finance. Where such institutions exist, efforts have in most cases been not to strengthen but to dismantle them.

A lack of attention to the implications of prudential norms for development finance is bound to compound the problem. The approved New Basel Capital Accord or the Basel II has, as one of its main objectives, an encouragement of internationally active banks to adopt risk sensitive models so that credit and other risks can be more accurately measured. However, the use of risk sensitive models may exclude small borrowers from banks' portfolio of clients, to the extent that credit to them becomes prohibitively expensive, due to higher capital requirements. This would happen because small borrowers would be judged as riskier ones, due to lack of (or more costly) information on them for an accurate risk assessment – information on small borrowers is more costly, especially in developing countries where they are in their large majority in the informal sector.

To summarise the main points made so far, this chapter takes the view that 1) Financial systems do not provide credit to different segments in an efficient way, due to market failures and information deficiencies. As a result, credit to the poor in particular is affected. 2) Prudential norms for the financial sector may help ensure stability of the system, but it does not contribute to an increase in credit provision to the poor. That is the main concern of this study. In the specific case of Basel I and II, which is the focus of this book, the new rules may potentially have a negative effect on development finance, and even on financial stability.

2.3   Possible impacts of Basel I on the macro-economy and credit: A brief review of the literature

This section reviews an empirical literature that addresses the following question: to what extent have efforts by banks in developed and developing countries to meet the Basel capital adequacy requirements affected credit provisions for the private sector?

A basic hypothesis which underlies the literature is that the risk-weight structure of banks' asset-portfolio as has been introduced by Basel I brings about a shift in the portfolio composition of banks when facing the specific regulatory pressure of meeting the minimum capital requirements. This happens because, whilst credit to the private sector has risk weight of 100 per cent for capital requirement purposes, government bonds have a 0 per cent risk weight. Banks can thus meet their capital adequacy requirements without actually raising their capital provisions.

The debate on whether the minimum capital requirements based on weighted-risk assets may cause a reallocation in banks' portfolio away from assets with high risk weights started in the US with the recession of the early 1990s, which many believe was characterised by a major credit crunch, coinciding with the implementation of Basel I in the country.

Berger and Udell (1994) noted that a shift in US banks' portfolio away from commercial loans and towards treasuries was observed in the early 1990s, offering the hypothesis that the newly adopted Basel rule on capital to risk weighted asset ratio – or the risk based capital (RBC) – played a major role in the reallocation of banks' portfolio assets and thereby caused a credit crunch at that time. But they also raised the point that if the credit crunch, understood as a shift in the supply credit curve to the left – really existed, other concurrent factors might have also have a role in it. One factor may have been the leverage requirement, which in the US was introduced together with the RBC requirements. It consisted of stipulating a minimum percentage of capital in relation to unweighted bank assets. Because the minimum percentage was decided at the discretion of the regulator, banks may have been induced not only to shift their composition of assets away from assets perceived as riskier but also to reduce the assets altogether. Non-regulatory explanations for a credit crunch provided by Berger and Udell (1994) include the existence of a steep slope of the term structure which encouraged banks to acquire treasury bonds. Berger and Udell also point at the existence of demand factors at play, such as the long-term decline in the demand for bank loans in face of growing competition from non-bank credit suppliers – the so-called secular decline hypothesis.

The authors tested empirically the factors that may have led to the credit crunch, and the empirical results were more supportive of the role of demand-side factors in explaining a decline in bank lending in the early 1990s than supply – and within it rules-based – factors.

In contrast, using a sample of US banks in New England, Peek and Rosengren (1995) find empirical evidence that the new regulatory framework caused a capital crunch in New England banks over that 1990–1991 period which, in turn, may have caused a credit crunch. The reason their work was limited to New England banks is that it was a way to control for the macroeconomic factors, which were common to all banks of a same region.

Ediz, Michael and Perraudin (1998) looked at the regulatory effects on UK banks, focusing on two questions: first, the impact of capital requirements on bank capital, especially when the capital ratio is close to the minimum required, and second, whether and how banks adjust their balance sheets when they raise their capital ratios. They gather information on UK banks to show that when banks are close to the minimum capital requirements, they tend to increase their capital adequacy ratios; moreover, they change their asset portfolio composition away from corporate loans, albeit just slightly. The measure they use for closeness to the minimum capital requirement is the difference between the actual capital adequacy ratio (CAR) and the minimum requirement, divided by a CAR volatility measure – as they reason, the likelihood of hitting the minimum required depends both on the distance between actual and regulatory minimum capital, and on CAR's variability over time. Their findings are based on descriptive data analysis. To provide more solid statistical evidence, the Bank of England researchers used a multivariate dynamic panel model based on quarterly data from 94 UK banks over 1980–1995. In this model, the dependent variable is changes in capital ratios, which is regressed on the lagged variable in levels, a number of conditioning variables on the nature of the banks' business and their financial health, and a regulatory pressure variable.

Their econometric results show that the regulatory pressure variables do indeed cause an increase in banks' CAR. However, the evidence is also that a higher corporate lending to total capital ratio leads to higher capital provisioning. The reasoning provided by the authors is that a riskier portfolio calls for the need of stronger capitalisation. It is therefore implied by this result that banks increase their CAR not through portfolio shifts away from riskier assets but by raising new capital. However, it is important to notice that in their exercise CAR is the dependent variable and corporate lending to total assets ratio is the independent variable, that endogeneity problems between these two variables is not addressed, and that banks' specific effects are not taken into account.

Shrieves and Dahl (1992) examine the relationship between changes in capital and risk to see which strand of the theoretical literature empirical evidence supports. The authors use a system of simultaneous equations based on a two stage least square (2SLS) estimation method for nearly 2000 US banks over the 1985–1987 period. The authors discuss the various theoretical frameworks supporting one or another hypothesis – that the utility maximising mean-variance framework as set out by Kim and Santomero (1988) suggests that capital and risk bear a negative relationship, while the theories of regulatory costs (put forward by Buser, Chen and Kane, 1981), unintended effects of minimum capital standards [Koehn and Santomero (1980); Kim and Santomero (1988)], bankruptcy cost avoidance (see Orgler and Taggart, 1983) and managerial risk aversion (Saunders, Strock and Travlos, 1990) will tend to result in a positive relationship between changes in capital and risk. The authors' empirical findings support the latter sets of hypotheses, that changes in capital and risk bear a positive relationship.

Using a similar methodology as that of Shrieves and Dahl (1992) but working with a muti-country context, Van Roy (2005) examines the impact of the Basel Capital Accord on changes in capital and credit risk for six OECD countries – which include Canada, France, Italy, Japan, United Kingdom, and United States – using an unbalanced panel and a simultaneous equation approach based on a three stage least square (3SLS) estimation method over the 1988–1995 period. In testing for the equality of coefficients across countries, the null of equality was rejected. The author therefore chose to estimate equations separately, classifying the countries into three groups: the US banks, the Japanese banks and the banks of the remaining four countries. Looking at the regulatory pressure and the variation in capital and in credit coefficients, what it found is that overall regulatory pressure did lead to an increase in capital, whereas results for the impact on risk is uncertain. As for the impact of changes in capital on risk and vice-versa, results are dissimila across groups of countries: positive though insignificant coefficients were observed for banks from the European countries plus Canada, a positive and significant coefficient for the impact of changes in capital on changes in risk among Japanese banks, and negative and significant coefficients for the impact of changes in capital on risk and vice-versa among US banks. The latter results confirm some of the results on the behaviour of US banks in response to the adoption of Basel I in the early 1990s.

Looking at the behaviour of internationally active banks in Japan both for the periods pre- and post-Basel, Montgomery (2005) finds that, for the post-Basel period 1988–1999, poorly capitalised international banks tend to have a slower growth of total assets and of loans in particular. When the pre-Basel period is included so that the sample cover the 1982–1999 period, a dummy Basel is introduced for the post-Basel period. The main result is that for international banks the Basel coefficient is statistically significantly negative, indicating that for the post-Basel period regulatory pressure resulted in a slower growth of risky assets.

All the empirical studies discussed so far focus only on developed countries. Hussain and Hassan (2005) focus on developing countries instead. The authors use Shrieves and Dahl (1992) simultaneous equation model for a group of eleven developing countries[1] over a period of five years starting from the dates when Basel was implemented in each country.[2] Contrary to most of the theory and many of the empirical results on the relationship between capital ratio and risk, the authors find a negative relationship between these two variables. Moreover, contrary to the results of Roy (2005) reported above, they find a negative and significant coefficient for the regulatory pressure variable both in the capital ratio and risk equations. This indicates that poorly capitalised banks did not increase capital when faced by regulatory pressure, and did reduce risk. The authors selected only the large banks of the sample countries, amounting to a total of 300 banks. Their model includes macroeconomic variables to control for country effects, but the authors do not use country dummies to control for remaining country effects.

What we have seen above is that the findings from the literature are conflicting with each other. What moreover stands out is that the findings are very sensitive to model and sample specifications, and that in virtually all studies it is extremely hard to control for all the factors that may, in one way or another, affect capital ratios and credit to the private sector. Thus, although it may be possible to detect trends in capital ratios and risk moving in opposite directions, it is difficult to establish a causal relationship. However, this does not provide a reason not to be watchful of possible impacts of capital regulation on credit patterns.

2.4   The impacts of Basel I in Brazil and India

Under Basel I, internationally active banks were expected to meet a total capital requirement of at least 8 per cent in relation to their risk-weighted assets, as mentioned earlier. Assets (and off-balance sheet exposures) are assigned weights according to their relative riskiness, ranging from 0 per cent to 100 per cent (applied over 8 per cent of capital).

Both Brazil and India made efforts to comply with higher capital requirements in their banking systems in the 1990s and early this century. In Brazil, Basel I was introduced in 1994, with regulators initially requiring banks to meet capital adequacy requirements of 8 per cent, as recommended in Basel I. In 1997, this limit was raised to 11 per cent (see Chapter 3). In India, the 8 per cent requirement was introduced in 1992 and increased to 9 per cent in 2000, in response to the recommendations of the 1998 Narasimha Committee Report (see Chapter 4). As a result, overall capital adequacy ratios went well above the minimum of 8 per cent, as recommended by the Basel Committee. In Brazil, for the largest five banks, the Basel index went up from 9.8 in December 1995 to 13.6 in 2001. For the banking system as a whole, the Basel index reached 19 per cent in December 2003. In India, the Basel index for the group of scheduled commercial banks (SCBs) went up from 10.4 per cent during the financial year 1997 to 11.8 per cent in the financial year 2004.

For Brazil, efforts by banks to meet the minimum capital requirement had two main effects:

1. It contributed to reinforce banking concentration in the country.

   Between 1999 and mid-2004, the percentage of assets held by the largest 10 banks in the total assets of the financial system went up from 52 per cent to 66 per cent; when the largest 20 banks are considered, the percentage of assets went up from 62 per cent to 77 per cent (Gottschalk and Sodre, 2007). These findings are similar to those obtained by Troster (2004), using the Herfindahl index to measure banking concentration.

   It is true that Basel I was adopted as part of a bigger package of banking reforms undertaken in the second half of the 1990s and early this century, which encouraged banking concentration. But Soares (2002) claims that Basel I itself played an important role in it

To explain how that happened, in Brazil the capital rules were even more stringent than recommended by Basel. Banks had to meet not just the 8 per cent requirement (and later 11 per cent, as mentioned above), but a minimum absolute requirement in a short period of time, regardless of the size of banks. Given that the smaller banks could not do that (due to their size and little capacity to raise capital in the capital markets), they were taken over by the larger banks.

2. It contributed to a steady decline in total credit as a proportion of the country's GDP, from 36 per cent in 1994 to 26 per cent in 2004. This trend was reversed between then and 2008, when the global financial crisis hit Brazil.

There are a host of factors that explain why credit as a proportion of GDP was and still is so low in Brazil – high levels of public financing requirements, the country's high levels of interest rates and spreads (which did not come down with the entry of foreign banks in the banking system), high insolvency levels among private borrowers, financial taxes, high levels of deposit rates with the Central Bank, and bankruptcy law and a judiciary system tilted towards the interests of the debtors (Gottschalk and Sodre, 2007).

However, these factors do not fully explain why credit declined between the introduction of Basel I in Brazil in the mid-1990s and 2004. An evidence that Basel I seems to have played an important role in it is the fact that the share of credit in banks' total assets declined sharply between 1994 and 2004, from 50.6 per cent to 29.7 per cent. This evidence is consistent with the simulations run by Barrel and Gottschalk (see Chapter 6) using a macro-econometric model for Brazil, which show that an increase in banks' minimum capital requirements brings about a fall in banks' credit to the private sector, and an increase in the levels of government bonds held by banks. The shift in portfolio assets composition happens because whilst credit to the private sector has risk weight of 100 per cent for capital requirement purposes under Basel rules, government bonds have a 0 per cent weight – that is, these assets are risk-free. One might argue that the shift in banks' portfolio towards government bonds was due to high interest rates. However, a similar shift in banks' portfolio took place in India following the adoption of Basel I in that country, under very different macroeconomic circumstances.

Data on the Basel index of capital ratios are not available in aggregate terms for the 1990s. But for three of the largest five banks in Brazil – Banco do Brasil, Caixa Economica Federal and Unibanco – data are

Table 2.1   The Basel Index and the credit-total assets ratio – selected banks (in %)

	Banco do Brasil		Caixa Economica Federal		Unibanco	
	Basel Index	Credit to assets ratio	Basel Index	Credit to assets ratio	Basel Index	Credit to assets ratio
Dec 1995	7.9	42.4	9.8	48.8	17.3	30.0
Sep 2004	15.6	31.9	18.4	18.7	15.4	34.9

Sources: Brazil's Central Bank.

available both for 1995 – the first year of Basel I in Brazil, and 2004. These are displayed in Table 2.1. The Table shows that an inverse relationship exists between the Basel index and the credit-total assets ratio for all the three banks.

High real interest rates from 1995 onwards may partly explain the change in banks' asset composition away from credit, and towards federal government bonds. But clearly, efforts to comply with Basel I has also been an important factor in explaining the change in banks' portfolio composition, as it induced banks to acquire risk-free government bonds, which makes easier for banks to meet the minimum capital requirements.

The biggest effort of adjustment by banks to the Basel rules occurred mainly in the second half of the 1990s. As mentioned above, for the largest five banks, the Basel index went from 9.8 in December 1995 to 13.6 in 2001. For the whole banking system, the index, available from December 2001 onwards, showed further increases between then and December 2003, from 16.4 per cent to 19.0 per cent – see Figure 2.1, which displays the trend in the Basel index for the Brazilian banking system for this latter period, on a quarterly basis. But, unlike the previous period, the credit to total assets ratio for the banking system exhibited stability, remaining at around 30 per cent over the 2001–2003 period – see Figure 2.2.

But were trends across banks uniform – that is, the portfolio composition remained constant as capital requirements continued to go up, as the overall data suggests? To see if trends across banks were uniform or whether for some banks at least these were downwards in response to higher capital allocations, we tested for the correlation between the Basel index and the credit-total assets ratio for the 50 largest banks in

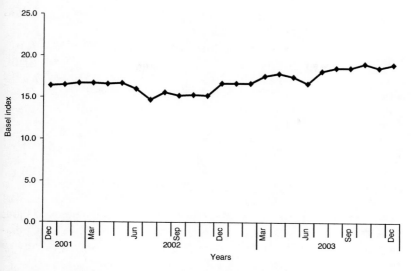

Figure 2.1   The Basel index in Brazil – Dec 2001–Dec 2003
Source: Central Bank of Brazil.

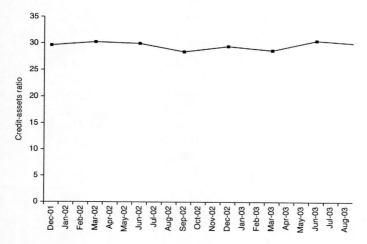

Figure 2.2   Credit to assets ratio for the Brazil's banking system
Source: Central Bank of Brazil.

2001 for the Dec-2001-Sep 2004 period, for which data are available on a quarterly basis for individual banks.

Changes did occur, and the direction of change across banks was rather mixed, which conforms with the aggregate pattern of credit-total asset ratio stability, as trends in opposite directions probably have cancelled each other. But can we draw a coherent story by grouping the individual banks in broad banking categories, and thus looking at trends across these different categories?

The answer is clearly positive. Among public banks, the correlation is positive for some, negative for others. Apparently, this was the case because some public banks succeeded in raising their capital requirements through government re-capitalisation. Among foreign banks, a mixed picture is also found; but most importantly, for the majority of private domestic banks, a negative correlation is found, which indicates that for this category of banks, further portfolio adjustments took place in response to their efforts to further increase their capital adequacy ratios.

In India, the capital rules also led to a shift in banks' portfolio towards government bonds and away from credit to the private sector. Between the financial years 1999 and 2004, the share of government securities in total assets of the portfolios of commercial banks went up from 24 per cent to 32 per cent.[3] Similar to Brazil, the reasons for this trend are: first, the capital adequacy ratio against government securities is just 2.5 per cent (to account for market risk; it was 0 per cent until 1998), thus very low compared to other assets; second, while the returns on these assets are generally low, they are virtually risk-free, thus having little chances of becoming non-performing assets (NPAs). Thus, government securities provided banks with a steady source of risk-free income while dispensing the need to provide for capital adequacy or provisioning (see Chapter 4 in this book).

A major implication of the change in composition of banks' asset portfolios was a slowdown in credit expansion in India. In 2004, while aggregate deposits of India's commercial banks increased by 17.3 per cent, and investments in government and approved securities went up by 24.1 per cent, bank credit increased by only 14.6 per cent. The public sector banks (PSBs) in India for their part have also avoided any possible lending problems including risk of default by investing in government debt, a management strategy that has been reinforced by Basel I. These banks' conservative lending strategy is highlighted by Banerjee and Duflo (2005), who have shown that credit disbursal in Indian public sector banks is largely based on past behaviour, thereby leaving rapidly growing firms credit constrained.

Together with the slowdown in credit expansion, credit to the SMEs by commercial banks fell sharply relative to total credit – for example, among the SBI and Associates, if fell from 10 per cent to 5 per cent between 2000 and 2007 (see Chapter 4 in this book). The reason for the latter had less to do with capital requirements, as these under Basel I did not vary according to the type of credit borrower, but to more stringent credit risk assessment systems adopted by banks which was part of efforts to comply with the prudential norms.

2.5   Basel II: Main changes and implementation in Brazil and India

As mentioned earlier in this book (see Chapter 1), the main change in Basel II in relation to Basel I is the fact that internationally active banks will be able to adopt their own models for risk assessment. As a result, these banks will no longer need to follow the risk-weight system established by the Basel Committee for determining capital requirements. The new rules for capital requirements are embodied in the so-called Pillar 1 of the New Accord, which concerns minimum capital requirements for banks. In addition, Basel II has also Pillar 2, on banking supervision, and Pillar 3, on transparency and market discipline, as explained in Chapter 1.

To the extent that the use of the internal models permit banks to determine their own risk-weight system, this will give them greater flexibility. But not all banks will be able to use internal models for capital requirements. As discussed earlier in this book, under the standardised approach, a specific risk level is designated for each type of asset. As has been suggested by the Basel Committee, the rating agencies will be charged with determining the risk levels. It will be up to the regulatory authorities in each country to decide which approach banks will be permitted to adopt for determining capital requirements.

Basel II also distinguishes itself from Basel I in that it requires capital for operational risk, in addition to capital for credit risk. As will be seen in Chapter 3, the need to allocate capital for operational risk may penalise, in particular, those banks that will adopt the standardised approach, given the lack of flexibility that this approach implies, a flexibility that would be important to compensate for increases in capital requirement for operational risk.

Depending on how Basel II is implemented by banking regulators in their own jurisdictions, the new capital accord could have undesirable implications for the banking system concerning its role in supporting growth and of credit provider, especially to the SMEs. In this chapter, we discuss three implications. As mentioned earlier these are (i) inequality with risk of banking concentration; (ii) loan portfolio concentration and (iii) increased bank credit pro-cyclicality.

The inequity issue had been raised before by the Basel Committee when Basel I was created. Their concern was that if Basel I did not ensure a minimum degree of homogeneity of rules across different jurisdictions, this could grant competitive advantage to internationally active banks based in certain jurisdictions against banks based in others. The point was that if rules were applied differently across different jurisdictions, some banks would end up facing higher capital requirements than others, for reasons of geography rather than risk. There was the further risk that these differences could be magnified by specific tax, accounting and other rules across jurisdictions.

Basel II provides a menu of options for calculating capital charges and this can also cause the inequity problem mentioned above, or banks working with different levels of capital requirements. But in this case that would happen not only among banks across countries but also within countries. For example, in the same jurisdiction there could be banks adopting one of the IRB approaches along with others adopting the standardised approach. But those banks adopting one of the IRB approaches could be at advantage in relation to the others. This is because the IRB approaches are likely to result in lower levels of capital requirements.

The Fifth Quantitative Impact Study (QIS 5) conducted by the BIS shows that for different groups of banks within and outside the G-10 the Advanced Internal Rating Based (AIRB) approach would bring the largest falls in capital requirements – by 29 per cent for one group of banks and over 26 per cent for two other groups, followed by the Foundation IRB (F-IRB) approach. At the same time, the standardised approach would either imply similar levels of capital or, for at least one group of banks, a substantial increase, of nearly 40 per cent (Basel 2006 p. 2, Table 1).

The larger and more sophisticated banks are more likely to adopt one of the IRB approaches and therefore to benefit from it, to the detriment of smaller banks, which are more likely to adopt the standardised approach. This type of inequity could, in turn, lead to banking concentration (through take over) favouring the larger banks, and in the case of many developing countries, it could favour the foreign banks.

An important implication of banking concentration for credit to the SMEs and the poor is that larger banks typically lend to bigger corporations – that is, they adopt 'cherry-picking' strategies. Moreover, to the extent that the smaller banks are absorbed by the larger ones, information on specific categories of borrowers in which smaller banks are specialised may be lost.

The second problem – of possible portfolio concentration – is likely to occur within the credit portfolio of banks adopting the internal models for risk assessment. The use of risk measurement techniques to determine the amount of capital to be allocated for different types of assets is likely to result in both more expensive and rationed credit to borrowers perceived as of higher risk, and more and cheaper credit to borrowers perceived as of lower risk. For reasons such as information asymmetry, small borrowers such as SMEs and the poor are likely to be judged as of higher risk than the larger ones, such as large companies. This happens because less information on smaller borrowers is available, or even that the sort of information needed to feed risk assessment models do not exist at all. The problem is even more acute among borrowers operating in the informal sectors of the economy. This can cause a concentration in banks' loan portfolio away from small borrowers and towards the larger companies.[4]

The third problem, of credit pro-cyclicality, is also related to the use of risk-sensitive models. These models are likely to detect an increase in the probability of default during economic downturns. As a consequence, the assets of a portfolio will be downgraded and lead to higher capital charges. Empirical evidence supports the claim that the use of the IRB approach to measure risk may have the effect of a higher variation in the capital charge over the business cycle, as compared to the use of Basel I type of rules for measuring risk (see Goodhart and Segoviano, 2005). This in itself may lead to both increased cost and reduced quantity of credit during economic slowdowns. Furthermore, the fact that it is harder to raise capital during economic downturns may reinforce the tendency in credit reduction, ultimately leading to a credit crunch and a deepening of the economic downturn, with further impacts on banks' portfolios. This is what seems to be happening in the current international financial crisis.

A reason why the measured risk by these models tends to be so much time-variant is that even when they are forward-looking, their time horizons often are limited to one year (see Borio et al, 2003). These models therefore result in assigning borrowers ratings in light of their current (or over a limited time-horizon) status. That is what is called the 'point-in-time' approach. But if models could instead look 'through-the-cycle', so as to reduce or eliminate variations in the ratings caused by changing conditions during the cycle, then their pro-cyclicality effects could be avoided or at least significantly reduced.

Higher credit pro-cyclicality does not affect development finance directly. However, developing countries face higher macroeconomic volatility than developed countries, and Basel II, by enhancing pro-cyclicality of credit, would contribute to increased macroeconomic volatility.

2.6   Conclusions

The Brazilian and Indian governments in their efforts to tackle poverty are taking a number of initiatives to provide banking services to larger segments of the country's population, and credit to micro-business. These initiatives are welcome in light of the reduced levels of credit in Brazil and India, and to counteract possible negative effects on credit expansion of the New Capital Accord. But we hold the view that the new regulatory framework for the banking system should be better aligned with the governments' policy aims.

Our assessment is that this is not the case at present. The New Basel rules, as Brazil's and Indian regulators intend to apply in their countries, may have at least two effects that can affect credit to the SMEs and the poor negatively: further banking concentration and banking portfolio concentration away from the SMEs. Moreover, the New Accord may lead to increased credit pro-cyclicality. These possible effects are currently not part of the concern of Brazilian or Indian regulators. But it is important that this be so.

Looking at Basel I as adopted in Brazil and India, it is possible to see that, in the case of Brazil, these rules have contributed to the banking concentration, to a decline in the share of credit in banks' portfolio of assets – and related to that, to a decline in credit as a proportion of total GDP in the ten years since the mid-1990s. In India, there too credit share in banks' total assets declined for a while following adoption of Basel I; moreover, credit to small enterprises has declined relative to total credit.

The effects of Basel I both in Brazil and India thus clearly demonstrate that changes in the regulatory framework for banks can have important effects on the structure of the banking system and on credit patterns. It is therefore important to avoid a repeat of the negative consequences that often accompany the introduction of new banking rules. Particularly at a time when international efforts are being made to reduce poverty worldwide, it is important to raise awareness – and encourage the debate, for the SMEs and the poor on the possible negative implications of the new capital rules which include Basel II – intended to be implemented by many countries around the world between 2007 and 2015. The debate could help create a consensus around measures that could be implemented to address the shortcomings of the new rules; in particular, measures that can help remove or at least reduce their potential bias against credit, especially to the neediest and no less productive segments of the economy.

Notes

1. The countries are: Argentina, Brazil, Chile, Hungary, India, Korea, Malaysia, Slovenia, Thailand, Turkey, and Venezuela.
2. Hussain and Hassan (2005) draw on data from Bankscope, a database of bank information produced by Fitch IBCA and Bureau Van Dijk .
3. A reversal in this trend has been observed since then – see chapter 4 in this book.
4. Of course, banks should also take into account the fact that lending to SMES even if judged riskier leads to portfolio diversification, which is important for overall portfolio risk reduction.

3
Basel Rules in Brazil: What are the Implications for Development Finance?

Ricardo Gottschalk and Cecilia Azevedo Sodré

3.1 Introduction

The main findings from the previous chapter – that adoption of Basel I in Brazil in the mid-1990s contributed in the following ten years to a fall in the share of banks' credit assets in their total assets, and to a declining trend in total credit as a proportion of the country's GDP – are worrisome trends, given that in Brazil total credit as a proportion of GDP is fairly low compared to other countries at similar stages of economic development. The adoption of Basel I in Brazil has probably also contributed to a higher degree of banking concentration. This fact can have negative implications for the provision of credit to the SMEs as the large banks in Brazil have little incentive to cater for this segment of the market.

This chapter builds upon Chapter 2's analysis of the impacts of Basel I on credit in Brazil by discussing in more detail Basel I implementation in the country, and then analysing changes in credit patterns observed in subsequent years. The chapter then reports the views in Brazil about the implementation of the Basel rules in the country. These views are based on interviews conducted by the authors in the second half of 2004.[1] It will be seen that the most worrisome among the findings are that, despite international consensus, the new Basel rules (known as Basel II) may restrict credit to the SMEs. At the time, little thought was given in Brazil to what could be done to mitigate this effect, once new rules came into effect. A negative impact on development finance could happen mainly through further banking concentration and the concentration of banks' credit portfolio away from SMEs and toward big companies. Moreover, little was being done to address a further likely implication – the increase in the pro-cyclicality of bank credit, a concern that has gained renewed attention since the 2007–2009 global financial crisis.

The chapter is organised in six sections. Section 3.2 reports how Basel I was adopted in Brazil, and describes the impact of Basel together with banking reforms on credit levels. Section 3.3 discusses changes in credit patterns between Basel I adoption and 2004, and the countervailing force directed credit played in the period. Section 3.4 describes how Brazil's regulators have planned to introduce Basel II in the country. Section 3.5 discusses how Brazilian banks are preparing themselves for the New Capital Accord. It discusses possible implications of Basel II for development finance, as well as the views and concerns of both the public and private banking sectors on the matter. Section 3.6 concludes the discussion.

3.2   The adoption of Basel I in Brazil

Brazil adhered to Basel I in September 1994 through the Resolution 2099 of Brazil's Central Bank.[2] The resolution established that to appropriately address credit risk, Brazil's financial institutions had to meet a minimum level of capital of 8 per cent in relation to risk-weighted assets. Later in 1997, the 8 per cent limit was raised to 11 per cent,[3] thus higher than the 8 per cent recommended by the Basel Committee. This decision was justified on the grounds that Brazil's financial institutions were subject to higher macroeconomic volatility and shocks than financial institutions based in the rich countries. In addition, the risk weights assigned to different categories of assets were slightly adapted (see Table A.3.1 in Annex). The Central Bank established in addition capital requirements for market and other types of risks, following advice from the original Basel Capital Accord document and subsequent ones that addressed these other types of risks in greater detail.

The reason given for the adoption of Basel I in 1994 was that Brazil's domestic banks were increasingly exposed to the international financial markets, and therefore there was a need to adjust regulation to this new reality. But, in retrospect, it can be said that Basel I in Brazil was part of a bigger package of banking reforms undertaken in the second half of the 1990s and early this century.

The country's compliance with Basel I and the broader restructuring process have dramatically altered the regulatory and financial system landscapes in Brazil. Each of these elements was part of an agenda of reforms that contributed significantly to the improved solidity of the financial system. That is a view broadly shared in Brazil, from top regulators to private and public bank representatives, and financial consultants.

How have the implementation of Basel I, and the reforms more broadly, affected the levels of credit in the country?

Figure 3.1 shows that total credit as a proportion of the country's GDP declined gradually between 1994 and 2002. However, the majority view held in Brazil is that Basel I did not affect the total level of the country's credit, or even credit to the rural sectors, the micro-enterprises or SMEs. The reason provided is that historically credit to the private sector has been very limited in Brazil – around 25 per cent, although it has been higher than that in recent years – and that other factors explain better why this is so. As mentioned in the previous chapter, these include high levels of public financing requirements, which makes government bonds the most important asset held by banks; the country's macro-economic conditions characterised by high levels of interest rates and spreads (which did not come down with the entry of foreign banks in the system), high insolvency levels among private borrowers, the existence of government taxes (what Brazilians call the ' fiscal wedge'), high levels of deposit rates with the Central Bank, and bankruptcy law and a judiciary system that are tilted toward the interests of the debtors.

Although we accept that a number of factors explain why credit has historically been so low in Brazil, the fact is that it declined between 1994 and 2002, and Basel I seems to have played an important role in

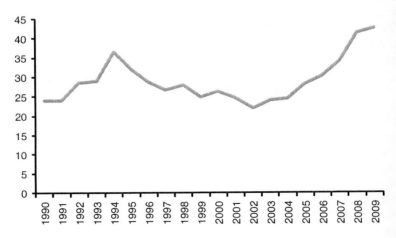

Figure 3.1   Credit in Brazil 1990–2004 as a proportion of total GDP %
Source: Central Bank of Brazil.

that decline, as discussed in Chapter 2. If credit was not even more so affected, this was due to the fact that efforts toward meeting the minimum capital requirements took place mainly through banks' re-capitalisation (see Gottschalk and Sodre, 2007) thereby reducing the need for credit cuts or cuts in the riskier types of credit. As can also be seen from Figure 3.1, since 2003 credit has expanded very rapidly, reaching 42 per cent of Brazil's GDP in 2009. This rapid expansion is independent of Basel I and is explained by a number of factors, including macroeconomic stability and lower interest rates.

As regards credit allocation, it is difficult to judge what happened to credit to SMEs or the poor, due to lack of information. But information about rural credit, is available. It shows that rural credit patterns are strongly determined by directed credit schemes, which has historically been a key government policy instrument to support the rural sector. This policy instrument clearly has countervailed any negative impacts Basel I may have had on rural credit.

The next section discusses in some detail how credit in Brazil was allocated across sectors between the mid-1990s and mid-2000s, and the role directed credit played as a countervailing force.

3.3   Credit allocation across sectors: What impact on the SMEs and the poor?

In the context of overall credit decline between 1995 and 2002, how was total credit distributed across sectors? Which sectors increased their share in total credit, and which sectors lost access to credit?

Tables 3.1, 3.2 and 3.3 show respectively how total, private and public credit is distributed across different sectors of activities, and how distribution shares evolved between 1994 and 2002 – when financial reforms started and Basel I was adopted.

It can be seen from Table 3.1 that the share of total credit from the financial system to the public sector fell dramatically between 1994 and 2002 – from 15 per cent to 4 per cent – while the share of credit flowing to the private sector increased from 85 per cent to per cent 96 per cent over the same period. The decline in the share of credit to the public sector, in the context of overall decline in credit as a percentage of the GDP, can be explained mainly by the reduction of public banks, which were the main lenders to the public sector, which constrained the ability of governments, especially at the sub-national levels, to borrow from the financial system. This happened along with new fiscal rules constraining the state-level governments' capacity to borrow. The latter is evidenced by the fact that lending to the public sector

Table 3.1   Total loans from the financial system – distribution by sectors[a] (as % of total)

	Public Sector	Private Sector						
		Industry	Housing	Rural	Commercial Activities	Individuals	Other Services	Total
1994	15.2	22.4	21.2	9.4	11.4	8.3	12.1	84.8
1995	14.9	23.9	19.8	9.6	13.1	6.5	12.1	85.1
1996	17.9	23.9	19.0	7.5	11.2	8.9	11.6	82.1
1997	9.5	26.0	19.4	8.6	11.2	13.1	12.2	90.5
1998	7.6	26.2	19.6	9.0	9.2	12.6	15.7	92.4
1999	6.1	29.3	18.5	8.9	10.0	13.9	13.3	93.9
2000	3.9	26.8	17.5	8.5	9.9	19.0	14.4	96.1
2001	3.0	29.7	7.2	7.9	10.9	23.3	18.0	97.0
2002	3.6	30.6	6.4	9.2	10.5	21.6	18.2	96.4

[a] December – balance end of period.
Source: Central Bank of Brazil.

Table 3.2   Loans from the private financial system – distribution by sectors[a] (as % of total)

	Public Sector	Private Sector						
		Industry	Housing	Rural	Commercial Activities	Individuals	Other Services	Total
1994	2.0	29.4	12.1	2.9	18.9	13.9	20.8	98.0
1995	3.0	33.4	10.2	2.7	21.9	9.8	19.1	97.0
1996	2.6	34.7	8.8	3.8	19.3	14.5	16.3	97.4
1997	1.8	33.1	7.1	4.5	17.5	20.5	15.6	98.2
1998	1.2	33.2	7.4	4.3	15.1	21.9	16.9	98.8
1999	0.9	34.0	6.4	3.8	15.6	21.0	18.3	99.1
2000	1.0	29.5	5.6	4.5	14.3	25.7	19.4	99.0
2001	0.9	28.9	4.3	4.8	13.2	27.7	20.2	99.1
2002	1.1	28.7	3.6	6.1	13.4	27.0	20.1	98.9

[a] December – balance end of period.
Source: Central Bank of Brazil.

by private banks also declined during the period – see Table 3.2. The decline also reflected the fact that a large number of public enterprises were privatised. The increase in the share of credit to the private sector benefited mostly individuals (e.g., consumer credit, others) and other services (telecommunications, transport, education and culture, press informatics) with their shares in total credit going from 8 per cent to

Table 3.3 Loans from the public financial system – distribution by sectors[a] (as % of total)

	Public Sector	Industry	Housing	Rural	Commercial Activities	Individuals	Other Services	Total
				Private Sector				
1994	25.3	17.0	28.2	14.4	5.6	4.0	5.5	74.7
1995	24.6	16.3	27.6	15.1	6.1	3.9	6.4	75.4
1996	30.1	15.3	27.2	10.4	4.8	4.5	7.7	69.9
1997	16.7	19.4	31.0	12.5	5.3	6.1	9.0	83.3
1998	12.8	20.6	29.4	12.8	4.5	5.1	14.8	87.2
1999	11.1	24.7	30.3	13.9	4.5	7.1	8.5	88.9
2000	7.7	23.3	32.8	13.6	4.3	10.3	8.0	92.3
2001	6.9	31.2	12.6	13.6	6.7	15.0	14.1	93.1
2002	7.6	33.7	10.8	14.2	5.8	12.8	15.1	92.4

[a] December – balance end of period.
Source: Central Bank of Brazil.

22 per cent and 12 per cent to 18 per cent, respectively. Another sector where share in total credit increased was the industrial sector (which may be a statistical effect due to privatisation). Credit to housing, which refers mainly to mortgage lending, fell sharply.

These trends are broadly similar between private and public credit, except that credit from private banks to the industrial sector was maintained at roughly constant levels, while from public banks, credit rose steadily; and credit from private banks to other services was maintained at a constant level, while from public banks, it increased sharply.

It is difficult to say whether the SMEs and the poor benefited or not from these trends. But it is possible to suggest cautiously that the increase in the share of credit to the rural sector and to individuals may have benefited small rural producers, and reached less wealthy individuals. At the same time, commercial activities lost financing from the private banks. More revealing, credit to the industrial sector declined steadily between 1999 and 2002, thus more than reversing an increase observed in the initial period of the analysis. This may have harmed the SMEs. So, it could be said that the redistribution of credit across sectors seems to have been in the form of a slight shift from productive and commercial activities to consumer credit. Thus, a preliminary hypothesis is that, first, Basel I – together with broader financial sector reforms – has affected the level of total credit negatively. Second, the redistribution of credit across sectors may not have discriminated against the less favoured households, though it may have affected the SMEs negatively.

3.3.1   The role of directed credit as a countervailing force

Whilst it is difficult to assert how new credit distribution patterns affected the SMEs and the poor, one clear fact is that the changing patterns closely follow what happened to directed credit in Brazil. This sort of credit accounts for a large part of total credit. In the period between 2000–2002, it averaged 39 per cent; if directed credit to the housing sector is excluded, it stayed around 30 per cent.

As can be seen from Table 3.4, directed credit explains why total credit to the housing sector fell so dramatically between 2000 and 2002, and why rural credit was maintained constant. Also, the Banco Nacional de Desenvolvimento Economico e Social (BNDEs), which figures as the largest development bank in Brazil, accounting for about 20 per cent of total directed credit in the country,[4] may well explain why credit from the public sector to the industrial sector expanded between 2000 and 2002 (see Table 3.3). It is important to notice that the BNDEs traditionally lends to large projects and companies, not the SMEs (although resources it lends through other banks and development agencies may reach the SMEs).

So, where credit may have benefited the SMEs and/or the poor, this was due to directed credit. In the case of SMEs, there is no directed credit in Brazil.[5] In the case of the poor, small rural producers may have benefited from directed rural credit. However, this is hard to gauge, due to lack of available data. Having said that, information on credit by size of credit, which bears some correlation with size of the rural producer, suggests that, at least for 2000–2002, small sized loans increased very sharply, while large sized loans declined (see Table 3.5).

The main message is that directed credit in Brazil is a powerful factor in determining credit patterns in the country, and may have had an important countervailing role in credit decline as a result of financial reforms and Basel I. Moreover, although the credit share by public banks (including development banks) has been drastically reduced, they still

Table 3.4   Directed credit as a proportion of total credit – 2000–2004 (%)

	Housing	Rural	BNDES[a]	Other	Total	Total minus Housing
Dec–2000	15.7	8.5	17.8	2.0	44.0	28.3
Dec–2001	6.4	7.9	19.7	1.6	35.6	29.2
Dec–2002	5.7	9.2	22.4	0.8	38.1	32.3

[a]Includes both direct resources and resources passed to other banks.
Source: Central Bank of Brazil.

Table 3.5 Total and free rural credit, by size of loans[a]

Share of total credit by size of loans %

	I	II	III	IV
2000	0.1	3.3	3.8	92.8
2001	40.9	21.3	7.0	30.8
2002	35.8	25.1	8.9	30.1

[a] Category I, II, III and IV correspond respectively to the ranges 0 to 40.000 Reais; 40.000 to 150.000 Reais; 150.000 to 300.000 Reais; and above 300.000 Reais; for the year 2003, the value 40.000 is increased to 60.000.
Source: Central Bank of Brazil.

seemed to have a crucial role in credit provision for productive urban sectors and rural activities.

3.4   Implementation of the new Basel rules in Brazil

Brazil's regulators established the procedures for implementing Basel II in December 2004. In 2007, the chronogram was updated and lengthened, extending the ending from 2011 to 2012. The new rules are intended to be adopted gradually over a period of 8 years – from 2005 to 2012 (see Table 3.6). During this period, those banks with significant weight in the domestic financial system and with international exposure are to be permitted to adopt the IRB approach (and the advanced IRB approach at the end of the transitional period as well) for credit risk, while the remaining banks must adopt the standardised approach. Contrary to what has been suggested by the Basel Committee, the standardised approach does not draw on external ratings for determining credit risk. It consists of an upgrading of the Basel I approach, through the incorporation of new risk buckets by the Central Bank. Finally, banks have to allocate capital for operational risk, a package component that has been widely debated in Brazil due to the degree of complexity that measuring this type of risk involves.

The Central Bank suggested that, initially, banks should adopt the basic indicator method for measuring operational risk. By the end of 2012, the largest banks will be permitted to adopt the internal models for operational risk. In our judgement, the proposed gradual approach in 2004 and further lengthening in 2007 are appropriate, as well the decision not to utilise the rating agencies for the standardised approach.

Table 3.6   Basel II in Brazil – announced Chronogram for implementation

Period	Measures/Action
Until end of 2005	Review of capital requirements for credit risk under the standardised approach; new capital requirements for those market risks still not covered by current rules; impact studies regarding operational risk
Until end of 2007	Establishment of capital requirement for operational risk.
2008	Eligibility criteria for adoption of internal models for market risk; establishment of the layout of the database for the internal models for credit risk.
2009	Authorisation of the use of internal models for market risk. Eligibility criteria for adoption of internal models for credit risk
2010	Authorisation of the use of the F-IRB approach for credit risk.
2011	Authorisation of the use of the A-IRB approach for credit risk. Eligibility criteria for use of internal models for operational risk.
2012	Authorisation of use of internal models for operational risk.

Source: Central Bank of Brazil (2004 and 2007).

3.5   The views on the new Basel capital accord – Basel II

The main purpose of the New Basel Capital Accord, approved in June 2004, was to further strengthen the soundness and stability of the international banking system, through encouraging banks to improve their risk management practices.

The approach to Basel II as planned by Brazil's authorities and described above is broadly consistent with what Brazil's top regulators had indicated during our interviews on what they would do. First, only the larger banks – in the regulators' words, between 12 and 15 – would be permitted to adopt the IRB approach at some stage, thus following the U.S. approach to Basel II. Second, the standardised approach to be adopted by the majority of banks would be indigenised to better suit Brazil's needs. Third, the basic indicator method whereby capital charge for operational risk should be calculated as a percentage over the banks gross revenues would be adopted – although as we can see, the proposed approach indicates that this would be the case only during the first years, as a timetable exists for the adoption of internal models for measuring operational risk. Finally, all banks, public and private, and regardless of their liability structure or mission, would be subject to Basel II rules.

The phased approach that Brazil's regulators proposed for the adoption of the new regulations looks appropriate for a developing country where banks probably need time, resources and capacity building to be able to adopt Basel II in full. However, the proposed framework lacked any countervailing mechanisms or instruments to address any of the issues outlined in Chapter 2 – issues of banking concentration, portfolio concentration away from SMEs, and increased pro-cyclicality. All these issues have clear macroeconomic, systemic and developmental dimensions, but lacked appropriate acknowledgement by Brazil's regulators.

This begs the question of whether Brazil's regulators, in not addressing the three issues just mentioned, were not excessively focused on micro-prudential risks (e.g., the risk facing individual banks), but not paying sufficient attention to macro risks, such as shocks or large swings in the business cycle, which are common to the whole banking system (Borio, Furfine and Lowe, 2003). Macro risks can be exacerbated by a banking system that has concentrated portfolios and that uses risk models that accentuate credit pro-cyclicality.

It is important to note that the 2007–2009 global financial crisis did not affect Brazilian banks to the extent it has affected developed country based banks. However, that is not to say that the higher degree of solidity found among the former reflects a stronger regulatory framework for banks in Brazil. It is more likely to reflect the fact that Brazilian banks are less developed – and thus less engaged in the international circuits of credit derivatives. Therefore, they are less susceptible to the risks and problems developed country banks suffered in the past couple of years.

3.5.1 Views of the private sector (and academics) and what steps they are taking

A large number of financial market participants were interviewed (both private and public).[6] The questions asked included: how are they preparing themselves for the new framework? Are they considering adopting the IRB approach? What challenges will they face in the process? How do they think Basel II may affect the financial system? What will be the welfare impact?

At the time the interviews were conducted, the private sector saw the adoption of Basel II rules in Brazil as a positive development. It believed it would lead to a strengthened capacity by banks to assess and manage different types of risk and as a result contribute to the solidity of the banking system.

By mid-2004, the largest banks were already taking steps to adopt the internal models to assess credit risk, and to measure operational risk. The three largest private banks – Bradesco, Itaú and Unibanco – had already established Directorships of Risk Management, charged with the developments of both credit and operational risk management models, and specifically in regard to credit risk, their expectation was to be able to adopt the advanced IRB approach.

Like the larger banks, the medium-sized banks expressed interest in adopting internal models for both credit and operational risk, but accepted that whether they would be able to use these models depended on permission granted by the supervisory authorities.

Brazilian banks perceived as a major challenge how best to address operational risk – specifically how to quantify this kind of risk, and the necessary capital required to protect against it. Although a good deal of loss arising from operational risk is clearly identified by banks – losses associated with labour, civil litigation, and fraud – a whole universe of unidentifiable losses still exists, making their measurement very difficult.

3.5.2   Views of the Public Banks and what steps they are taking

A good number of Brazilian banks still remained public by the mid-2000s, despite the banking restructuring and banking privatisation in the preceding years. These were mainly federal banks with large retail base and development banks, although a few state-level banks still existed.[7] All of them were taking steps to be prepared for the new capital rules. Like the private banks, the largest retail public banks held a favourable view of Basel II, and believed that these rules could be adopted in Brazil in its entirety to the benefit of the financial system. The new instruments of risk and managerial controls and increased transparency were seen as positive developments, among other reasons because they could contribute to reduced political influence on lending decisions and thereby to greater efficiency.

But a number of medium-sized and development banks held a more cautious position. Whilst acknowledging certain benefits, such as the strengthening of a risk management culture, they pointed to the operational difficulties in implementing Basel II, the high costs involved especially for the smaller banks, the potential conflict between new supervisory control on managerial practices and the social purpose of certain lending programmes, and the impact of capital requirement for operational risks on the cost and level of credit. Moreover, they acknowledged the fact that the new rules may constrain credit to the group of borrowers perceived as of higher risk, which typically are the small businesses. Therefore, a much higher degree of heterogeneity of views was found among public banks than among private banks, and within the former group this reflected a divide along the lines of size and nature of the banking activity.

Banco do Brasil (BB), which until the merging of the second and the third largest banks, were the largest bank in the country, took a favourable view of Basel II, and was seen as leading the process in developing internal risk assessment models both for credit and operational risk. Regarding credit risk, they claimed to be, at that point in time, at a considerably advanced stage in developing a model. They were also investing considerable amount of resources in developing a VAR model to measure operational risk, and in preparing the database, expected to have a 5-year period coverage by 2007.

Other banks were also taking steps to be prepared for Basel II. The public banks at the state level were improving the managerial practices of their credit portfolios, through upgrading their credit risk assessment models and pursuing modelling design for operational risk. They intended to adopt internal risk models in the future and were hoping to have them fully developed and tested by 2007. Other banks had only created risk departments short before the interviews were conducted, and therefore were running behind other banks in developing risk assessment models, particularly for operational risk, and in building the required data base, admittedly a task of great complexity, especially for medium-sized and small banks, which face high fixed costs in relation to the scale of their operations.

The public federal banks other than the BB – Caixa Economica, Banco da Amazonia (Basa), Banco do Nordeste do Brasil (BNB), were also attempting to improve their risk assessment systems, and intended to adopt internal models for credit and operational risk assessment. Given their limited internal capacity, they were working on these areas with the assistance of external consultancies. But even with external help, they pointed to the difficulties they were facing in taking these steps. A particular difficulty relates to how to map and quantify operational risk, and especially how to disentangle operational risks from other types of risk, including credit risk. Some institutions also feared the risk of investing in the development of internal models for risk assessment, but not having them validated by the Central Bank.

Both groups of banks – federal and state-level ones – shared a number of concerns. In addition to their difficulties in developing and putting in practice new risk assessment models, and the costs that these tasks involve, especially for the smaller banks, they raised a number of other pertinent points.

First, they believed the use of internal risk models would imply less capital requirement, and that if they ended up not adopting these models they would find themselves at disadvantage in relation to those banks adopting them, as it would imply allocating higher levels of capital and therefore higher costs. A study by Carneiro, Vivan and Krause (2004) based on simulations for Brazil, shows that the use of the IRB approach by banks would, for the majority of banks, imply a reduction in capital requirements between 0 per cent and 40 per cent. For a few banks, the needs would be reduced even more, by up to 82 per cent. This indicates that the risk envisaged here, of a few banks gaining substantial competitive advantage through use of the IRB approach, is very real.

Second, banks were worried that the capital requirement for operational risk, by increasing the banks' total capital requirement, would lead to higher costs, which are likely to be reflected in more expensive credit. The larger banks might be permitted to adopt the most advanced model at some point, which requires less capital. But the smaller banks would have little alternative but to adopt the basic indicator method (i.e., capital required corresponding to 15 per cent of banks' gross revenues) and therefore would face higher capital requirements, both in absolute terms and relative to other banks adopting a more advanced method. There were therefore two problems arising from the need to allocate capital for operational risk: 1) overall higher level of capital requirements with banks facing higher costs as a result,[8] and 2) the competitive effect affecting negatively those banks adopting the simplest approach.

Third, some of these banks (especially the retail ones at the state level) believed they had a relatively homogeneous portfolio of clients to which credit extension is in many cases consigned, which reduce the credit risk they face. Their risk controls may not be among the most sophisticated ones, but were deemed as sufficient in light of their customer profile. However, to the extent they attempted to expand their client base to include clients with different and riskier profiles, they fear that the new risk control systems would inhibit this process from taking off. That is, the system would delimit the sorts of products offered by the bank and therefore affect its business activities. There would thus be a heightened conflict between different areas of the bank. This indicates that elements of Pillar 2, such as stricter supervisory controls and monitoring, are likely to restrain credit expansion policies. (In relation to Pillar 3, banks pointed out that there was a need to clarify better what sort of information needs to be disclosed, and within that, to clearly separate strategic information and information that can be made available to the markets. The underlying concern was that excessive information disclosure might be harmful to banks and the system as a whole.)

Fourth, public banks have a social mission. In line with that, many of their lending programmes derive from Federal and State level social policies. But the new Basel rules are likely to exacerbate the tension between profit maximising and social objectives, as the latter should be expected to involve activities deemed as of higher risk. As it is put in a IADB report, '[p]ressures for profitability may induce public bank managers to deviate from their social mandate and mimic private banks in their credit allocation criteria' (IADB, 2005, p. 144, footnote 8, based on De La Torre, 2002). Moreover, the new rules may also constrain the ability of public banks to play a counter-cyclical role, when needed.[9]

A final point that relates closely to the previous one is that development banks, such as the BNDES, Basa, BNB and BDMG, believed they should be given a differentiated treatment. They recognised that the restructuring process involving cleaning and recapitalisation in previous years provided public banks with conditions to compete with private banks on an equal basis, but they firmly believed there was a need to recognise the specific features of development banks, such as their distinct liability structure and their development financing role. Accordingly, it would be important to make the Basel rules more flexible to this group of banks. That could include a lower capital adequacy requirement, whose minimum level in Brazil is higher at 11per cent compared with the 8 per cent determined by the Basel Committee for the G-10. The BNDES went further to propose that the bank should not be subject to the new Accord, partly due to its liability structure based on compulsory savings, partly because its lending operations consisted in large measure of passing resources on to other financial institutions (banks and development agencies) which are the ones that ultimately bear the risk.

The banks management believed that there was a lack of debate in the country on a number of important issues, such as the need for differentiated treatment across the banking system, and the impact of Basel I on the system and on credit provision in particular. There was a feeling that Brazil's regulators missed the opportunity to raise these issues more forcefully in international fora and with the Basel Committee. There was a debate of some of these issues domestically within the Febraban (Federation of Brazilian Banks), as well as at national and international fora, but it was limited. It was therefore felt that more needed to be done.

Thus, the views between the private sector and public banks on the potential benefits but especially costs of Basel II diverged fairly significantly. This divergence reflected their differences in terms of size, capacity to adopt more advanced risk assessment approaches, and their nature and purpose. But a particular concern that emerged very strongly and that reflected public banks' social concerns was that credit can be affected by Basel II rules through a variety of mechanisms.

3.6   Conclusions

This chapter has discussed in some detail how Basel I was adopted in Brazil, and described the changes in credit patterns following Basel adoption. It then discussed how Brazilian regulators planned to adopt Basel II in the country, and reported the views and concerns of different stakeholders in Brazil on the subject. The chapter first finds that credit patterns in Brazil following Basel I adoption and bank reforms were strongly influenced by directed credit and the preservation in Brazil of public and development banks.

Thus, from the analysis of credit patterns, it is possible to affirm that financial reforms and Basel I did not have a major impact on credit allocation in ways that harmed the poor or the SMEs – at least not in a major way – due to the maintenance of two key institutional factors that have historically strongly featured in Brazil's financial system: large public and development banks, and directed credit. Whilst the presence of public banks in Brazil has been downscaled, directed credit remains an important instrument for credit promotion and allocation toward the less favoured segments of the economy.

This is so much the case that, in the early 2000s, the Brazilian government undertook a number of initiatives in support of micro-business and the poor in Brazil, such as creating a number of mechanisms that include directed credit to individuals and micro-business. However, scepticism was raised at the time as to whether private banks would really use this type of directed credit as a starting point to penetrate the SMEs market, or whether they would simply deposit the resources with the Central Bank. The question thus still remains as to how to make mainstream lending more widespread across income groups, and how to ensure that the new regulatory framework for capital adequacy does not work as a limiting force to the expansion of credit in Brazil, especially to the SMEs and the poor.

Regarding the views of Brazilians on the Basel capital accords, whilst their views are, on the whole, that these accords have positive elements, this assessment is tempered by some sectors of the banking community in Brazil. Whilst recognising concrete benefits stemming from Basel I, such as the development of a credit risk assessment culture, some bankers from the public sector warn that the specific Basel rule on capital requirement is likely to affect public institutions' lending capacity. In the specific case of development banks, some argue that these banks should not be subject to the Basel capital requirements, since their liability structure is based on compulsory savings, not bank deposits, and that compliance with Basel is therefore not only unnecessary but counter-productive. Its implementation has the (admittedly unintended) effect of restricting these banks' capacity to support financing for developmental projects, which are at the heart of their mission. For this reason, in their view the homogeneous treatment given across private and public banks that differ in their liability structures and purposes should be reviewed.

Specifically in regard to Basel II, a number of concerns were raised by bankers from public banks, including: banks using the standardised approach would find themselves at competitive disadvantage in relation to banks adopting the internal risk models; the use of the standardised model would not offer capital relief as would the internal risk models, seen as important to offset the need for more capital with the introduction of capital requirements for operational risk; new risk control systems could delimit the sort of products banks may be able to offer to expand their markets; and that a tension was likely to increase between risk and social objectives public banks are expected to pursue. Thus, what emerges from this chapter and in particular from the views of those directly involved in the banking industry in Brazil, is the need to adapt Basel II to incorporate social and developmental concerns.

Appendix 3.1

Table A.3.1   Basel I in Brazil: Risk weights for different categories of assets

Weight (%)	Loans to/Investment in
0	• Brazil Central Government's bonds • Foreign currencies deposited with the Central Bank • Compulsory deposits with the Central Bank
20	• Bank deposits in other banks • Gold • Deposits and credits in foreign currencies • Tax related credits (then raised to 300 per cent in August 1999, through Circular no. 2916).

Continued

Table A.3.1   Continued

Weight (%)	Loans to/Investment in
50	• Government bonds outside the Central Government • Inter-bank deposits with own resources • Foreign currencies abroad • Mortgages
100	• Private bonds with own resources • Investments in variable income assets • Investments in commodities • Operations linked to stock exchanges and future markets • Exchange operations • Diverse credits

Source: Annex IV, Resolution No. 2.099 of 17/08/1994. Available at: www.bcb.gov.br

Notes

The authors thank Gerson Romantini for his valuable comments and inputs into this chapter.

1. The interviews were conducted as part of a DFID-funded project on 'Codes and Standards of International Best Practice and Development Finance'.
2. Central Bank of Brazil (1994).
3. Specifically, in June 1997 the minimum capital level was raised to 10 per cent (Central Bank of Brazil, 1997a) and later in November of the same year, to 11 per cent (Central Bank of Brazil, 1997b).
4. This includes both direct resources provided by the BNDEs and those resources the bank distributes via other banks.
5. It should be noted that, in 2003 directed credit to micro-businesses was implemented, which may from then on have reached small business, through credit to individuals.
6. Most interviews were conducted in July and August 2004.
7. This picture has not changed much since then, as Brazil had at the time the left-leaning Lula's government, which won a second mandate for the period 2007–2010. This government has never shown an appetite to carry on with the privatisation process, initiated by the previous administrations.
8. It has been noted that banks adopting the IRB approach for credit risk could end up requiring less capital for this type of risk, thus offsetting the added capital for operational risk. But banks adopting the standardised approach would not be able to generate this balancing effect – see IADB (2005, chapter 16).
9. This point has been made mainly by academics. Moreover, an IADB study presents evidence that public banks in Latin America are less pro-cyclical than private banks in extending credit (IADB, 2005, p. 23 and chapter 11).

4
Basel Norms on Capital Adequacy, the Banking Sector and Impact on Credit for SMEs and the Poor in India

Sunanda Sen and Soumya Ghosh

4.1 Introduction: The context and a summary of the arguments

The new Basel norms for capital adequacy have been drawing a lot of attention in India, not just in banking circles but also among the general public and the media. Much of this revived interest is due to the changes with the introduction of Basel II. In this environment, one observes an over-emphasis on financial stability as a goal in itself, even when it goes contrary to distributional norms as well as growth potentials of the economy, which are no less relevant.[1]

The history of the Basel Core Principles relating to minimum capital adequacy for banks goes back to 1988 with the developed countries' initiative to protect the Organisation for Economic Cooperation and Development (OECD) banks from the financial crises common during the 1980s. The capital adequacy norms were to protect the depositors' money by raising capital from the market up to at least eight per cent of the risk-weighted bank assets. The assets, consisting of advances and securities, were attributed a three-tiered credit-risk ranging from zero to 100 per cent. Generally, government-held debt (securities) carried a zero risk while bank borrowings and other loans were respectively at 20 per cent and 100 per cent risk categories.

With securities overpowering the global market for bank credits by the 1990s, the notion of risk was no longer confined to credit alone. Risk today includes the possibilities of capital losses due to movements in prices or interest rates or even exchange rates in the market, in addition to operational risks.

To counter the potential risks associated with market volatility, a group consisting of central bank governors and the heads of bank supervisory authorities of a group of ten (G10) countries arrived at a consensus on the International Convergence of Capital Measurement and Capital Standards in 2004. Popularly called as Basel II, the new capital rules framework sets out the details for adopting more risk-sensitive models for minimum capital requirements for banking organisations. The norms of Basel II is currently being implemented in the banking industry. As at the moment while Basel I had been impacting the bank balance sheets in India since the late 1990s, Basel II is on way to be implemented and this may further change the composition of bank portfolio with further effects on the sectoral deployment of credit. Although not mandatory for non Basel II countries including India, the majority of them expressed the intention of implementing Basel II.

In the new model of risk-weighted capital adequacy for banks, the risk-weight of bank assets is judged either by an external agency through the standardised approach (SA) or by banks themselves through an internal rating based (IRB) model. The New Basel rules thus aim to bring in financial discipline for banks and greater degree of financial stability.

The Indian monetary authorities, as in many other developing countries, have made efforts to comply more broadly with the Basel Core Principles since the early and mid-1990s. The Scheduled Commercial Banks (SCBs) in the country experienced, as a direct consequence, a noticeable drop in their non-performing assets (NPAs) between 1997–98 and 2003–04. There was even an absolute decline in these NPAs during the 2003–04 financial year. Encouraged by these results, from 2004 onwards the Reserve Bank of India (RBI) as well as the major commercial banks in the country have started to prepare a road map for Basel II which is more comprehensive than Basel I in that it covers a number of important areas of the Basel Core Principles, and not just capital requirements as was the case with Basel I.

In retrospect, the improvement in the NPA performance of banks can be related to several developments, including a demonstrated preference on the part of the SCBs to hold risk-free government securities far in excess of the stipulated Statutory Liquidity Requirements (SLRs). Holding the risk-free government securities enabled banks to meet more easily the capital adequacy requirements while providing opportunities for reaping trading gains with declining yields and rising prices of government bonds in a soft-interest rate regime.

The improved NPA of banks was also made possible by the higher provisioning, as warranted by the RBI's new prudential rules. With the switchover from the earlier 180–day to the 90–day NPA norms by the RBI in accordance with international practice, the SCBs raised provisions towards NPAs by as much as 40 per cent in 2003–04. By the end of 2003–04, the cumulative provisions of the SCBs accounted for 56.6 per cent of the gross NPA.

However, the Basel norms and more generally the prudential rules for the banking system, have implications that go far beyond the performance criteria of banks, such as the reduced NPAs. One needs to look at the changes in the composition of bank assets, which have a strong bearing on the distribution of bank credit. A key example discussed in this chapter is the priority sector credit to the small-scale industries (SSI). Lately, this type of credit has declined as a percentage of total priority sector credit, as more than two-fifths of the priority sector credit has been offered to cover the 'other segments.' These segments typically comprise small business, retail trade, small transport operators, professional and self-employed persons, housing, education loans, micro credit, housing, and so on. Between 2000 and 2008, the percentage loans to SSI sector in total priority sector fell from 36 per cent to 21 per cent. However, judged by the relative size of the net NPAs on net advances, it is not correct to say that loans to SSIs have been less creditworthy as compared to other priority and non-priority sector loans.

According to the Third Census of Small industries, shortage of working capital remains a major factor behind weaknesses in the SSI sector. Much of the so-called risk-aversion of banks with regard to loans to the small and medium industries have their origin in the quick adoption of the Basel-approved credit risk adjusted ratios (CRAR) for capital. Implementing Basel II will further accentuate the ongoing trend by moving credit away from the deserving industrial units in the small sector. We can mention here the basic fact that employment generated by the organised sector of the manufacturing industry is only 14 per cent compared with 86 per cent by the unorganised sector of which small and medium enterprises remain the major component. Moreover, small and medium enterprises, which include the SSIs, currently contribute 40 per cent of the total industrial production and over 34 per cent of national exports for the country. In contrast, labour intensity of output in the organised big industries is alarmingly in the downtrend, as a result of technological upgrading and the adoption of labour market flexibility.

One thus observes, with serious concern, the limitations of the guiding principle of the Basel norms for the banking sector in a country like

India, where credit needs to be re-directed to units which are deserving, not only in terms of productive contribution but also in terms of social priorities.

The present chapter is an attempt to review the impact of Basel I and II norms on credit flows to the SMEs and the poor in India. But it takes a broader focus by also discussing the parallel process of financial system reforms in India and compliance with the Basel Core Principles and changes in credit patterns, some of which are related to the Basel norms. The chapter then reports what steps the Reserve Bank of India is undertaking in relation of Basel II, and presents the views of different financial market participants on the possible impacts and challenges in connection with the implementation of the Basel norms in India. These views were gathered by the chapter authors in a series of interviews conducted in late 2004, thus after the approval of Basel II in June the same year.

Following this introduction, Section 4.2 discusses the changing structure of the banking system in India, the impacts on assets and liabilities, and aspects of the banking reform related to adherence to the capital adequacy ratio under Basel I. Section 4.3 discusses Priority Sector lending in India, in light of the banking sector reforms and implementation of Basel I. Section 4.4 discusses the challenges and concerns related to Basel II implementation, including possible implications for credit to the SMEs and the poor, as seen by different Indian stakeholders. Section 4.5 concludes with an overall assessment of the prudential norms in India

4.2   The Changing structure of the banking industry in India: The transition from regulation to liberalisation

4.2.1   The transition

Indian banks prior to 1991 functioned in a tightly regulated and controlled environment, with an administered interest rate structure, quantitative restrictions on credit flows, high reserve requirements and the channelling of a significant proportion of lendable resources towards the 'priority' and government sectors.

To evaluate the problems of the banking industry, the Government of India set up in 1991 a Committee on Financial Systems, under the chairmanship of N. Narasimham. The Committee Report, submitted towards the end of 1991, contained far-reaching recommendations for reforms in the banking sector, providing important inputs to the overall economic reforms of the 1990s. The main features of these bank-related reforms in 1991 included the following:

- Introduction of stricter income recognition and asset classification norms;
- Introduction of higher capital adequacy requirements;
- Introduction of higher disclosure standards in financial reporting;
- Introduction of phased deregulation of interest rates;
- Lowering of statutory liquidity ratio (SLR) and cash-reserve ratio (CRR) requirements.

A second banking reform committee, set up under Narasimham again, recommended in 1998 a further tightening of the capital adequacy norms for the banking system. In addition to capital adequacy ratio (CAR) requirements, other measures included:

A risk weight of 20 per cent for investment in government guaranteed securities issued by Public Sector Undertakings (PSUs);
- 20 per cent risk weight on State Government guaranteed advances, which remained in default as on March 31, 2000, and 100 per cent weight in the case of continued default after March 31, 2001;
- Risk weight of 2.5 per cent to account for market risk for Government and approved securities;
- 100 per cent risk weight on the foreign exchange open position limit.

From 1992 onwards, the interest rate structure was progressively deregulated. The rates were gradually freed, and at present, the interest rate on term deposits has been completely deregulated. The only administered interest rate that remains is on savings deposits, with a prescribed interest rate at 3.5 per cent per annum.

As for loans and advances, between 1988–89 and 1994–95, the RBI switched backwards and forwards, from a ceiling rate at 16.5 per cent to a maximum lending rate, initially fixed at 16 per cent, later increased to 19 per cent in 1991–92, but, subsequently lowered again to 14 per cent in 1993–94.

It is relevant here to point out that rates on priority lending were set more freely after 1992. Thus, lending rates on loans exceeding Rs. 0.2 million were freed in October 1994. In April 1998, rates on loans under Rs. 0.2 million were also freed provided they did not exceed the Prime Lending Rate (PLR) of the banks.

Another major reform measure, largely in a bid to augment liquidity in the system, has been the gradual reductions in the Cash Reserve Ratio (CRR) and the Statutory Liquidity Ratios (SLR) requirements. However, while the reduction in CRR has resulted in an increase in investible funds with the banking system, the impact on advances in general to the small sector and the poor in particular, has remained limited.

In terms of banking structure, a more competitive environment has been created and banks today not only compete within the industry but also with players outside the banking industry. While existing banks have been allowed greater flexibility to expand their operations, new private sector banks are allowed entry, and have already gained a significant presence in the financial sector.

As part of the reforms, the government has allowed equity dilution in nationalised banks, but it has not ceded management control. Equity dilution has largely been a capital raising exercise, without greater non-governmental shareholder supervision.

With the enactment of the Insurance Regulatory and Development Authority (IRDA) Act of 1999, banks and Non Banking Finance Companies (NBFCs) have been permitted to enter insurance business, thus permitting new forms of non-banking income.

The facts presented above on the restructured pattern of the bank balance sheets in India indicate the following:

- Indian banks have been able to improve their CAR ratio, but this may have resulted in a much faster growth in investment in government securities as compared to growth in advances.
- Banks in India today can venture out to non-bank operations like insurance and the security-related transactions, which provide them with non-bank sources of income.
- Intensified competition in the banking sector has encouraged banks to obtain these alternate sources of income.
- Finally, the options to invest in risk-free government securities on the one hand and to fix interest rates on advances including the small ones on the other hand are factors which may have affected the volume as well as the terms of credit to those who are only marginally bankable like the poor and the SMEs.

4.2.2   Changing structure of the banking industry in India: What impacts on assets and liabilities?

An overview of the changing structure of the banking sector in India demands a sketch of the credit market structure in the country.

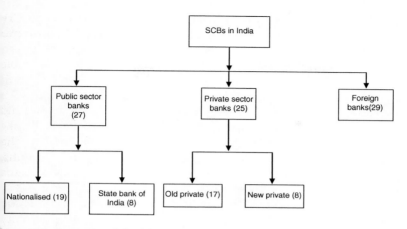

Figure 4.1 Structure of the SCBs as on FY2008

Source: RBI Report on Trends & Progress of Banking in India [various years].

In India, given the relatively underdeveloped capital market and the limited internal resources that corporate entities can plough back, the latter rely, to a large extent, on financial intermediaries to meet a large portion of their financial requirements. The major institutional intermediaries in India include banks and non-bank financial institutions (that is, developmental financial institutions or DFIs), other financial institutions (FIs), and non-banking finance companies (NBFCs). The non-institutional or unorganised sources of credit include indigenous bankers and moneylenders, information on which is limited. As for the term structure of credit, while banks and NBFCs predominantly cater for short-term needs, DFIs provide mostly medium and long-term funds. However, the role of DFIs has been shrinking, which has constrained the ability of the financial system to provide long-term and development finance to the economy.

Banks in India can broadly be classified as scheduled commercial banks or SCBs, regional rural banks or RRBs, development banks and co-operative banks. These banks can be grouped into the following four categories:

Public sector banks or PSBs, which include the State Bank of India (SBI) and its associates, and other nationalised banks.

Private sector banks (old and new).

Development banks of different vintage, including the Industrial Development Bank of India (IDBI), Industrial Finance Corporation

(IFC), Industrial Credit and Investment Corporation of India (ICICI), Small Industries Development Bank of India (SIDBI) and Co-operative Banks.
- Foreign controlled banks.

At the end of FY2008, the SCBs had a network of 61,129 branches, with total assets worth Rs. 43265 billion, thus making them the most active and dominant financial intermediaries in the country (See Figure 4.1 on the structure of SCBs in 2008). In this section we will concentrate on SCBs only.

Over the last few years, the banking industry has witnessed significant drop in concentration, largely due to the presence of new domestic private and foreign controlled banks.

Trends in the structure of the banking industry thus can be described as follows:

- A declining concentration in the banking industry with major players (top 5 or 10) controlling a smaller proportion of assets held by the SCBs as a whole.
- A gradual but steady erosion of public sector/nationalised banks in terms of their presence in the deposit market.
- SBI and its associates continuing as major players in the asset market, in possession of more than 1/4th of bank assets. However, the SBI and associates have the capacity to extend branch business with tendencies for centralising credit creation within this group.
- New private banks in a position to attract business, often at cost of other nationalised as well as old private banks.

These trends can have a great deal of significance in terms of the access of bank credit for the SMEs and the poor, as will be pointed out later in this chapter.

4.2.3   Aspects of banking sector reforms with special reference the Capital Adequacy Ratio (CAR)

The CAR provides a means to monitor the financial solvency of banks. The minimum CAR was raised to 9 per cent on March 31, 2000, in response to the recommendations of the 1998 Narasimham Committee Report. However, the overall CAR of SCBs in India has improved even more than the stipulated norms, going up from 10.4 per cent during FY1997 to 13.0 per cent during the FY2008. The CAR of PSBs improved from 10 per cent during FY1997 to 12.5 during FY2008.[2]

Table 4.1 shows the level of CARs across different categories of banks between 2002 and 2008.

Table 4.1   Level of CAR (Number of banks)

	FY2002			FY2004			FY2008		
	4% but less than 9%	Between 9%–10%	Above 10%	4% but less than 9%	Between 9%–10%	Above 10%	4% but less than 9%	Between 9%–10%	Above 10%
State bank group	None	None	8	None	None	8	None	None	8
Nationalized banks	2	2	15	None	None	18	None	None	19
Old private	None	2	19	None	1	20	None	1	17
New private	1	1	6	1	None	8	None	None	8
Foreign	None	2	33	None	None	33	None	1	29
Total	3	7	81	1	1	87	None	2	81

Source: RBI Report on Trends & Progress in Banking, various issues.

The CAR for the PSBs has increased partly because of capital infusions by the government and equity capital through the capital market. By FY2003, the government had already injected Rs. 230 billion towards re-capitalisation of 19 nationalised banks. Some banks had to resort to repeated doses of capital infusion to achieve the capital adequacy requirements, and also to provide for loan loss provisioning.

As pointed out earlier, the government's ownership of the PSBs has been gradually diluted with several PSBs making public offerings of their equity shares. PSBs were first able to raise capital in the domestic equity markets in the early 1990s, with the SBI as the first PSB to raise resources through an initial public offering (IPO) in December 1993. In the following years as many as 16 PSBs raised Rs. 82 billion through public issues between 1993 and 2004. The pressure on banks for accessing the capital markets is expected to accelerate as government funding for recapitalisation tapers off over the coming years, as well as because of the Basel implementation.[3]

A major impact of the tightened CAR requirements in India (which was consistent with financial liberalisation and the implementation of Basel norms) has been that banks, and especially the PSBs, have increased their investments in government securities far in excess of their SLR requirements. In the mid-2000s, it was estimated that the banks were holding 42 per cent of the net demand and time liabilities in government securities, against the statutory 25 per cent requirement.

Investments in government securities are expected to benefit banks in the following manner: First, the CAR requirement against government securities is either nil or very low as compared to other assets. Second, while the return on these investments is generally low, these assets are virtually risk-free, thus having very little chances of creating NPAs. Thus, government securities provide banks with a steady source of risk-free income while dispensing the need to provide for capital adequacy or provisioning. These investments also do not entail priority sector commitments, whereby a PSB has to set aside 40 per cent of its advances as loans for the priority sector. Finally, in the soft interest rate regime of the previous decade, banks stood to gain with appreciated values of these assets.

Banks naturally prefer to lend to the government at market-determined rates rather than to make loans to the private corporate sector (and even less to the small borrowers), which are considered as risky (especially in terms of Basel II). Even strong SCBs have voluntarily invested in excess of SLR requirements. This was a bid to minimise credit risk while increasing profitability and also to avoid priority lending. Furthermore, a fall in interest rates results in an increase in prices of government securities. In years of declining interest rates, the SCBs significantly increased their profitability by investing in government securities.

Between 2004 and 2008, the trend was reversed, as the growth rate of loans and advances increased at a significant rate as compared with that of the pre-2004 period, while banks' investments in Government securities slowed down considerably. However, as we will see later, a significant portion of these incremental loans and advances were made to the retail sector, in particular housing, education and consumer loans. The increase in loans to the housing sector is also reflected in higher priority sector target achievement on an overall basis (since housing loans up to a threshold limit of Rs 10 lakhs is categorised as priority sector). These trends are consistent with the changing asset profile of the SCBs, as shown in Table 4.2.

Summing up the impact of the recent prudential reforms relating to Indian banks, one can offer the following observations:

- A noticeable improvement in the CAR, which far exceeds the 9 per cent norm.
- A large part of this rise in CAR was, however, contributed by capitalisation on part of the government in the initial years; in particular, the weak banks received substantial financial support from the government.

Table 4.2 Asset profile of scheduled commercial banks(%)

% of total assets	FY2008	FY2007	FY2004	FY2003	FY2002
Cash and bank balances with RBI	7.5	5.6	5.7	5.1	5.7
Balances with banks and call money	2.6	4.6	4.2	4.4	7.7
Investments of which	27.2	27.5	40.6	40.8	38.2
Government securities	21.4	21.8	32.4	31.6	27.9
Total Advances	57.3	57.3	43.8	43.5	42.1
Fixed assets	1.0	0.9	1.1	1.2	1.3
Other assets	4.6	4.1	4.7	5.0	5.0

Source: RBI Report on Trends & Progress in Banking, various issues.

• The asset composition of banks was heavily weighed in favour of government securities pre 2004, as investment in these assets enables banks to meet the CAR and avoid the priority credit stipulations. Holding of government securities also fetched capital gains under the low interest regime of the previous two decades. However, post 2004, the investments in government securities have declined significantly, with lending outstripping these investments. It may be noted that with the onset of the global turmoil in 2008, banks have again started to invest in government securities.

4.3   Priority sector lending and credit to the SMEs

Looking at the history of priority lending in India, no specific target was fixed during the initial years of bank nationalisation. Banks were for the first time advised in November 1974 to raise the proportion of priority sector credit to one-third of aggregate advances by March 1979. In March 1980 the target, to be achieved by March 1985, was revised upwards to 40 per cent, which has been maintained since then.

A major consequence of the banking sector reforms has been the changing norms relating to priority sector credit. These were reinforced by the implementation of the Basel norms, with Basel I having had an impact on banks' balance sheets in India since the early 1990s.

Beginning in the 1990s, the 40 per cent priority sector lending requirement for net bank credit (NBC) continued but its burden on banks was sought to be eased by freeing the interest rates on loans above Rs. 0.2 million, raising the rates on small loans and making additional types of credit available. For foreign banks the priority sector credit requirement was increased to 32 per cent in 1993. As of end-FY2004, all the bank groups seem to have met their priority sector lending targets. However, fulfilling the 40 per cent target of priority credit does not necessarily ensure that these are directed to those sectors that are cash–starved most.

For instance, no target is set for lending to the small sector industry (SSI) other than it being a residual after other priority credit targets are met. Specifically, advances to agriculture and to weaker sections are set respectively at 18 per cent and 10 per cent of NBC, which effectively leaves 12 per cent as a residual for SSIs. Sub-sectoral targets for tiny and other units of SSIs are, however, set at specified percentages of SSI advances from PSBs. It is not clear on what basis these allocations are made. For foreign banks, advances to the SSIs and to the export units are respectively set at 10 per cent and 12 per cent of their NBC – see Table 4.3.

Despite the specified targets for SCBs as a whole (public, private and foreign), the actual disposal of priority credit has declined as a percentage of NBC over the years. Moreover, the 9 per cent CAR norm of Basel I implemented from FY2000 onwards seems to have had an impact on the flow of credit to the SMEs. For instance, from FY2000 onwards there has been a steady decline in SME credit as a percentage of NBC by the public and private banks as indicated below in Table 4.4.

The priority sector norms were revised in April 2007. According to these, the priority sector definition was to include not only sectors that impact large sections of the population (e.g., the weaker sections and sectors which are employment-intensive such as agriculture, and tiny and small enterprises) but also retail trade in essential commodities, consumer cooperatives stores, micro credit, education loans and housing.

As regards the SCBs, while there is no specific target for lending to the SSI, even the sub-targets are not met. As Table 4.5 shows, the percentage of lending to the tiny segment of SSIs as a percentage of total sums lent to the SSIs fluctuated between 42.3 per cent and 11.7 per cent between FY 2001 to FY2004 (FY2000 is taken as the cut-off point as the CAR of 9 per cent norm was made applicable from this year only).

In general, the percentage share of loans to the SSI sector in total priority sector loans has been significantly squeezed over the years – see Figure 4.2. One possible reason for this may be the fact that loans to other priority sectors (for instance housing loan up to Rs 10 lakh) has witnessed a steep jump over FY2000–2008.

Table 4.3 Targets and sub-targets under priority sector lending

Categories of advances	SCBs (excluding Regional Rural and Foreign banks)*	Foreign banks in India**	Regional Rural banks (RRB)	Co-operative Banks
Aggregate advances to priority sector	40% of NBC	32% of NBC	40% of outstanding advances	60%
Of which Agricultural advances	18%	No Target	No Target	
Indirect	Should not exceed 4.5% of NBC*	No Target	No Target	
Of which SSI advances		Not less than 10% of NBC	No Target	
Tiny (investment < Rs 0.5 mn)	40% of total credit to SSI	No Target	No Target	
SSI (> 0.5 mn < 2.5 mn)	20% of total credit to SSI	No Target	No Target	
Other (>2.5mn)	40% of total credit to SSI	No Target	No Target	
Export credit		Not less than 12% of NBC	No Target	
Of which Advances to weaker sections	10% of NBC	No Target	10% of outstanding advances	25%
Advances under differential rate of interest / DRI	1% of previous year's NBC	No Target	No Target	
Scheduled Caste/Tribe	40% of total advances under DRI			
Through rural and semi urban	66 2/3% of DRI			

Note: *Advances in excess of 4.5 per cent are not counted as 18 per cent earmarked as agricultural advances. Banks having shortfall in lending to agriculture are allocated amounts for contribution to Rural Infrastructure Development Fund / RIDF established in NABARD. Shortfall in any target to be made good by depositing with SIDBI.

Source: RBI guidelines on priority sector lending.

Table 4.4   Share of SME in total credit by SCBs

	SBI & associates	Nationalised banks	Private banks	Foreign banks
FY2000	10.0	8.6	7.6	1.6
FY2001	9.1	7.4	6.5	2.4
FY2002	7.1	6.3	4.1	1.5
FY2003	6.3	7.1	3.3	1.4
FY2004	5.6	6.3	2.4	1.1
FY2005	5.8	5.4	2.2	2.8
FY2006	5.5	4.8	1.8	1.4
FY2007	5.0	4.6	2.3	1.2

Source: RBI Report on Currency & Finance, 2008.

Table 4.5   Sub-targets for SSI lending by SCBs to tiny SSI

	No of Accounts	Amount Outstanding	
	In lakhs	Rs bn	As a % of SSI credit
FY2001	21.55	240.87	40.1
FY2002	9.27	73.4	11.7
FY2003	15.38	269.37	42.3
FY2004	9.79	102.45	14.3

Source: Basic statistical returns, RBI, various issues.

A number of factors led to the growth of the retail segment, includ ing diversification (banks shifting from traditional to broad-based lending), declining interest rates, low levels of NPA, and fiscal incen tives of the government (housing loans are allowed for tax exemption) However, official studies suggest – and the global financial crisis o 2007–2009 demonstrates that well – retail lending may also pose vari ous risks, having adverse implications for banks' asset quality (RB 2004; 2008).

4.4   Implementation of Basel II in India

In India, the Reserve Bank of India (RBI) has decided that all banks wil follow the standardised approach. It thus opted for the adoption of

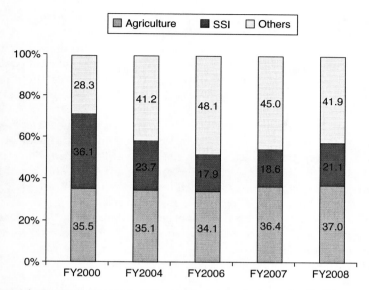

Figure 4.2 Percentage loans to SSI sector in total priority sector (in %)

Source: RBI, Report on Trends & Progress of Banking in India various issues.

more cautious strategy than that of Brazil's Central Bank (see Chapter 3). The focus, as in Brazil, is on Pillar 1 rather than on Pillars 2 and 3 which deal with banking supervision and market discipline. One recognises that this decision is despite the fact that Indian banks seem to be less prepared than Brazilian banks for the adoption of internal models, and that India has not advanced as much as Brazil in the areas of banking supervision and market discipline. But it also reflects a traditionally more cautious attitude in India regarding financial regulation, as has been the case with external financial opening.

In contrast to Brazil, the Indian authorities proposed that, under the standardised approach, rating agencies be used for determining credit risk and that banks submit a road map for the adoption of the new rules, particularly regarding adoption of management risk systems (Pillar 2) and information transparency (Pillar 3). In the case of internationally active banks, these were to be able to propose a road map for eventual adoption of internal models.

RBI officials thus clearly recognise that Indian banks are not ready yet to Basel II implementation in full. In relation to Pillar 1, they expect that most banks will adopt the standardised approach. It will be seen below that bankers in India also adhere to this view.

Interestingly, banking analysts have projected a capital plunge (rather than a climb) in post Basel II. They expect that between 2–3 per cent of their CAR will be shaved off under the new norms. This is also because the 'one-size-fits-all' will no longer exist. The RBI wants banks to adopt the standardised (SA) approach for credit risk and a 'basic indicator' approach for operational risk. The latter will certainly imply a significant increase in capital requirements, which may more than offset the capital freed by the adoption of the SA and the IRB approaches for credit risk. While the majority of banks already have done public issues, other banks will tap the market soon to raise capital, if needed. Thus, two opposite trends will be at play. While the requirements of capital for market as well as operational risk will tend to shoot up, those with quality assets will need less provisioning for credit risk.

In our judgment, in the event of some banks adopting the IRB approach while others adopting the SA, those with the IRB approach will be much more risk sensitive than the banks on the SA, since even a small change in the degree of risk might translate into a large impact on capital requirement for the IRB banks. As a result, IRB banks could avoid assuming high-risk exposures. Since banks adopting the SA are not equally risk sensitive and since the relative capital requirement would be less for the same exposure, banks on SA could be inclined to assume exposures to high risk clients, which will not be financed by the IRB banks. As a result, high-risk assets could flow to banks on the SA, which need to maintain lower capital on these assets than the banks on the IRB. Simultaneously, low risk assets would tend to be concentrated with IRB banks, which need to maintain lower capital on these assets than the SA banks. Hence, due to concentration of higher risks, SA banks may become vulnerable at times of economic downturns. Also not all banks, and especially the small ones, will have the capacity to devise and follow an IRB method. Issues as above demand policy responses from the supervisory bodies.

Regulatory initiatives taken by the RBI in regard to Pillars 2 and 3 have been more specific and operational as compared to those for Pillar 1. These are to ensure that banks have suitable risk management framework and are oriented to meet their requirements as dictated by the size and complexity of business, risk philosophy, market perceptions and the expected level of capital. Banks are expected to adopt frameworks which are adaptable to changes in business size, market dynamics and introduction of innovative products in the future. The RBI has already initiated Risk Based Supervision (RBS) in 23 banks on a Pilot basis. Also it has been encouraging banks to formalise their Capital Adequacy Assessment Programme (CAAP) in alignment with business plans and performance budgeting system. The above, together with the adoption of the RBS, is expected to help in factoring in the Pillar II requirements under Basel II.[4]

As for the implementation of Pillar III, banks in India are actively encouraged to enhance disclosures, so as to have greater transparency of their financial position and risk profile while improving their standards of corporate governance.

On the whole, implementation of Pillar I, as compared to the measures taken to implement Pillars II and III, shows lower degrees of preparedness at the time of writing this chapter. Apart from the request for a road map, all that the RBI has done so far is to insist on capacity building. The latter is to ensure that the regulators are able to identify and permit eligible banks to adopt the SA and the more advanced measurement approaches. Thus, Basel II needs time to enable the supervisors at the RBI to prescribe higher than the minimum capital levels for banks, to identify slackness and to assess/quantify the extent of additional capital which may be required to be maintained by such banks. The magnitude of this task with India having as many as 100 banks, is daunting.

4.4.1   Issues concerning implementation of Basel II

We put forward below the impression we gathered from our interactions with banking regulators and financial market participants in India, of the impact of the Basel norm implementations.

Representatives of the Reserve Bank of India (RBI) make a positive assessment of Basel II in relation to the emphasis the new rules place on the need to cover different types of risks, particularly operational risk and those linked to financial innovations.

Basel I, according to the official position of the RBI, has lost its relevance and appropriateness in the changed scenario of the money and capital markets since it was launched in 1988. The reasons include the rather simplistic, one-size-fits all formula to assess credit risk. Describing it as a single pillar approach, top regulators at the RBI pointed at its inadequacy to handle operational risks as well as risks connected with the financial innovations in the market (though amendments to Basel I were made in the 1990s to address these latter types of risks as well).

The RBI and most of the banks we have interviewed held the view that the banks in India are likely to follow the standardised approach (SA). There is a feeling that there exists a data gap in India to run and validate the IRB models. There is also the question of technical capability, which apart from a few select banks, is absent in most of the banks. At the time of the interviews, the RBI had clearly pointed out there was no pressure on banks from the RBI other than the requirement to provide the road map for the SA (and if possible also the IRB).

In regard to the SA approach, the RBI has recommended that borrower's level of risk is determined by rating agencies (unlike Brazil's and other developing country regulators in Africa – see the other chapters of the book). Doubts, however, were expressed by the RBI officials themselves on the feasibility of even the SA under Pillar I of Basel II. An issue seen as critical is the lack of reliable information at the micro level that can permit an objective calculus of risk.[5] Among bankers, concerns about the adoption of the SA approach include the fact that the capital requirements for banks are bound to be much higher due to their recent market exposures. It was however admitted that most large banks have already achieved a fair margin in terms of provisioning which, as we have pointed out earlier, is often more than the regulatory minimum.

For the implementation of the SA, India has three established rating agencies in which leading international credit rating agencies are stakeholders and to which they extend technical support. However, the level of penetration of these agencies is not very effective as, so far, ratings are restricted to issues and not issuers. While Basel II gives some scope to extend the rating of issues to issuers, this would only be an approximation and it would be necessary for the system to move eventually to the ratings of issuers. However, the above may prove to be a challenge to the rating agencies.

Under the SA approach, banks believe there is a risk of adverse selection, due to doubts related to the capacity by these agencies to assess risk. In addition, banks foresee that credit may turn even more procyclical with the use of rating agencies. Indeed, the risk of intensified credit pro-cyclicality has been debated in India. There, the sentiment that Basel II may turn credit more pro-cyclical is expressed more strongly than in other developing countries – see the other chapter in this book.

However, if the SA approach has its complications and possible undesirable effects, Indian regulators believe that the adoption of internal models by banks would be even more challenging, given the need to upgrade the risk management apparatus.

As regards the operational risk, banks in their majority will adopt the basic indicator method, which is the simplest among the three proposed methods. Banks in India generally feel that measurement of this type of risk is a necessary condition, since a large number of co-operative bank frauds have taken place in India in recent times. Also, one bank said that there is an incentive to go from the BI to the AMA approach (even though this will require significant investment), as the capital required under the latter will be much smaller.

As for credit to the SMEs, one bank official interviewed said that that the total number of small borrowers between Rs 25000 and Rs 2 lakhs has been falling over time. To come to an overall position, there seems to have been a decline in credit flow to the SMEs, not just with the adoption of Basel I but also with the contraction of subsidised credit as a result of financial liberalisation that started in India during the early 1990s.

A number of factors explain why credit to the SMEs has declined. One of them, and perhaps the most important one, is the perceived higher risk among for the SMEs. Higher quality loans from Indian banks are significantly under-priced reflecting the perceived lower risks. According to some estimates made available by the Indian public sector banks, the result of this disparity in perceptions is that the interest rate differential between a large and a small borrower is as much as 2 per cent. Some of the bankers that we met in India follow a strict credit rating appraisal system. For instance, one of the banks that we met said that it follows a system of credit allocation whereby close to 100 parameters are considered under factors like industry overview, financial performance of the borrower, management, ability and competence and security of the borrower. Another banker said that the determination of the interest rate remains a function of the value of the account, the probability of losing that account, how long their business is, non-fund business and the like. These credit appraisal systems, the banks feel, are a result of the Basel I norms and may have affected the flow of credit to the SMEs.

However, even though there was a decline in credit flow to the SMEs, there was also a spurt in credit flow to mid-sized corporate. The credit market in India could thus be best described as one with an increasing competition so much so that clients were dictating terms (so the quantity of credit was not the problem). Herein lies the problem with the SMEs, as it is believed that economies of scale and absence of transparency are not allowing them to have access to bank loans. The large and mid-sized corporates do not belong to the SMEs and the small corporates who may be synonymous with SMEs do not have the ability to obtain loans. One of the bankers interviewed felt that these SMEs need some sort of scheme as is prevalent in other industries in India Technology Upgrading Fund or TUF).

Moving on to agricultural credit, we also interviewed the major agricultural bank in India, NABARD, which supervises the co-operative banks. In addition, we spoke to the official in charge of agricultural credit. These credit flows are often controlled by the co-operative banks, having no formal link to the RBI. Given this, the co-operative banks are not concerned about the Basel norms. These credit flows are significant for the poor in the countryside. Still on agricultural credit, our interview with a public sector bank based in Northern India and very aggressive in areas of lending to agriculture indicated that it is not correct to say returns are low. For example, while typical returns on agriculture were 9 per cent, the cost of funds was 5 per cent. Thus the spread was comfortable. However, this bank maintained that in the course of lending it ensured that there was a proper mechanism to generate incomes from such activities, so that those loans did not turn non-performing. This bank also emphasised that in India the priority of banks was not separable from the goal of development banking. Also, as far as Basel I was concerned, until then there was no problem with the Indian banks as the Government of India recapitalised these whenever needed. However, with Basel II coming up there could be the problem of additional capital requirements. In a similar vein, one more bank based in Eastern India was of the opinion that diversification in areas of lending, for example, to rural areas, helped to minimise risk.

Perhaps the most startling revelations came from this supervisory body – that there is a clear conflict between the regulatory bodies. For example, NABARD looks after only the supervision of regional rural banks but cannot do anything apart from improving their performance. Respective state governments control the management of these banks and more often than not there is political interference. The RBI looks after the urban co-operative banks. In a similar vein, the co-operative banks are under the supervision of co-operative societies. Interestingly only portions of the Basel norms have been made applicable to these banks.

Finally, one of the persons interviewed spoke about the history of public banks in India and said that in the past high cost of financial intermediation had plagued the Indian banking system. The implementation of Basel I norms improved the asset quality and aligned the capital with risk weights in the 1990s. However, given the social conditions, imperfect markets and lack of infrastructure, we have to see how the new Basel norms may be integrated into the Indian markets.

4.4.2   Basel II norms and the merger of banks

We need to mention here an issue, which is currently debated in the context of Basel II. This relates to the merger of banks. Two concerns related to mergers are particularly important. The first relates to the implication or loans to small business and agriculture. Banks find it expedient not to meet the norms for priority sector lending if options like investment in government securities, lending to top grade corporates and retail loans are open to them. There are reasons to fear that this trend could be accentuated with mergers as a result of which many banks may acquire the critical minimum size that enables these to service the larger corporates. This does come into conflict with the objectives the government has in mind in terms of social responsibility for banks. The other concern has to do with the local character of some of the banks. To cite the most glaring example, SBI's associates such as State Bank of Patiala, State Bank of Indore and others have a strong local or regional flavour to their operations that could be eroded if they were to be merged with the parent. Not only have the subsidiaries preserved their local character, they have been successful. In 2003–04, all of SBI's seven subsidiaries had a return on assets, which was more than that of the parent. Lastly, mergers will also take away the 'relationship route', to the extent this exists under the formal banking sector. That is, loss of information in specific markets would happen with the disappearance of the smaller banks.

4.5 Conclusions

While the pattern as well as the magnitude of bank credit in India has been subject to drastic changes since the beginning of liberalisation of the country's financial sector, the recent revival of interest in the risk-management techniques of banks, as have come with the introduction of Basel II in 2006, are equally responsible for those changes.

One observes, with serious concern, the limitations of the guiding principle of the Basel norms for banking system in a country like India where credit needs to be re-directed to units which are deserving, not only in terms of productive contribution but also in terms of social priorities.

With the steady implementation of the capital adequacy norms under Basel I and the on going efforts made for the introduction of Basel II, one observes a number of changes in the structure as well as the functioning of the Indian banking industry. An important change has been the holding of risk-free government securities, which enabled banks to meet more easily the capital adequacy requirements while providing opportunities for reaping trading gains. A large part of this rise in CAR was also made possible by capitalisation on part of the government; in particular, the weak banks received substantial financial support from the government.

However, the restructuring of the banking sector with the Basel norms, and more generally the prudential rules for the banking system, has had implications that go far beyond the performance criteria of banks, such as the improved CARs. More than two-fifths of the scheduled priority sector credit has at some point been directed to 'other segments' which typically comprise small business, retail trade, small transport operators, professional and self-employed persons, education loans and micro credit, and housing. This is a positive development in that such credit is probably reaching the poor, especially in the informal sector. However, the process by-passes the fairly productive SSIs and SMEs who are not less credit-worthy as compared to the other priority and non-priority sector loans.

Advances to the priority sector also have been liberalised. The result has been the stiffening of the loan terms for the SSIs. Norms for priority sector lending by the SCBs have the anomaly that no target is set for lending to the small sector industry (SSI) other than it being a residual after other priority credit targets are met. Thus, meeting the 40 per cent target of priority credit does not necessarily ensure that these are directed to those sectors that are cash–starved most. From FY2000 onwards, there has been a steady decline in SSI credit as a percentage of NBC by the public and private banks. One possible reason for this may be the fact that loans to other priority sectors (for instance housing loan up to Rs 10 lakh) have witnessed a steep jump over FY2000–2008. Given the fact that the small units compare reasonably well with other borrowers in terms of either credit-worthiness or productivity, no amount of 'rationality' on the part of the banks can explain the shrinking size of bank credit to the small sector.

As for the changing structure of the banking industry in India in recent years, especially with the implementation of Basel I norms, one notices a gradual but steady erosion of public sector/nationalised banks in terms of their presence in the deposit market. While the SBI and its associates, the major PSBs in India, continue as major players in the asset market, these have a reduced capacity to extend branch business with tendencies for centralising credit creation. In contrast, the NPB are attracting business, often at the expense of other nationalised a well as old private banks. One notices the PSBs as a whole as well as the old private banks are gradually losing market share to the NPBs. Aspects as above can have a great deal of significance in terms of the access of bank credit for the SMEs and the poor.

As regards implementation of Basel II, all SCBs were instructed to work out a 'road map' towards a transition to Pillar I. However, bank which are internationally active were also to follow an assessment of risks with an Internal Rating Based (IRB) approach, using their own expertise. However, doubts have been expressed by the RBI officials on the feasibility of even the standardised approach (SA). As for the IRB approach, it is expected that it will be even more difficult to implement Basel II given the need for the upgrading of the data as well as risk management apparatus. Also there lies the hurdle of a lack of reliable information at a micro level, which permits an objective risk calculation.

In our judgment, in the event of some banks adopting the IRB approach while others adopting the SA, those with the IRB approach will be much more risk sensitive than the banks on the SA, and thus prone to concentrate lending towards big companies and away from SMEs. In addition, they will become more pro-cyclical in their lending operations. Issues as above demand policy responses from the supervisory bodies. Regulatory initiatives taken by the RBI in regard to Pillars 2 and 3 have been more specific and operational as compared to those for Pillar 1. The RBI wants most banks to adopt the SA for credit risk and a 'basic indicator' approach for operational risk. The latter will certainly imply a significant increase in capital requirements, which may more than offset the capital freed by the adoption of the standardised approach for credit risk. On the whole, implementation of Pillar I, as compared to the measures taken to implement Pillars II and III, shows lower degrees of preparedness. Apart from the request for a road map, all that the RBI has done so far is to insist on capacity building.

Issues currently debated in India in the context of Basel II point at its implication for loans to small business and agriculture. Concerns are also that a declining trend in credit to the above areas could be reinforced with the current wave of mergers. This possible outcome would come into conflict with the objectives the government has in mind in terms of social responsibility for banks.

At the policy level a trend as above is of a serious concern, with the un-organised industry which includes the small and the medium units providing more than 4/5th of employment, 1/3rd of exports and 2/5th of industrial output. The matter thus calls for remedial measures, not just with a social concern but also on genuine economic grounds.

Attempts in the form of fiscal support to enhance credit flow to these sectors are not enough to correct the imbalances and inequities emerging from the process of Basel compliance. While it is a little early to have a judgment on the success of these new prudential regulations in terms of the long term stability and growth of the country's banking sector, one can duly have some reservations regarding the possible contractionary effects with changing composition even within the targeted priority credit itself. Supplementary finance, as available from outlets like the SIDBI, Co-operative Banks or even the direct fiscal measures do not fill in the void left in terms of the unfulfilled demand for finance on the part of the SMEs. As for the poor, meeting the minimum target by banks may not deliver what is needed by those who are not even considered 'bankable' by the banks themselves.

Notes

1. See Sunanda Sen, Global Finance at Risk: On stagnation and Instability in the Real Economy Palgrave Macmillan 2003 and OUP (paperback) 2004.
2. RBI Report on Trends & Progress of Banking in India.
3. This point was made by a senior public sector banker based in Delhi. Also, due to the need to raise capital in the face of the ensuing Basel II norms, during FY2008, a total of Rs 300 bn was mobilised from the equity market.
4. RBI website: http//www.rbi.org.in/
5. See for a discussion of risk calculation under Basel norms in the context of the loan waiver scheme, Sen, Sunanda and Ghosh, Soumya Kanti, 'Missing link in the loan waiver scheme'*Mainstream*, V.46(No.23), 2008(24.5.2008): P.8–10. See also, Sen Sunanda and Ghosh Soumya,'Basel Norms, Indian Banking Sector and Credit to SMEs and Poor' (co authored) *Economic and Political Weekly* 19th March 2005.

5
Basel II Implementation in Low-Income Countries: Challenges and Effects on SME Development

Ricardo Gottschalk and Stephany Griffith-Jones

5.1 Introduction

This chapter examines the implementation of Basel II in low-income countries (LIC).[1] The aims are to assess the low-income countries' views and concerns on Basel II, whether and how they intend to implement the new Basel Capital Accord, and the challenges they may face in doing so. The chapter in particular discusses the possible implications of Basel II implementation for competitiveness of LIC banking sectors and financial inclusion.

Specifically, the chapter[2] addresses the following questions:

To what extent will Basel II be implemented by LIC regulators? What approaches are being proposed for adoption? What are the main obstacles for implementing the different approaches? Are possible variations being considered?
* What are the main challenges facing regulators – lack of human, financial resources? If a LIC is planning to implement the Internal Ratings Based (IRB) approach, is there sufficient capacity to validate models? Should the focus be on other regulatory issues, which need to be addressed previous to implementing Basel II?
* What about banks' preferences regarding the adoption of Basel II?
* Would banks that adopt the IRB approach (usually international banks) have competitive advantage over banks that adopt, or are asked to adopt, the standardised approach? Is it a concern that this

might cause a division of labour between banks, with small and riskier borrowers migrating to banks (usually national ones) that use the standardised approach?

- What can be done to mitigate possible negative impacts of implementation of Basel II on access to credit by the poor and SMEs?
- To what extent do LIC regulators/others feel Basel II should be adapted to their own needs and circumstances?

Drawing on a survey conducted in late 2006 involving low-income countries, mainly from sub-Saharan Africa, the chapter finds that most LICs are adopting a very cautious approach toward Basel II. Their intentions are first to understand better how Basel II works and to have a better grasp of their possible implications, in order to be able to adopt an informed decision on the issue. It is a 'better wait' approach. Furthermore, several LIC countries feel that they have previous tasks to complete within Basel I or more generally within banking regulations before they tackle Basel II. The IMF and the Basel Committee say they share this caution and do not push LICs to adopt Basel II. However, there seems to be pressure from international consulting firms, rating agencies and others for countries to adopt Basel II.

A few other LICs are already signalling a move toward Basel II. However, they intend to do so in a gradual fashion. For some countries, gradualism means starting with Pillars 2 and 3, and later moving to Pillar 1. For other countries, it means adopting first a simplified version of the standardised approach under Pillar 1, with no clear timetable for moving on to more sophisticated approaches later on.

The LICs' cautious attitude reflects their awareness about the complexities that Basel II involves, and their lack of human and financial resources to deal with these complexities. Major challenges comprise the need to build extensive and reliable databases to run sophisticated risk assessment models, and to build supervisors' capacities to assess, validate, and monitor the use of such models. But the challenges LICs face are not exactly the same. They can differ across countries according to the country's size (population, absolute GDP) and whether the country harbours foreign banks in its jurisdiction.

With regard to size, obviously large countries, such as India, do not face extreme constraints in human resources and thus, were able to consider adopting Basel II soon after it was approved in 2004 (although through starting with the less complex approaches; see Chapter 4). In contrast, Lesotho (not strictly a LIC), is a small country and therefore faces limited availability of human resources. Therefore, the country had not decided at the time of the survey whether to implement Basel II, even though its per capita income may be higher than India's.

As for the presence of foreign banks, a continuum among LICs can be found as regards the presence of foreign banks in their jurisdictions. At the one end, we can find countries with no foreign banks while at the other end, there are countries where all banks are foreign. Ethiopia, for example, has no foreign banks, which implies it does not face the pressing issue of how to deal with foreign banks keen to adopt the most sophisticated approaches, and therefore can take the time to build capacity for Basel II implementation. At the other end, one can find Botswana and Lesotho (not LICs but small), where all commercial banks are foreign. These countries would have therefore to deal with Basel II issues even if they decided not to adopt the new capital accord in the foreseeable future, as foreign banks would wish to adopt this approach globally. Though formally, LIC regulators have the freedom to require all banks in their jurisdiction to follow a certain regulatory approach, foreign banks have great deal of leverage given their option of pulling out, if national regulations are not convenient for them. This could become a serious problem for LIC economies.

Given the pressing need for building up capacity to deal with Basel II, at the time of the survey LICs' efforts were concentrated on building such capacity through participation in various activities and events such as local and foreign seminars, and training programmes. This left little space for discussion on possible broader negative implications of Basel II for their banking systems. This was the case even when LIC regulators were aware of these implications as a result of their own reflections and learning process.

Further important findings reported in this chapter are that, first, in countries with foreign banks there was scant evidence of collaboration between home and host regulators. This despite the fact that host regulators know collaboration is crucial and that Basel II documents emphasise the need for such collaboration; and second, that very little technical assistance (TA) was being provided at the time the interviews were conducted.

The remainder of this chapter is organised as follows. Section 5.2 provides a global picture on what countries intended to do, which is then contrasted by Asia's and sub-Saharan Africa's picture. Section 5.3 provides country-specific information on what options are being considered in sub-Saharan Africa regarding Basel II implementation. This is based on interviews with banking regulators from sub-Saharan African countries. Because South Africa is a middle-income country facing issues that are more similar to countries such as Brazil and India than other sub-Saharan African countries, Basel II implementation in South Africa is discussed separately. Section 5.4 presents what the main issues facing LICs are. Section 5.5 discusses the further issue of whether Basel may inhibit financial innovation for financial inclusion, an issue that has been hardly explored in the debates on possible Basel impacts on development finance. We conclude with Section 5.6.

5.2   What do countries intend to do in terms of Basel II implementation?

5.2.1   Global versus regional pictures

The Financial Stability Institute (FSI) conducted a survey in 2004 and follow-up surveys in 2006 and 2008 on implementation of Basel II in non-Basel Committee member countries (see Financial Stability Institute, 2008). The 2008 survey obtained responses from 101 jurisdictions, out of 130 jurisdictions to which the survey was sent – that is, a rate of response of 78 per cent. The survey shows that, at the time it was conducted, 91 per cent of all respondents worldwide had implemented or were planning to implement Basel II between 2007 and 2015 – see Table 5.1. These intentions are higher than what the 2006 survey found – by then 84 per cent of all respondents intended to implement Basel II at some point.

Table 5.1   Number of countries intending to adopt Basel II

Regions	Number of Respondents		Respondents intending to adopt Basel II		Total (in %)	
Year	2008	2006	2008	2006	2008	2006
Africa	16	17	12	12	75	71
Asia[a]	18	16	17	16	95	100
Caribbean	9	7	8	4	89	57
Latin America	14	14	12	12	86	86
Middle East	9	8	9	8	100	100
Non-BCBS Europe	35	36	34	30	97	83
Total	101	98	92	82	91	84

[a] Excludes Japan as BCBS member-countries were not included in the survey.
Source: Financial Stability Institute (2008).

As can be seen from Table 5.1, the results are aggregated on a regional basis and do not distinguish among countries with different levels of development.

Including the 13 BCBS countries, at the end of 2007, 31 countries had already adopted Basel II, and 26 other countries intended to have it adopted by the end of 2008 (FSI, 2008).

Of the total of 57 countries that intended to have implemented Basel II by the end of 2008, 34 countries are from Europe, 10 countries from Asia and 8 countries from the Middle-East. But in the Americas, only three countries intended to have Basel II implemented by the end of 2008, and in Africa only two countries. Thus, although intentions to implement Basel II have been widespread around the world, effective implementation has been skewed toward Europe and Asia, and against the Americas and Africa.

Although the number of countries already implementing Basel II is already fairly large, it is possible that the increase in numbers effectively adopting Basel II will decelerate markedly in the next few years, as it is expected that many developing countries will postpone their initial timetable due to technical obstacles and other considerations.

Under Pillar 1, the standardised approach is expected to be the most widely used option of the three credit risk methodologies available for calculating capital ratios – 87 per cent of respondents planning to adopt Basel II intend to use this approach, while 65 and 61 per cent of all respondents intend to adopt the FIRB and AIRB approaches respectively. As regards operational risk, the basic indicator method is expected to be the generally adopted framework – an intention expressed by 84 per cent of the total respondents. But 73 and 53 per cent of all respondents also intend to adopt the standardised approach and the Advanced Measurement Appproaches (AMA) until 2015. Finally, many countries are expected to implement Pillars 2 and 3 before the end of 2015. Curiously, according to the Surveys' respondents, the speed by which countries intended to implement Pillar 2 has slowed down considerably between the 2006 and 2008. As the FSI report points out, there probably has been a realisation by countries that Pillar 2 requires more preparation than originally envisaged. (Financial Stability Institute, 2008).

5.2.2   Basel II by regions

This sub-section reports the FSI Survey results for Asia and Africa – the two regions of the world where most low-income countries are located.

Table 5.2   Number of Asian countries (out of 18 Respondents) adopting the different credit risk approaches over 2007–2015

	2007	2008	2009	2010–2015
Standardised	2	12	13	13
FIRB	1	6	6	11
AIRB	0	4	6	11

Source: Financial Stability Institute (2008).

In Asia, 95 per cent of respondents intend to implement Basel II at some point over 2007–2015. This is quite striking given that a fairly large number of low-income countries are located in Asia. But more detailed information from the FSI survey shows that intention of adopting Basel II does not necessarily mean doing it now. According to the survey, only 2 out of a total of 18 respondents had adopted the standardised approach by 2007, while only 1 adopted the FIRB approach and none the AIRB approach in that year. This means that 3 countries at the maximum (but probably less than that) out of 18 had implemented Basel II in 2007 through adopting one of the three options offered under pillar 1. However, a big jump in numbers can be observed for the year 2008, when 12 respondents expressed intention of adopting the standardised approach, 6 the FIRB approach, and 4 the AIRB approach (see Table 5.2).

5.2.3   Basel II in Africa

In Africa, 75 per cent of respondents intend to implement Basel II. This figure is lower than the other regions, but still fairly high.

However, looking more carefully at the results from the FSI survey, we can see that implementation of Basel II in Africa will be very gradual. In 2007, no country intended to move to Pillar 1 at all. By 2009, only three countries (out of a total of 16 survey respondents) were planning to have implemented the standardised approach for credit risk. The number of countries adopting the standardised approach then increases gradually to nine – or 56 per cent of the total – in the period 2010–2015 (see Table 5.3). Adoption of the FIRB and AIRB approaches are intended to start in 2008, with a total of respectively 4 countries adopting them until 2015 (see also Table 5.3). Curiously, the implementation speed of the Pillar detected by the 2008 survey was slower than that of the 2006 survey, indicating that African countries were encountering higher obstacles than initially anticipated in their efforts to implement Basel II.

Table 5.3 Number of African countries adopting the different credit risk approaches over 2007–2015

	2007	2008	2009	2010–2015
Standardised	0	2	3	9
FIRB	0	1	3	4
AIRB	0	1	3	4

Source: Financial Stability Institute (2008).

The FSI 2008 Survey also shows that intentions regarding the implementation of Pillars 2 and 3 in the near future have declined dramatically in Africa – for example, while in the 2006 survey, nine African countries (of the 16 respondents) intended to have adopted Pillars 2 and 3 by 2009, in the 2008 Survey intentions decline to five.

The FSI results are fairly consistent with our own survey, based on selected interviews with banking regulators in sub-Saharan Africa and information available on their websites, except that the interviews did not capture the fact that countries would face more difficulties in implementing Pillars 2 and 3 than initially thought.

Those banking regulators from Africa we interviewed that intended to implement Basel II in the near future expressed plans to start either with pillars 2 and 3 first, or start with pillar 1 by adopting first the standardised approach. It will be seen below that the possibility of moving to the more advanced approaches under pillar 1 is left for the long term.

A more complete study conducted by the FSI in 2004 shows that the main reason cited by banking regulators for this cautionary approach is lack of capacity; therefore, building capacity through expertise upgrading and information-sharing are seen as very important for effective Basel II implementation (FSI, 2004).

5.3   Findings from our country interviews

Our findings are based on interviews conducted with eight countries in total, all from sub-Saharan Africa. These were: Botswana, Ethiopia, Ghana, Kenya, Lesotho, Tanzania, Uganda and Zambia. In addition, detailed information has been obtained about India by drawing on previous studies and press reports, and an interview was conducted with an ex-banking regulator from the Caribbean, who reported the current thinking in the region and challenges for implementing Basel II.

We believe these findings probably resonate with what countries from other developing sub-regions are experiencing in regard to Basel II implementation. This may be particularly the case in South Asia, where most countries are low-income, and Central Asia, where most countries are either low-income or lower-middle income, with still fairly low levels of financial development.

What have we found?

On the basis of our sample of countries, it is possible to affirm that one of the biggest challenges facing LICs is lack of human skills and resources to deal with Basel II issues. In light of that, most bank regulators had not decided yet when or how they were going to implement Basel II in their countries. At the time of the interviews, they were still trying to understand how Basel II works and to have a better grasp of their possible implications, in order to be able to adopt an informed decision on the issue. It is a 'better to wait and see' approach.

But some countries had already decided how to move forward. Basically, they intended to adopt a gradual approach. This approach reflects a cautious position, due to the difficulties and challenges that implementation of Basel II involves. A couple of country regulators, for example, said they would start with pillars 2 and 3. Starting with Pillars 2 and 3 makes sense because many LICs have not fully complied with the BCPs yet, and Pillars II and III do embed many elements of the BCPs. At the same time, the challenges facing LICs are huge, even if the initial focus is not on Pillar 1 but on Pillars 2 and 3. Pillar 2 in particular requires a considerable amount of resources and capacity for implementation. This explains why the FSI Survey just discussed shows that between 2006 and 2008, low-income countries slowed down considerably in their plans to adopt Pillars 2 and 3.

Given the challenges facing LICs in regard to Pillars 2 and 3, a move to Pillar 1 would be made in a second phase, with the adoption of the simplified standardised approach. Adoption of the IRB approach would only happen once they had built a database and capacity within the Central Bank. A timetable for adoption of the various phases was not set yet. Other countries had set a date for implementing the simplified standardised approach – Ghana regulators for example, intended to adopt the simplified approach in 2008. Table 5.4 below reports the timetable for implementation of Basel II for selected low-income countries.

Table 5.4 Timetable for implementation of Basel II in low-income countries (as of 2006)

Country	Credit risk			Operational risk		
	STA	FIRB	AIRB	BIA	SA	AMA[a]
Vietnam	End–08	Q4–08	End–08	Q4–8	Q4–08	Q4–08
Bangladesh	Jan–09	Not decided	Not decided	Jan–09	Not decided	Not decided
Botswana[b]	Not decided	Not decided	Not decided	Not decided	Not decided	Not decided
India	Apr–09	Not decided	Not decided	Apr–09	Not decided	Not decided
Nepal	Jan–07	Not decided	Not decided	Jan–07	Not decided	Not decided
Pakistan[b]	Jan–08	Jan–10	Jan–10	Jan–08	Jan–08	Not allowed
Ethiopia	Not decided	Not decided	Not decided	Not decided	Not decided	Not decided
Ghana	2008	Not decided	Not decided	End–06	End–09	Not decided
Kenya	Not decided	Not decided	Not decided	Not decided	Not decided	Not decided
Lesotho[b]	Not decided	Not decided	Not decided	Not decided	Not decided	Not decided
Sierra Leone	Not decided	Not decided	Not decided	Not decided	Not decided	Not decided
Tanzania	Not decided	Not decided	Not decided	Not decided	Not decided	Not decided
Uganda	End–10	Not decided	Not decided	End–10	Not decided	Not decided
Zambia	End–08	Not decided	Not decided	End–08	Not decided	Not decided

[a] Standardised Approach (STA); Foundation Internal Ratings Based (F–IRB) Approach; Advanced Internal Ratings Based (A–IRB) Approach; Basic Indicator Approach (BIA); Standardised Approach (SA); and Advanced Measurement Approach (AMA).
[b] Middle-income country.

Sources: Standard Chartered Bank; Central Banks' websites; interviews and email communication.

5.4   What are the issues?

The vast majority of countries were adopting the 'better wait' and the gradual approaches, in face of the huge challenges posed by Basel II.

5.4.1   Capacity to validate models and monitor their use

A major challenge facing LIC regulators is a lack of sufficient technical capacity to validate the more complex models (F-IRB and A-IRB models) that Basel II proposes for use, and to monitor their use. Related to this is the lack of a sufficiently detailed and reliable database available to banks, including international ones, to be able to run the models adequately. This is the main reason why LIC regulators, if and when they implement Basel II, do not intend to adopt the more complex approaches.

In addition to the more complex models, the Basel Committee also proposes the use of the standardised approach. This approach differs from the more complex ones in that it relies on credit rating agencies to determine the risk level for different categories of borrowers. But because LICs do not have domestic rating agencies (and if they have them their penetration is very low) and the process of establishing credit bureau systems is only at the initial stages, they are not even considering adopting the standardised approach. Instead, their intention is to adopt a simplified version of such an approach – the so-called simplified standardised approach – in which the risk weights for different categories of assets are fixed and pre-determined by the regulatory authorities. This latter approach, which can be found in Annex 11 of Basel II documents – see Basel (2006), is very similar to Basel I, but differs from it for having more risk elements.

It should be emphasised that the issues facing LICs are not simply – or even mainly – technical. There are also broader issues, such as competitiveness of national and foreign banks, access to credit by SMEs, potential increased pro-cyclicality of bank lending resulting from Basel II and their macro-economic impact, discussed below.

5.4.2   Presence of Foreign banks

Although most countries intend to postpone implementation of Basel II or opt for the simpler approaches for determining credit risk, these are not easy options. The main reason is that most LICs have foreign banks (see Table 5.5 for Africa), and these banks intended to adopt the most complex approaches (F-IRB and A-IRB) in the countries where they operate through their subsidiaries and branches.

Table 5.5 Variation in ownership structure in African countries, where available

Mainly govt	Mainly foreign	Foreign+govt	Equally shared	Mainly local
Eritrea	Botswana	Burkina Faso	Burundi	Benin
Ethiopia	Central Afr Republic	Congo, Dem. Rep.	Ghana	Mali
Togo	Chad	Sierra Leone	Kenya	Mauritania
	Côte d'lvoire		Rwanda	Somalia
	Gambia		Senegal	Sudan
	Guinea-Bissau			Zimbabwe
	Liberia			
	Madagascar			
	Malawi			
	Mozambique			
	Niger			
	Tanzania			
	Uganda			
	Zambia			

Note: Mainly government (foreign; private) means more than 60 per cent of total assets are held by banks which are majority-owned by government (foreign; local private) shareholders.
Foreign + government means these two together concentrate more than 70 per cent.
Equally shared is a residual category (in Senegal, foreign plus private local add to more than 70 per cent).
Source: World Bank (2006).

For South and Central Asia, the presence of foreign banks is somewhat less prominent. Perhaps with the exception of India and the Maldives, where fully owned foreign banks exist, foreign bank presence in the countries of these sub-regions takes the form mainly of joint ventures (up to 49 per cent participation – see Table 5.6). This suggests that decisions regarding implementation of Basel II are in the hands of nationals. Related to this, a question is whether Basel II will speed up opening of the banking sector in developing countries. To the extent that countries start permitting full banking ownership by foreigners, then the issues raised in this sub-section become relevant for this group of countries as well.

The question then is: how should LIC regulators deal with these banks?

Botswana and Lesotho (not strictly LICs) can be cited as extreme cases in that these countries have only foreign commercial banks in their jurisdictions. By the end of 2006, neither country had decided whether

Table 5.6   Foreign banking ownership in South and Central Asia (as of end of 2007)

South Asia	Foreign participation	Central Asia	Foreign participation
Afghanistan	22% total assets with foreign branches	Kazakhistan	No information available
Bangladesh	12 banks with foreign participation, of a total of 28 financial institutions	Kyrgyz Republic	1 foreign bank (from Pakistan)
Bhutan	Joint ventures, with foreign participation	Tajikistan	1 foreign bank (out of 9 banks)
India	33 foreign banks (7% of total assets)	Turkmenistan	1 foreign bank (from Pakistan)
Maldives	4 foreign banks and 1 local	Uzbekistan	1 foreign bank
Nepal	6 joint ventures out of a total of 23 banks		
Pakistan	No information available		
Sri Lanka	No information available		

Source: Authors' elaboration, based on Central banks' websites.

or how to implement Basel II. They still had a number of pre-requisites to meet before moving to Basel II in a major way. Botswana for example still had to fully comply with the Basel Core Principles, put in place a risk-based supervision – Pillar 2 of Basel II – and build an adequate legal and regulatory framework.

Moreover, neither Botswana nor Lesotho has domestic rating agencies. Therefore, it is most likely that, if and when they adopt Basel II, it would seem to justify adopting the simplified approach (Annex 11). Allowing foreign banks to adopt the F-IRB or A-IRB would imply loss of supervisory power in their jurisdictions, as they still do not have the technical capacity to validate these models or monitor their use.

Of course, countries where foreign banks co-exist with local ones would face similar problems. If they adopted the simplified approach for local banks, while letting foreign banks adopt the more complex approaches, this too would imply loss of supervisory power over the foreign banks. In light of this, the most appropriate response might instead be to enforce the simplified approach to all banks, local and foreign. But would this be feasible?

Compliance with the simplified approach to meet the regulatory requirements in the host country implies that foreign banks would have to have a double reporting system – one for the home regulators, the other for the host regulators. European banks are already unhappy with the lack of regulatory homogeneity between the U.S.and Europe (see Chapter 1), as it implies higher challenges, and certainly oppose to it happening again between their home countries and LICs where they have subsidiaries. Undoubtedly, this is an area of potential conflict between foreign banks and host regulators. Moreover, the simplified approach is expected to require higher capital levels, thereby creating further tensions between foreign banks and host regulators as well as the competitiveness issues with national banks, discussed below.

The tension could be mitigated by the home regulators, depending on how they set the rules for global versus country allocations of capital. For example, it might be the case that if capital requirements are higher in a specific LIC due to the imposition of the simplified approach, the bank might be able to accommodate this higher requirement without an impact on the bank's global capital allocation. But this depends on how the global allocation rules are set by the home regulator, and also on the banks' portfolios. Presumably, banks with their credit portfolios concentrated in developed countries will have more room to absorb higher capital requirements in LICs without an impact on its global capital requirement levels than banks with stronger presence in the developing world.

Although formally, LIC regulators have the right to tell foreign banks which approach (e.g., standardised) they should follow, foreign banks also have the option of pulling out of the country. This may be particularly relevant for large foreign banks, mainly active in developed economies, for whom the scale of operations in an individual LIC country is very small in relation to their total operations. Reportedly, this would be less the case for international banks more concentrated in operations in LIC countries.

Furthermore, the threat of possible withdrawal, especially if the foreign bank holds an important part of the banking system's assets and liabilities, may be highly problematic and put pressure on host regulators to comply with banks' regulatory preferences (e.g., bias toward IRB). Therefore, LIC regulators need not just technical assistance but also more 'political' support for their negotiations on regulations with international banks to ensure that their regulatory regime is consistent with national aims for both financial stability and sufficient credit, especially to SMEs.

5.4.3   Collaboration between home and host supervisors

It would probably help if home and LIC host regulators could try to address the issue of divergent regulatory regimes together.

However, a worrisome finding is that, among those LIC regulators interviewed, no communication or any sort of collaboration was taking place between them and their counterparts in the home countries to discuss this and other Basel II-related issues. As the above implies, collaboration is essential even if the country decides not to adopt Basel II at all. LIC regulators know it is important to collaborate with home regulators, and have reported that although collaboration was not the case, they expected it would take place in the future.

5.4.4   Competitiveness issue

It has been mentioned above that one main potential problem facing LIC regulators is loss of supervisory power over foreign banks in their own jurisdictions if they propose the simplified approach to local banks while permitting foreign banks to adopt the more complex ones. However, a further possible negative implication of such a dual regulatory regime is that allowing foreign banks to adopt the F-IRB or A-IRB approaches may grant these banks competitive advantage over local banks, which would have to adopt the simplified approach and which would be far away from being able to adopt the internal risk based approaches at some point in the future.

This would happen because, as said before, the F-IRB and A-IRB approaches are likely to result in less capital requirements. At the same time, the standardised approach would either imply similar levels of capital or a substantial increase (see the results of the Fifth Quantitative Impact Study (QIS 5) conducted by the BIS and reported in Chapter 2 in this book). A competitive advantage obtained through the adoption of the F-IRB and A-IRB approaches could, in turn, lead to banking concentration favouring foreign banks to the detriment of local ones.

5.4.5   Credit portfolio concentration and access to SMEs

The use of risk-based IRB models by foreign banks to determine the amount of capital to be allocated for different types of borrowers is, moreover, likely to result in both more expensive and rationed credit to borrowers perceived as of higher risk, and more and cheaper credit to borrowers perceived as of lower risk, as argued earlier in other chapters of this book. For reasons such as information asymmetry, small borrowers and SMEs are likely to be judged as being of higher risk than the larger ones, such as large companies. This can cause a concentration in banks' credit portfolios away from small borrowers and toward the larger companies.

Foreign banks using the IRB approach would have the incentive to concentrate their portfolio in the upper end of the market as this would save them capital, and thereby would allow them a competitive advantage to lend to 'good' companies over local banks using the standardised approach. The latter group of banks would, in turn, be pushed toward lending to the riskier segments of the markets, making them potentially riskier. This would create a division of labour between foreign and local banks that would not bode well for the stability of the entire financial system. It is true that such a division of labour may already exist where foreign banks co-exist with local banks, but in introducing a dual-regime Basel II would reinforce this pattern. Although LIC regulators are aware of some of these possible implications, there is hardly any discussion of these within their jurisdictions, as their efforts are concentrated on trying first to improve their understanding of the technical issues on Basel II.

5.4.6 Pro-cyclicality

The use of risk-sensitive models under the IRB approach is bound to result in these models detecting an increase in the measured probability of default during economic downturns. In LICs, pro-cyclicality may be somewhat mitigated with the adoption of the simple version of the standardised approach, in which risk weights are fixed over time. However for this to be the case, the host regulators would have to be able to enforce its adoption among foreign banks. There is, however, uncertainty about whether and how they will be able to do it (see discussion above).

5.4.7 Skills shortage

A major challenge facing developing countries, but especially low-income countries and small countries, is their regulators' insufficient capacity to validate the more complex (F-IRB and A-IRB) models that Basel II proposes for use, and to monitor their use. Public and private banks in these countries also face human capacity problems to implement the more complex models. This is a main reason that regulators in these countries are considering moving to Basel II, through adopting the standardised approach rather than the more complex ones. It is hoped that the skills shortage faced by banks can be reduced over time through investments in capacity building. However, regulators may take the decision to give permission to foreign banks and, in the case of emerging market economies, the large domestic banks, to adopt the more complex approaches while instructing the remaining banks to adopt the standardised approach. In this case, the risk is that banks going for the more complex approach will poach human resources from the country's regulatory cadre. This will erode badly needed resources for effective banking supervision and regulation.

5.4.8   Technical assistance

Although LIC regulators are keen to learn about Basel II, little technical assistance has been provided on it – at least to those we have interviewed. There is no common view on what sort of technical assistance might be useful. But one idea floated by a LIC regulator is that they may greatly benefit from spending some time (say a month) in a home country central bank to see how things work. In the absence of TA, LIC regulators are trying to learn as much as they can by attending local and international seminars, and by organising awareness forums with their banks and counterparts in neighbouring countries. But even attending such events is not always straightforward. Low-income country regulators face budgetary constraints to attend seminars in which they could learn more about the issues with which they are grappling.

The SADC

To what extent are issues raised in the context of SSA and low-income countries more broadly similar to or different from those facing the sub-grouping of countries that are part of the Southern African Development Community (SADC)?

Two points can be made in that respect. First, SADC comprises a quite diverse group of countries. It includes South Africa (which is an emerging country and is thus discussed separately in Box 5.1), natural resource-rich countries such as Angola and DR Congo, and very small countries such as Lesotho and Swaziland.[3] Second, looking at Table 5.5 above on banking ownership, it is obvious that all SADC countries listed on the table have mainly foreign banks (except Zimbabwe). These facts indicate that the issues discussed above for the SSA sub-region are relevant for SADC countries, particularly capacity implementation issues related to small country size and presence of foreign banks, which can lead to regulatory conflicts and banking concentration in favour of foreign banks and to the detriment of local banks. Finally, it should be noted that the SADC grouping includes two countries where all banks are foreign owned (Botswana and Lesotho), a fact that exacerbates some of the issues just mentioned.

Box 5.1 Basel II implementation: What issues does South Africa face?

South African regulators have proposed implementation of Basel II in South Africa from beginning of 2008.[4] Unlike Brazil and India, it has been left to banks themselves to decide which approach to adopt under Pillar 1 – the standardised, the F-IRB or the A-IRB approach. In 2006, of a universe of 33 banks – national and foreign – operating in South Africa, seven banks indicated they intended to adopt the A-IRB approach, one the F-IRB approach and 25 the standardised approach. Among the locally registered banks – 19 in total – four expressed intention of adopting the A-IRB approach and one, the F-IRB approach.[5]

In terms of banking structure and development, South Africa is in the same position as other emerging market economies, rather than being a part of the SSA countries. Banking concentration is high, as, by end of 2006, the four largest banks held 84 per cent of banks' total assets.[6] These larger banks intend to adopt the more complex approaches. Thus, for South Africa, the issues raised regarding possible banking concentration and asset portfolio concentration, are pertinent in terms of larger versus smaller banks – as is the case in Brazil and India, rather than in terms of foreign versus local banks, as is the case for SSA countries.

South African regulators, therefore, have been less strict than Brazil's and India's regulators in that they have given more freedom as to how banks can go about adopting Basel II rules. This, in turn, opens up the possibilities for undesirable developments. Although banking concentration in the country is already high, Basel II could reinforce it, if banks' behaviour post-Basel II implementation is not adequately monitored and actions not taken to avoid undesirable trends and impacts. A specific concern relates to financial innovation, which has played an important role in mass market expansion in South Africa, but which could be inhibited by possible undesirable developments, such as further banking concentration (see section below).

In regard to concerns about financial inclusion, South African regulators have undertaken the initiative to create banking regulations which support access to finance, namely the co-operative banking regulatory framework.[7] However, this initiative has yet to be fully implemented and thus, is still untested. Moreover, it clearly is not sufficiently broad in that it does not include the whole banking system, which is what could truly support access to finance on a large scale. Although there seems to be voices in South Africa in favour of the notion that banking regulation should not be limited to ensuring the stability and efficiency of the financial system, but also about facilitating development of financial markets and pursuing developmental objectives,[8] it remains to be seen to what extent this sort of thinking will be able to help push policy-making toward policies and initiatives that are effective for financial inclusion.

5.5   Can banking innovation be inhibited by Basel II?[9]

This section discusses a further issue that has been virtually unexplored, either in this book or elsewhere: the possibility that Basel II inhibits financial innovation. Innovation that is of interest here is not the sort of new, very complex financial market products developed by highly sophisticated financial engineers – the sort who can be found in large numbers in investment banks in Wall Street and the City of London. Large and profitable banks are those more capable of encouraging and supporting such developments, as are banks facing fierce competition. Basel II through enabling these banks to save capital may reinforce their ability to invest in innovation in this conventional sense. Banking de-regulation in the past 25 years or so has been shown to be a key factor behind innovation in the international financial system.

The innovation that is of concern in this section is one that helps increase financial services to the poor: for example, through taking the form of new modalities of financial services which carry lower costs and are more attuned to the specific needs of the poor;[10] or through new ways of reducing default risks. It is probable that banks operating closer to the bottom end of the market, which in many countries tend to be the smaller banks, are the ones mainly interested in the latter type of innovation.[11]

The smaller banks' culture and greater flexibility are probably critical factors in their willingness to innovate. Moreover, competitive pressure is an important driving force behind searching for ways to expand market share, and to innovate to be able to penetrate new, untapped markets. For the provision of banking services, a general understanding of the targeted market segment is key for successful product development. In regard to credit provision in particular, what puts smaller banks in a strong position to innovate successfully probably is their better understanding of the markets they want to capture, and the risks they are willing to take to serve these markets. Local knowledge is certainly a key ingredient for innovation to support credit provision, which can best be held through proximity with potential customers, made possible through high degree of branch penetration.

To the extent that smaller banks are indeed those facing and holding these conditions and characteristics – greater flexibility, higher competitive pressure, local market knowledge and higher risk taking – they will be more likely to innovate. A regulatory framework that favours larger rather than smaller banks could affect innovation through banking concentration. Even if smaller banks do not disappear, they could close down their local branches to reduce operational costs due to competitive pressure. This in turn could lead to information loss and thereby make it more difficult for these banks to innovate.[12]

Can banking concentration have an impact on financial inclusion?

To a certain extent, this book has already addressed this question in previous chapters. Looking more carefully, it is important to examine the credit patterns across different types of banks, by size (large or small) and by ownership (foreign or national). In certain countries, research has indicated that larger banks tend to concentrate their business at the top end of the market and smaller banks in the middle segment, SMEs and poorer individuals (Gottschalk and Griffith-Jones, 2003). A possible explanation for this market segmentation between banks is that larger banks have a competitive edge (as a result of economies of scale among other factors), and therefore are better able to capture what is seen as the most profitable segments of the market. At the same time, smaller banks hold better knowledge of local markets and thereby have a greater ability to assess risks for a larger number of clients based in these markets. Where these conditions hold, banking concentration could imply less credit to the mid-to-bottom end of the market. In addition, it could cause the loss of local knowledge held by smaller banks, again with negative implications for credit provision to borrowers located toward the bottom end of the credit market.

Even if smaller banks are capable of resisting a takeover, they would still need to take action to face the regulatory-induced competitive advantage of larger banks. This could take the form of reducing the number of branches, particularly by closing down those located in rural, less densely populated areas where the poor are concentrated. The closing down of such branches would inevitably imply the loss of local knowledge and thereby reduce banks' ability to assess borrowers' risks and therefore to provide credit, in addition to other banking services.

Alternatively, smaller banks could try to adopt the more complex (IRB or A-IRB) approaches as well. However, in order to do this they would have to overcome at least two obstacles. First, they would have to have permission granted by the regulatory authorities. Second, even if permission were given, they would need to amass resources including the technical capacity required to deal with the complexity of the models and to build large database to run the models. Moreover, even if smaller banks were prepared for adoption of more complex models and permission were granted for that purpose, the regulators themselves may lack sufficient capacity to validate and monitor the use of models by a large number of banks.

It is difficult to ascertain whether a larger bank would, or not, expand its market base after a takeover. However, more complex approaches for capital allocation may not only help banks save capital and give them a competitive edge. It may also induce them toward credit portfolio concentration, as discussed elsewhere in this book.

Higher capital requirements following the global financial crises

It is possible that, as a result of the global financial crisis, national regulators around the world will require that banks hold higher levels of capital in absolute terms. Thus, exploring the possible consequences of Basel rules more broadly on financial innovation and inclusion, banks may become less inclined to increase operational costs to support an expansion strategy. Expanding access to financial services, penetrating new market areas, creating new physical forms of territorial presence, developing new forms of risk assessment that get around data information constraints, and developing new market products, are all activities that involve costs and that banks therefore may be discouraged to undertake under a regulatory environment in which both compliance and capital costs increase significantly. Thus, the supposed benefits of a regulatory framework in terms of a stronger and safer banking system must be weighed against the costs in terms of inhibiting business expansion to support financial inclusion, and innovation.

Basel II may inhibit innovation not only through possible banking concentration or higher capital costs. It may also hinder innovation through regulation specifically targeted at idiosyncratic activities, which are those activities considered bank specific. For example, the requirement for additional capital under Pillar 2 for activities that are bank specific may have the unintended consequence of penalising innovative forms of banking services to the poor. So it is important that bank regulators are capable of discerning between idiosyncratic activities and innovation. Finally, new risk control systems may inhibit attempts by banks to expand their client base to include clients with different and riskier profiles. These come under Pillar 2 in the form of stricter supervisory controls and monitoring, which could restrict the range of products banks could offer and thereby discourage product development (see discussion concerning Brazilian banks in Chapter 3 above).

5.6   Conclusions

This chapter finds that low-income countries face a number of challenges in implementing Basel II in their jurisdictions, including possible loss of regulatory power over foreign banks where these have a presence in the country, and possible competitive advantage being granted to foreign banks to the detriment of national banks, which can cause banking concentration, skew credit provision away from SMEs, and reduce banking stability.

The chapter also discusses the further issue of financial innovation for financial inclusion and the risk that Basel II may inhibit positive trends in this area taking place in developing countries. In discussing Basel II impacts on financial innovation, it focuses on pro-poor product development, affecting in particular smaller banks geared to the bottom end of the markets.

LIC regulators need to carefully assess these challenges, including possible impacts on financial innovation for financial inclusion, due to their far reaching implications. For example, Basel II impacts on credit policy have implications for macro stability and growth, and impacts on access to credit for SMEs have implications for employment, poverty reduction and equity.

A critical issue to be addressed is loss of regulatory power. In this regard, it is advisable that LIC regulators proceed cautiously in implementing Basel II. Political support is needed, so that LICs do not rush to implement the more complex approaches, which are favoured by the international banks. It is symptomatic of Basel complexities that LICs have slowed down the speed at which they initially intended to implement Basel II. This has been the case even among those countries that had planned to start with Pillars 2 and 3, which were considered less challenging than Pillar 1. Higher levels of technical assistance to LICs are thus required. In addition, regional collaboration is desirable, which may provide the option of searching for a uniform approach, and to forge a common position on specific issues.

All the above could help LIC economic authorities decide on pace and modality of implementing Basel II in ways most appropriate for their development objectives.

Notes

1. This chapter draws on work on Basel undertaken by the authors at IDS over the past several years, most of it funded by the UK Department for International Development.
2. Although the focus of the chapter is on LICs, it also discusses the cases of small middle-income countries such as Botswana and Lesotho, which share problems similar to those facing LICs. In addition, in the context of a discussion on the SADC sub-region, the chapter also covers in a box the case of South Africa, which is a large middle-income country.

3. The SADC are formed of: Angola, Botswana, Democratic Republic of Congo, Lesotho, Madagascar, Malawi, Mauritius, Mozambique, Namibia, South Africa, Swaziland, Tanzania, Zambia and Zimbabwe.
4. See Banks Amendment Act, No 20, 2007.
5. *SARB (2006)*.
6. In Brazil, by mid-2004 the largest ten banks held 66 per cent of total assets (see Chapter 3 in this book).
7. South African Reserve Bank, 2007.
8. Genesis (2004).
9. We would like to thank Anne-Marie Chidzero, Jenny Hoffman and Steven Goldblatt for discussions around the main ideas elaborated in this section.
10. For a discussion on innovation and the motivations driving it see, for example, Porteous (2004).
11. On the point that smaller players tend to be the most innovative ones, see Genesis Analytics (2004, p. 14).
12. Admittedly, the outcome could be just the opposite: to face up to competition, they would have to innovate further to be able to penetrate new markets and thereby expand their business and their total profits.

6
Capital Adequacy Requirements in Emerging Markets

Ray Barrell and Sylvia Gottschalk

6.1 Introduction

In 1988, the Basel Committee on Banking Supervision introduced an international standard of banking regulation, founded on a single measure of regulatory capital provisions for credit risk and straightforward credit risk categories. Its main objectives were to encourage international banks to boost their capital positions and to reduce competitive inequalities. In the late 1990s, international regulators became increasingly concerned about the impacts Basel I would have on emerging markets. Up until then, the main focus of the Basel Committee was the banking system of its members, even though some of the risk categories of the Capital Accord concerned directly loans to non-OECD countries. Two events contributed to this change. First, the disproportionate amount of one-year and interbank loans that flowed to Asia in years preceding the 1997 Asian Crisis led the Committee to investigate whether its simple credit risk structure was to blame for the crisis. Second, since the mid-1900s, many developing countries have been adopting its regulatory framework. And after the Asian Crisis, this happened with the support of the Basel Committee.

This chapter investigates the macroeconomic impacts of changes in capital adequacy requirements in Brazil and Mexico. Changes in the capital adequacy requirements of international and domestic banks are considered, since the former adopted the Basel Capital Accord in 1988 and the latter in the mid-1990s. Unlike most papers in the budding literature on the effects of the Basel Capital Accords in developing countries, this chapter adopts an empirical approach, grounded in a general equilibrium macroeconometric model, which allows us to examine indirect transmission mechanisms. The chapter first estimates a reduced financial block for Brazil and Mexico, which we integrate into the National Institute's General Equilibrium Model (NiGEM). The chapter then simulates a shock to domestic and international capital adequacy ratios.

There is ample macroeconomic evidence that a reduction in domestic bank lending has negative impacts on the real economy (see Bernanke 1983, amongst others). However, an industry-wide fall in domestic credit must occur for this to affect the real economy and it is difficult to see how all banks would be uniformly affected by the introduction or tightening of capital adequacy ratios. Even if some capital constrained banks cut back lending, the reduction must not be fully offset by increased lending either by better capitalised banks or by the issuance of debt or equity. In a paper examining the impacts of the 1988 Basel Capital Accord on the G10, Jackson et al. (1999) find evidence of imperfect substitution between bank lending and alternative sources of finance in the U.S. and Japan, which may have led to a credit crunch in the early 1990s. Regarding emerging markets, three factors indicate that tighter regulatory capital requirements are likely to cause a domestic credit crunch.

First, it is a well-documented fact that capital markets are quite shallow in these countries (Caprio and Honohan 1999, Barth, Caprio and Levine 2001, Powell 2004). Consequently, corporate debt and equity issuance do not constitute a realistic alternative to domestic or international bank lending. In Mexico, for instance, debt issuance represented less than 6 per cent of total private sector finance in 2000. This contrasts with the proportion of bonds in the liabilities of North American companies. Byrne and Davis (2003) report that in 2000 bonds constituted 13 per cent of corporate liabilities in the U.S. and 17 per cent in Canada. Second, the banking sector in emerging markets is usually quite concentrated. Data from the Central Bank of Brazil show that in 2004, 50 per cent of domestic credit in that country was provided by five banks. The 10 largest banks supplied 71 per cent of total domestic credit. Clearly, the reduction of credit by a few capital-constrained banks is likely to have a significant impact on domestic credit to the private sector. Finally, in most emerging markets, there is a marked presence of the government in the real economy, in the form of state owned banks and state-owned companies. Under the rules of the 1988 Capital Accord and of the standardised approach of the 2004 Revised Framework, public sector entities may be included in the zero credit risk category, along with the central government and the central bank[1]. In this context, a private bank subject to tighter capital requirements in an emerging market has several alternatives for increasing its capital ratios without raising additional capital. It may substitute its risk-weighted loans (to the private sector) by zero-risk loans to the central government, state-owned firms or state-owned banks.

Several papers examine the risks to financial stability from a macroeconomic perspective, Gottschalk and Sodré (chapter 3 in this book), Benito, Whitley and Young (2001), and Catalàn and Ganapolski (2005). Gottschalk and Sodré investigate whether the adoption of Basel I led to a private credit crunch in Brazil. Catalàn and Ganapolski (2005) integrate a financial sector within a dynamic stochastic general equilibrium framework to investigate whether capital requirements should be loosened during recessions. Benito, Whitley and Young (2001) build a detailed model of the U.K. financial sector that is incorporated into a macroeconometric model, the Bank of England's medium-term macroeconometric model (MTMM). Two distinct analyses of risks to financial stability are presented in the paper. The first consists of deriving probability distribution functions for keys financial variables, e.g., corporate debt, and then evaluate the chances of these variables assuming crucial values. For instance, there is only a 5 per cent chance that corporate debt will reach the levels of the early 1990s. The second approach investigates the sensitivity of the financial sector to unanticipated shocks, and is characterised by the authors as a 'stress test'. The first shock is a fall in U.K. house prices; the second, an increase in U.K. interest rates.

Catalàn and Ganapolski (2005) integrate a financial sector within a dynamic stochastic general equilibrium framework to investigate whether capital requirements should be loosened during recessions. The prevalent view, based on partial equilibrium analysis, suggests that tightening capital requirements during recessions provokes a credit crunch to firms, which intensifies the economic downturn. The authors found, amongst other interesting results, that tightening capital requirements during a recession has a positive impact on households' savings decisions. Since their savings are the main source of corporate finance, via bank loans, an increase in capital requirements ultimately leads to a faster economic recovery.

Our approach in this chapter is closer to Benito, Whitley and Young (2001), although our results cannot be directly compared to theirs. We estimate the behaviour of several financial variables, and incorporate the resulting equations into a macroeconometric model. We then simulate a positive shock in the international and domestic capital adequacy ratios, and analyse its impact on GDP and its components. Our main results are more comparable to, although they differ significantly from, those of Catalàn and Ganapolski (2005). First, household debt is non-existent in their model. Increases in interest rates translate exclusively into increases in household wealth. Here, household debt incurs interest payments that offset the interest paid on savings. Second, in Catalàn and Ganapolski (2005) banks are price-takers. The interest rate that remunerates deposits/savings is determined by the market. The lending rate is modelled as being state-contingent and tied to firm productivity. If the productivity of the firms banks lend to rises, the return on the loans also rises, and banks then increase their loans to firms. In Brazil and Mexico, banks are price-makers and we found that they increase their lending rate when capital adequacy requirements are tightened.

Our results show that an increase in capital adequacy ratios has adverse impacts on Brazilian and Mexican GDPs. A moderate credit crunch occurs in both countries and is accompanied by a rise in lending rates. However, there are important differences in banks' reaction to tighter solvency ratios in each country. In Brazil, domestic banks adjust their portfolios by switching from higher-risk loans (private sector) to zero-risk loans (sovereign and public sector), instead of increasing their capital provisions. Sovereign lending, and hence government spending thus rises sharply in Brazil. This offsets the negative impacts of the fall in private investment that follows the credit crunch. In Mexico, sovereign lending from domestic banks remains largely unaffected by changes in capital adequacy ratios, whereas foreign loans to the Mexican public sector decrease. However, the Mexican private sector bears the bulk of the adjustment of domestic and foreign banks to the new regulatory rules. These findings suggest the existence of a financial 'crowding-out', where government borrowing replaces private sector borrowing in domestic banks loans portfolios.

Consumer credit in both countries is not sensitive to changes in solvency ratios. Nonetheless, our simulations show that household consumption in Brazil and Mexico drops following a rise in capital adequacy ratios. The transmission mechanism is carried out through household net wealth. Higher solvency ratios lead to higher interest rates, which, other things unchanged, increase net interest payments of households and [thus] reduce their net financial wealth. In our model lower financial wealth results into lower consumption. Overall, GDP falls by 3.5 per cent in Brazil, and by 2.2 per cent in Mexico.

This chapter is organised as follows. After this Introduction Section 6.2 surveys the literature on the impacts of capital adequacy regulation in developing countries. Section 6.3 presents the model used in the simulations underlying the results of Section 6.4. Section 6.5 concludes and precedes the Data Sources (Appendix 1) and the Equations (Appendix 2).

6.2 The Basel capital accord and its impact on developing countries

The Basel Capital Accord was mainly aimed at internationally active banks, few of which can be found in developing countries and emerging markets[2]. However, an increasing number of countries are adopting the Basel capital accords, with direct consequences on their domestic provision of credit. For the most part, developing countries are affected by the accords through their effects on international capital flows.

Regarding the macroeconomic impacts on countries adopting Basel I or II, there is a belief among some researchers that capital requirements will not improve the stability of domestic financial sectors, and may even deteriorate it. De Juan (1996), for instance, remarks that although most Latin American countries adopted Basel I capital standards in the 1990s, some also experienced severe banking crisis during that decade. Rojas-Suarez (2003), at the same time, shows that changes in equity – the core of capital adequacy requirements under Basel I and II – are a poor indicator of the occurrence of a banking crisis. Real net equity increased by nearly 20 per cent in Malaysia, Mexico and Thailand in the year preceding the Mexican and Asian Crisis, whereas real net equity decreased by approximately 20 per cent in Norway and Sweden in 1991, a year before the Nordic financial crisis.

Caprio and Honohan (1999), Barth, Caprio and Levine (2001) and Powell (2004), amongst others, thus see deficient regulation as a more important determinant of banking crisis than the lack of adequate capital provisions. Caprio and Honohan (1999) argue that in all countries supervisors are generally less well paid than bankers, but that it is markedly so in developing countries, where the problem of retention of skilled supervisors in regulatory agencies is particularly acute. In this context, as Powell (2004) suggests, adopting the more sophisticated risk weight measurements proposed in Basel II will allow banks to bypass supervision easily. Powell (2004)'s main conclusion is that compliance with the so-called 'Core Principles' should be a pre-requisite for the adoption of Basel II.

The 'Core Principles' are guidelines for the regulation of banking activity. They were put out in an intricate document published by the Basel Committee, BIS (1997), and were meant to be a set of supervisory principles that could be adopted by any country, irrespective of the sophistication of its banking industry. Some were summed up in Pillar 2 of the 2004 Capital Accord. An empirical study by Podpiera (2004) examines the relationship between banking sector performance and the quality of regulation and supervision, as measured by compliance with the Core Principles. The basic question the author addresses is whether following the Core Principles creates a regulatory and supervisory environment that helps improve banking sector performance. Two of the common measures of banking sector performance are used: nonperforming loans (NPL) and net interest margins (NIM). A high level of NPLs is usually considered an indication of serious problems in the banking sector. Net interest margins are interpreted as a measure of efficiency, since they are an indicator of the cost of banking intermediation paid by customers. An econometric model for NPL and an econometric model for net interest margins are estimated as panels of 65 countries from 1998 to 2002. Podpiera (2004) finds that compliance with Basel Core Principles decreases the share of nonperforming loans in total loans and decreases the net interest margins. Nonetheless, a survey of financial standards of the member countries of the IMF and the World Bank indicates that only 50 per cent of them comply with 1/3 of the Core Principles set up in BIS (1997) (See International Monetary Fund and World bank 2002).

A very incipient research focuses on the effects the adoption of the Basel Capital Accords could have on the provision of domestic credit for the private sector in developing countries. Barajas, Chami, and Cosimano (2005) investigate whether the adoption of Basel I in Latin America caused a reduction of lending throughout the continent between 1987 and 2000. Of the 24 Latin American countries, 22 adopted Basel I between 1991 and 1997. Their empirical results show that most countries of the region experienced a credit slowdown during that period and that there is evidence – albeit weak – that Basel I was a contributing factor. Banks appear to have adjusted their capital requirements by increasing their risk-free, 0 per cent risk weight loans to the federal government, to the detriment of financing private firms.

There have been more studies on the impacts of Basel II on capital flows to developing countries, some of which is surveyed in Daoud (2003). This growing literature points to the negative effects the adoption of the new risk weights could have on international capital flows to these countries. Griffith-Jones (see next chapter in this book)[3], and Weder and Wedow (2002) argue that Basel II could lead to an international credit crunch for developing countries and emerging markets due to a combination of reduced volumes of credit and the increase in the pricing of loans, as regulatory capital requirements may feed through international lending rates.

6.3 Model structure

The National Institute's Global Econometric Model, NiGEM, is presented briefly in subsection 6.3.1, and in more detail in Appendix 2. Several papers using NiGEM as analytical tools describe the model, e.g., Barrel, Dury, Hurst and Pain (2000), Barrell and Dury (2000), Barrell, Byrne and Dury (2003), Barrell and Pina (2004), and Barrell, Holland, Choy and Gottschalk (2002). In Subsection 6.3.2 we present relevant macro-economic indicators of the Brazilian and Mexican economies, which will be included in the existing NiGEM models of these two countries. The equations for the banking sector of these two countries will be described in Appendix 2.

Table 6.1 The model structure

External Block

(1) $P^X = \Phi_1 (eP^w, P)$ (2) $P^X = \Phi_2 (eP^w, P)$

(3) $X = \Phi_3 (Y^W, P^X/eP^W, FDI)$ (4) $M = \Phi_4 (Y, P/P^M, FDI)$

(5) $FDI = \Phi_5 (Y, eP^W/P)$ (6) $TB = P^X X - P^M M$

(7) $CA = r^W NFA + TB$ (8) $NFA = NFA_{-1} + CA$

Supply Side

(9) $Q^* = \gamma[s(K)^{1-1/\sigma} + (1 - s)(L \star TP)^{1-1/\sigma}]^{-\sigma/(1-\sigma)}$

(10) $TP = \lambda_{time} \star TIME + \lambda_{FDI} ln(FDI) + \lambda_M ln(M/P)$

(11) $L = \Phi_6 (Q^*, W/P, TP)$ (12) $W/P = \Phi_8 (Q/L)$

(13) $K = (1 - \delta) \star K_{t-1} + I/P + \Delta FDI$ (14) $K^* = \Phi_7 (Q)$

Demand Side

(15) $C = \Phi_9 (Y_T, FW)$ (16) $FW = M1 + D + eNFA$

(17) $I/P = \Phi_{10} (K/K^*)$ (18) $Q = \Phi_{11} (Y + eP^M M/P)$

Prices and Money

(19) $P = \Phi_{12} (W, L/Q^*, P^M, Q/Q^*, M1/Y)$ (20) $M1/P = \Phi_{13} (Q, \Delta P)$

Government and GDP

(21) $G = \Phi_{14}(Y)$ (22) $T = \Phi_{15}(Y)$

(23) $D = D_{t-1} + G + T - \mu\Delta M1$ (24) $Y = C + I + \Delta FDI + G + TB$

Endogenous variables

P^X: export prices P^M: import prices

X: export volumes   M: import volumes

Continued

Table 6.1   Continued

FDI: stock of FDI	TB: trade balance
CA: current account	NFA: net foreign assets
Q^*: desired industrial output	TP: technical progress
L: labour	W: wages
K^*: desired capital stock	K: actual capital stock
C: consumption	FW: financial wealth
I: investment	Q: actual output
P: domestic prices	M1: narrow money aggregate
G: government expenditure	T: government receipts
D: government debt	Y: GDP

Exogenous variables

P^W: world prices	e: nominal exchange rate
Y^W: world demand	r^W: world interest rate

Parameters: γ and s, scale and distribution parameters of production function, respectively
σ: elasticity of substitution of production function. δ: depreciation rate of capital, λ_i: technical
progress parameter. μ: percentage of public debt monetised by the government.

6.3.1   NiGEM

NiGEM is a large scale macro-econometric model. Each country modelled separately is represented by 60–90 equations with around 30 key behavioral relationships. Unlike models such as computable general equilibrium models (CGE) these equations are econometrically estimated from actual data, rather than calibrated. This in turn implies that variations in each country model may arise. However, those are the result of genuine institutional or specific factors that emerge in econometric estimation, rather differences in theoretical approaches. Each individual model has demand and supply sides, and there is an extensive monetary and financial sector. As a macro model, NiGEM distinguishes itself from CGEs by the aggregation of the production sector into a representative profit maximising firm. Linkages between countries take place through trade, through interacting financial markets and through international stocks of assets. All markets in the NiGEM model clear, implying that all inflows of income must be matched by outflow of income from another sector or economy. The world current account must add up in order that global assets and liabilities match. The government is required to be solvent in the long run, implying that income taxes will adjust automatically in order to prevent the stock of government debt to explode in the long run. The NiGEM model is essentially New Keynesian in its approach. Economic agents – households, firms and governments – are presumed to have rational expectations and be forward-looking, at least in some markets, but nominal rigidities slow the process of adjustment to external events, such as changes in monetary or fiscal policy, changes in world commodity prices or oil price shocks. Most countries of the OECD, including Mexico, are modelled separately. Non-OECD countries fully modelled include Brazil, China, Estonia, Hong Kong, Latvia, Lithuania, Poland, Russia, Slovenia and Taiwan. There are regional blocks for East Asia, Latin America, Africa, OPEC, Developing Europe, and Miscellaneous Developing Countries. NiGEM incorporates models of regional trade or monetary agreements and country associations, with a separate block for NAFTA, the European Union, the European Monetary Union, the OECD.

NiGEM is widely used for forecasting and policy analysis. Policy analysis is conducted through simulations of the model under alternative scenarios. Typical simulations involve analysing the effects of changes in interest rates, government consumption in a single country or in a group of countries. Since NiGEM is a worldwide model and because there are multiple linkages between countries, it is possible to evaluate the global repercussions of the policies of a single country. A classical example is an increase in U.S. government spending, which is usually followed by a rise in U.S. households consumption, in U.S. imports of goods and services, and thus by an increase in world exports. NiGEM is the perfect tool for more complex policy analysis, such as an examination of the impacts of potential entry of the U.K. in the European Monetary Union (see Barrel and Dury 2000, Barrel, Byrne and Dury 2003, Barrel and Pina 2004). An investigation of the impacts of monetary and fiscal shocks on the Euro Area and the U.K. are presented in Barrell et al. (2004).

New countries or blocks can be easily incorporated in NiGEM. The fact that linkages between blocks and countries in NiGEM occur through trade and international financial markets allows a greater flexibility in modelling individual countries. The Hong Kong model, developed by the National Institute for the Hong Kong government, is a clear illustration of the degree of flexibility allowed in modelling individual countries Barrell et al. 2002).

We use NiGEM to evaluate the multiple impacts of changes in capital adequacy requirements in Brazil and Mexico. We have extended the existing models of Brazil and Mexico in NiGEM to incorporate a small banking sector, where banks receive deposits and savings from the private sector, lend to households and firms and make capital provisions for credit risk. The final model will depend on the importance of each variable in the economy of each country and on the availability of data. In both countries, for instance, loans to households represent a very small proportion of total domestic loans. So, it is unlikely that the implementation of banking capital requirements will have a major impact on loans to households.

6.3.2   Macroeconomic indicators: Brazil and Mexico

Figure 6.1 shows the solvency ratios of Brazil, Mexico and the OECD average[4]. We have included for comparison the Basel solvency ratio. Clearly, the capital requirements of all the countries considered in the figure are well above the Basel minimum. The solvency ratio for the OECD rises sharply from 9.5 per cent in 1991 to 12.5 per cent in 1992, and fluctuates around this value over the sample period (1991–2001). It declined slowly from 1992 onward to about 11 per cent in the year of the Asian Crisis (1997) and has been increasing ever since. The ratio for Mexico was below the Basel minimum in 1991, and increased steadily until 1999. A very sharp rise occurred right after the Mexican Crisis, from 9.5 per cent in 1994 to approximately 13 per cent in 1998, and again right after the Russian Crisis, when the capital adequacy ratio reached 16 per cent.

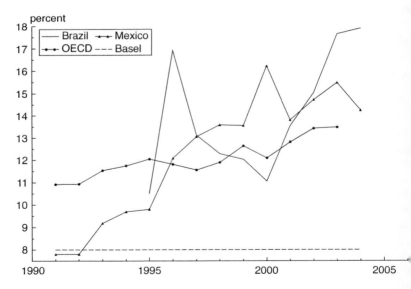

Figure 6.1   Capital adequacy ratios – Brazil, Mexico OECD
Source: Central Bank of Brazil and OECD.

The minimum solvency ratio for Brazil was set at 8 per cent by the Central Bank after the adoption of Basel I in 1994 and to 11 per cent in 1997. A 1996 amendment required banks to make capital provisions for interest rate and exchange rate risk, with consequent changes to be implemented until 2000. In 1999, the Brazilian Central Bank published an official classification of credit into nine risk levels with associated risk weights. Figure 6.1 reflects these developments. First, it should be noted that the data prior to 2000 concern only the five biggest Brazilian banks, whose assets represent 24.75 per cent of the assets of the whole sector. Data on solvency ratios for the whole banking sector are only available from March 2001. In 1995, these five banks had a solvency ratio of 10 per cent. It increased to 17 per cent in the aftermath of the Mexican Crisis, but declined steadily thereafter. A new step change occurs from 2001 onward, partly because the 1996 amendment mentioned above came into force. Banks started making capital provisions for interest rate risk and the capital adequacy ratio of the whole sector increased as a result. The recapitalization of failing state-owned banks by the government started in 1996, which may also account for this rise in capital adequacy ratio (Salviano Junior, 2004).

Brazil

Figure 6.2 shows the spread of Brazilian sovereign bonds over U.S. Treasury bonds, along with the annual inflation rate calculated quarter-on-quarter,

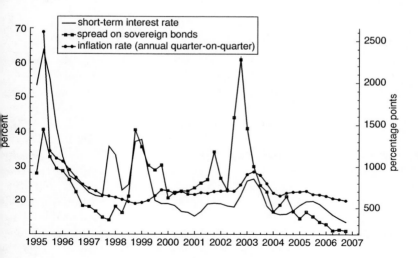

Figure 6.2 Interest rate, inflation and spread – Brazil
Source: IFS and Thomson Datastream.

and the short-term interest rate. The spread is in percentage points and graphed on the right-hand y-axis, whereas the interest and the inflation rates are graphed in percentage against the left-hand y-axis. A spread on sovereign bonds is the difference in percentage points between the interest rate paid by the issuing government and the interest rate paid by the U.S. government. Since U.S. government bonds are considered risk-free, spreads on sovereign bonds are thus a measure of the risk inherent to a certain country. Figure 6.2 shows a weak declining trend in the spread over the period 1995–2008, from 1500 percentage points in 1995 to less than 230 percentage points in 2007. This indicates that the 'Brazil risk' has declined over this period. Several explanations can be offered. The stabilisation plan of 1994 has been successful in reducing annual inflation rate from 2084 per cent in 1993 to 403 per cent in 1994 q1 (not shown on the figure), 81 per cent in 1995 q2, and 3.6 per cent in 2007. The Russian Crisis in 1998 had a strong impact on the perception of the 'Brazil risk', with a surge in the spread in the third quarter of the year. The huge increase in spread in the last quarter of 2002 can be accounted for by the results of the presidential election of November 2002, which brought to power a left-wing political party. The newly elected government pursued a moderate policy, and guaranteed the independence of the central bank in the management of the inflation target regime. This reassured international investors and sovereign spread declined accordingly.

Finally, the interest rate decreased noticeably over the decade, from around 60 per cent per annum in 1995 to less than 15 per cent per annum in 2007.[5] This fall reflects the success of the inflation moderation policy. The short-term interest rate rose sharply in 1997 and 1998, as a result of the Asian and Russian Crisis and their consequent speculative attacks on the Brazilian exchange rate, and again in 2003, following an acceleration of inflationary pressures.

Figure 6.3 presents the evolution of domestic credit in Brazil, by category of borrowers, as a ratio of GDP, from 1997 to 2007. Total domestic credit rises from 23 per cent to 30 per cent of GDP. Most of the rise can be attributed to the increase in household lending, which took off in the second half of 1997. After the Russian Crisis, lending to the public sector fell rapidly to 2 per cent of GDP, and remained around 1 per cent of GDP from 2002 onward. Private sector credit, which includes household borrowing, fluctuated around 25 per cent of GDP over the period. The participation of state-owned firms in banking finance remained very low over the period, with a declining trend.

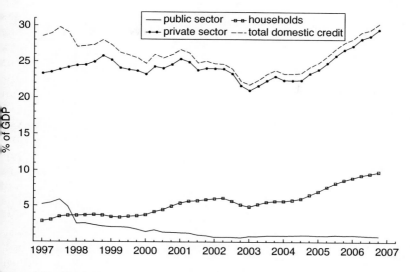

Figure 6.3 Recipients of domestic credit – Brazil
Source: Central Bank of Brazil.

Mexico

Figure 6.4 shows the spread of Mexican sovereign bonds over U.S. Treasury bonds, along with the annual inflation rate calculated quarter-on-quarter, and the short-term interest rate. As above, the spread is graphed against the right-hand y-axis, whereas the interest and the inflation rates are graphed in percentages against the left-hand y-axis. Unlike the spread on Brazilian bonds, the spread of Mexican bonds presents a very strong declining trend over the decade 1995–2005, with the exception of the surge in 1998, which resulted from contagion during the Russian Crisis. Interestingly, the Asian Crisis has very little impact, if any on the risk of Mexican bonds.

Figures 6.4 and 6.5 highlight several aspects of the credit sector in Mexico between 1997 and 2007. Figure 6.5 presents domestic and foreign credit to the private sector, as a percentage of GDP. Total credit to the private sector represented approximately 25 to 30 per cent of GDP over the period, a very similar ratio to Brazil. This similarity overlooks the difference between the developments of the financial sectors in these two countries. Legal restrictions were placed on the expansion of the Mexican banking sector in the 1980s, whereas the Brazilian banking sector was encouraged to develop by the government. Foreign

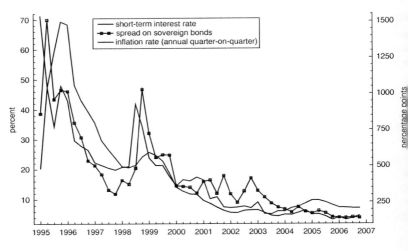

Figure 6.4   Interest rate, inflation and spread – Mexico
Source: OECD and Thomson Datastream.

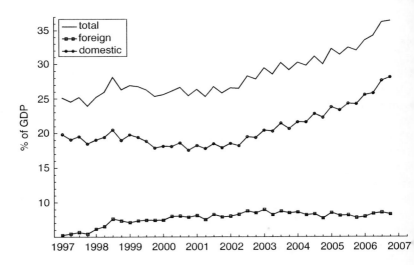

Figure 6.5   Sources of credit to the private sector – Mexico
Source: Central Bank of Mexico.

loans amounted to less than 10 per cent of GDP and remained largely unaffected by the Asian crisis. Moreover, the share of foreign credit in total credit rose noticeably over the period, from 20 per cent in 1997 to 36 per cent in 2007, reflecting the continuous increase in the confidence of international investors. Nonetheless, the bulk of banking credit to the private sector was provided by domestic institutions. Data from the Central Bank of Mexico not shown in the figure suggest that firms were the major recipient of banking credit, receiving about 79 per cent of total loans over the period. Household borrowing amounted to approximately 21 per cent of total loans to the private sector, and to 5 per cent of GDP. Figure 6.4 cast some light on the institutional sources of loans in Mexico. The participation of commercial banks decreased from around 80 per cent in 1997 to 40 per cent in 2006 q4, to the benefit of financial intermediaries like savings-and-loans institutions or cooperatives ('non-banks' in Figure 6.5). Issues of debt instruments increased in recent years, whilst financing from development banks decreased concomitantly.

6.4 Simulations of the model

This section presents the results of the simulations of a shock to domestic and international capital requirements on Brazil and Mexico. From the discussion in Section 6.2, we simulate an increase rather than a decrease in solvency ratios. The results are presented either as a percentage difference from base, or absolute difference from base (percentage points), if the variable is in percentage, e.g., interest rates. The base for the Brazilian and Mexican blocks is the value of the variables on the last available quarter, which is flattened forward to 2010 q4. As most financial variables and the components of GDP are quarterly, the base is their value in 2004 q4. Personal sector variables, such as net interest payments, dividends, non-wage personal income, are annual variables. Their base value is that of 2003. For the Mexican and OECD solvency ratios, the base is 2001. For Brazilian solvency ratios, it is 2004 q4.

6.4.1 Shock to national capital adequacy requirements

Figures 6.7 to 6.13 show the results of a positive shock of 0.5 percentage points in domestic capital adequacy ratios. The user cost of capital in both countries rises, by 0.15 percentage points in Mexico and by 0.35 percentage points in Brazil (Figure 6.7). Since this is the cost of lending for private firms, it follows immediately that domestic loans to firms will decline, as can be seen in Figures 6.7 and 6.10. Domestic

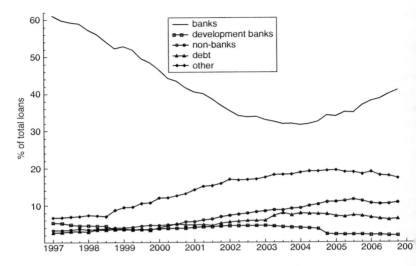

Figure 6.6   Institutional sources of credit to the private sector – Mexico
Source: Central Bank of Mexico

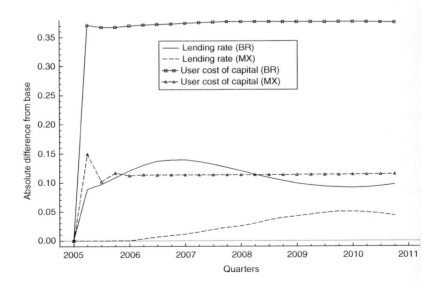

Figure 6.7   Impacts of domestic shock: Interest rates – Brazil

lending decline by less than 1 per cent in Brazil and approximately 1 per cent in Mexico. The impact on government lending in each country differs markedly. Domestic loans to government in Mexico remain unaffected by changes in domestic capital adequacy ratios, as can be expected from the Basel capital adequacy rules. However, as was seen above, banks have reacted to the implementation of capital adequacy rules by increasing lending to lower risk-weight borrowers, which in most cases, are the government and the Central Bank. This fact was documented in Brazil by Gottschalk and Sodre (2009) chapter 3 of this book and we found empirical evidence of it in the period 1997–2004, as can be seen in equation (32). The corresponding equation for Mexican government lending, equation (36) also shows no direct relationship between the domestic capital adequacy ratio and government lending. Figure 6.8 shows that domestic loans to the Brazilian government would rise by approximately 2 per cent above base following an increase in domestic capital adequacy ratio.

Before we examine the impacts on foreign lending, it is worth looking at Figures 6.10 and 6.11. Clearly, GDP and consumption rise in both countries, whereas exports tend to fluctuate around base. The fall in GDP relative to base reaches 3.5 per cent in Brazil and about 2 per cent

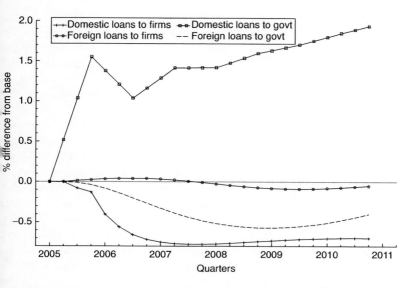

Figure 6.8 Impacts of domestic shock: Domestic credit – Brazil

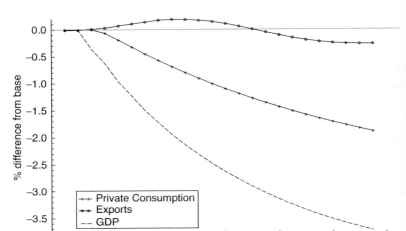

Figure 6.9   Impacts of domestic shock: GDP – Brazil

in Mexico, owing to the sharp decline in private investment. Equations (38) and (39) show a strong negative statistical relationship between total lending to firms and private investment. Finally, although capital adequacy ratios do not directly feed into household borrowing, equations (26) and (27), the net interest payments by households depend on them through the lending rate, as can be seen in equations (42) and (43). Consequently, the rise in the lending rate seen in Figure 6.7 increases households' net interest payments, which decreases their disposable income and hence reduces household consumption.

It is interesting to note that changes in domestic capital adequacy ratios have negative impacts on foreign lending to firms and government. This is an indirect effect, stemming from the fall in GDP. As can be seen in equations (24) and (25), foreign lending to Brazilian and Mexican firms are sensitive to the overall economic performance of the private sector, which is proxied by the growth rate of exports in the Brazilian equation and the level of exports in the Mexican equation. Consequently, since exports remain around base in Brazil, foreign loans to its private firms also fluctuate around base. In the Mexican case, we found that foreign loans are statistically extremely sensitive to changes in export performance, which account for the strong decline in foreign loans to Mexican firms when exports fall. An analogous argument applies to foreign lending to government, which depends on GDP.

As we found in the case of Brazil, changes in foreign capital adequacy ratios may have a potentially more damaging effect on the Mexican economy than changes in their domestic equivalent. Foreign lending may be reduced to a greater extent, which leads to a larger decline in private investment, consumption and ultimately GDP.

6.4.2 Shock to international capital adequacy requirements

Figure 6.10 summarises the impacts of an increase of 0.5 percentage points in capital adequacy ratio on Brazilian GDP, consumption and on foreign loans to Brazilian firms and government. GDP and household consumption fall by more than 3.5 per cent relative to base and slightly less than 2.5 per cent from base respectively. As above, the decline is household consumption results in the rise of the lending rate, which depends on the differential between domestic and foreign capital adequacy ratios, as can be seen in equation (35). Foreign loans to Brazilian firms are found to be irresponsive to changes in foreign capital adequacy ratios, which accounts for its fluctuations around base. Moreover, foreign loans to firms are inversely related to the Brazilian sovereign risk, proxied by the spread of sovereign bonds, which declines

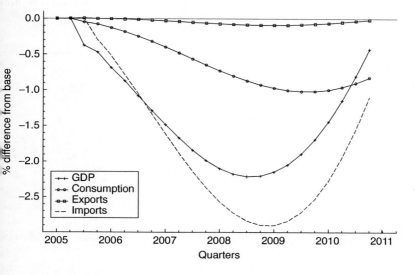

Figure 6.10 Impacts of domestic shock: GDP Mexico

slightly in the 8 quarters following the shock. Foreign loans to the Brazilian government, on the contrary, are sensitive to changes in foreign banks' capital requirements and decrease to by approximately 1/2 per cent below base three years after the shock.

A comparison of the impacts of a shock on domestic and foreign capital requirements (Figure 6.12) shows that the negative effects of the latter are larger than that of the former. The decline in GDP resulting from a foreign shock is about 2 percentage points bigger than the fall in GDP resulting from a domestic shock. This difference can be accounted for by the fact that an increase in foreign capital adequacy requirements leads to a fall in private investment and government expenditure, whereas a rise in domestic capital adequacy ratio decreases private investment but increases government lending and hence, government spending (equation 44).

Table 6.2 and Figure 6.13 show the impact of an increase in OECD capital requirements on foreign loans to Mexican firms, total loans to the Mexican economy and on Mexican private investment. It is clear that even a small increase in capital requirements will have negative impacts on the Mexican economy in the shortterm. Total loans will decline by approximately 1.7 per cent in less than a year, whilst loans to private firms will decline by 2 per cent in the first quarters following the shock. The impact of a rise in foreign banks' capital requirements

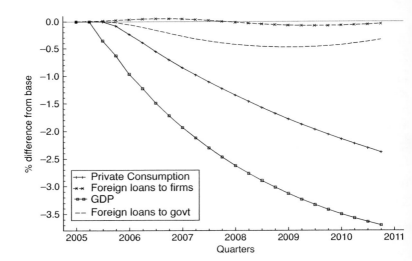

Figure 6.11   Increasing international capital requirements – Brazil

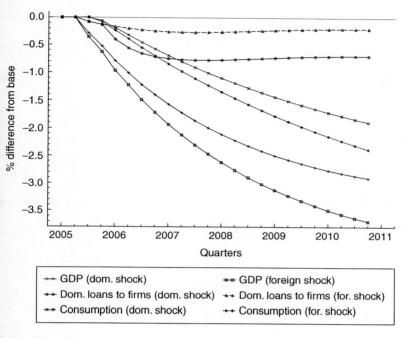

Figure 6.12 Comparing domestic and foreign shocks – Brazil

Table 6.2 Impacts of domestic and foreign shocks – Mexico

	Domestic shock		Foreign shock			
	Domestic loans		Foreign loans		National accounts	
Quarters	Firms	Government	Firms	Government	Consumption	GDP
Q1	0.000	0.000	0.000	−4.240	−0.015	−0.11
Q2	−0.180	0.000	−1.750	−4.630	−0.012	−0.07
Q3	−0.330	−0.002	−2.000	−8.670	−0.028	−0.17
Q4	−0.480	−0.001	−3.060	−9.400	−0.029	−0.14
Q5	−0.600	−0.005	−3.370	−8.900	−0.033	−0.12
Q6	−0.690	−0.013	−4.020	−9.510	−0.040	−0.14
Q7	−0.770	−0.028	−4.310	−9.110	−0.044	−0.13
Q8	−0.820	−0.047	−4.720	−9.630	−0.051	−0.16
Q9	−0.860	−0.072	−4.960	−9.320	−0.054	−0.15
Q10	−0.870	−0.240	−5.720	−9.710	−0.076	−0.19
Q11	−0.800	−0.520	−6.100	−10.080	−0.090	−0.21
Q12	−0.780	−0.900	−6.310	−10.440	−0.110	−0.22

All values in % difference from base.

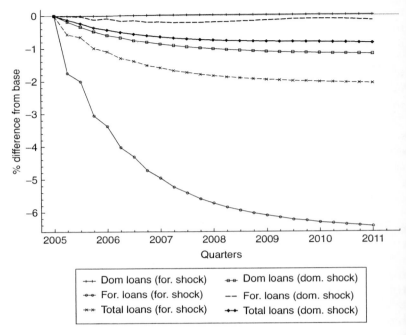

Figure 6.13   Comparing domestic and foreign shocks – Mexico

on Mexican private investment is rather mitigated, since foreign loans constitute a smaller proportion of Mexican firms' loans.

Finally, Figure 6.13 compares the shocks on domestic and foreign solvency ratios on Mexican loans to firms. The foreign shock has larger negative impacts on total loans and foreign loans, whereas the domestic has a bigger impact on domestic loans than on foreign loans. The decline in total loans resulting from a shock in foreign capital requirements is quite pronounced, and has fallen more than 6 per cent below base.

As we found in the case of Brazil, changes in foreign capital adequacy ratios may have a potentially more damaging effect on the Mexican economy than changes in their domestic equivalent. Foreign lending may be reduced to a greater extent, which leads to a larger decline in private investment, consumption and ultimately GDP.

6.5   Conclusion

The Basel Capital Accords came to light as a response to the increasing vulnerability of the international financial system to disruptions in national financial markets. As these became increasingly integrated from the late 1970s onward, it became more and more likely that failures of national financial institutions with international activities could build up into global crisis. The main objectives of the Capital Accords were thus the promotion of international cooperation of national supervisors and the implementation by its members of common prudential rules, and, in particular, of a common solvency ratio.

As the Capital Accords were originally designed to strengthen the solvency of internationally active banks, developing countries and emerging markets were not – and still are not – bound by its capital adequacy rules. However, countries such as Brazil, India and Mexico, have adopted the Basel prudential rules to regulate their domestic financial sectors in the late 1990s.

This chapter investigates the potential impacts of the adoption of capital adequacy rules from a macroeconomic standpoint. We show that changes in capital adequacy ratios in Brazil and Mexico may negatively affect households, firms and government, by rising lending rates and decreasing banking loans. We found that public sector finance in Brazil may rise as a result of an increase in domestic capital adequacy requirements to the detriment of private sector lending. Moreover, our results suggest that changes in foreign capital adequacy ratios may have a potentially more damaging effect than changes in their domestic equivalent. This can be accounted for by a portfolio redistribution effect. As government lending tends to increase with a rise in domestic solvency ratio, government expenditure rises, which helps sustain GDP.

Appendix 1   Data sources

1. Brazil

* Central Bank: total loans to non-financial private sector, total domestic loans, loans from domestic banks to private firms, loans from domestic banks to individuals, total loans from banks, total deposits and savings. M4. All variables available for the period 1991 q1–2006 q4. Capital adequacy variable (1995 q1 – 2007 q2).

  IBGE: National accounts data. (1) GDP and its components (GDP, consumption, private investment, government investment, government consumption, export volumes, import volumes, inventories); (2) National accounts by institutional sector: Households (distributed dividends, interest income, tax, compensation, transfers). All variables available annually for the period 1990–2003.

- IPEA: Stock of capital (1991–2003).
- IMF: deposit rate (instant savings rate), cost of borrowing (weighted average of rates charged by banks on loans with fixed interest rates and with own funds to individuals and firms. Weights are loan amounts), 3-month interest rate (money market rate, which is the average rate on loans between commercial banks). (IMF). All variables available for the period 1991 q1–2006 q4.
- Thomson Datastream: Spread of Brazilian sovereign bonds (JPMorgan EMBI) over U.S. Treasury bonds. 1994 q3–2006 q4

2. Mexico

- Central Bank: total loans to non-financial private sector, total domestic loans, loans from domestic banks to private firms, loans from domestic banks to individuals, total loans from banks. Total deposits and savings. All variables available for the period 1996 q4–2006 q4.
- INEGI: National accounts data. (1) GDP and its components (GDP consumption, private investment, government investment, government consumption, export volumes, import volumes, inventories) (2) National accounts by institutional sector: Households (net wealth of households, distributed dividends, interest income, tax, compensation, transfers; liabilities); (3) depreciation, GDP deflator. All variables available for the period 1993–2001.
- IMF: Average cost of funds (banks), deposit rate (weighted average rate payable to individuals on 60-day time deposits. Weights are deposit amounts), cost of borrowing (lending rate). Both variables available for the period 1980 q1–2006 q4. 3-month interest rate (Treasury bill rate) (1987 q1–2006 q4). [?]. Government domestic and foreign net borrowing (1980 q1–2005 q2). M4.
- OECD Statistical Compendium: Capital adequacy variables for OECD banks, risk-weighted assets, Tier 1 and Tier 2 capital, net capital. All variables available for the period 1991–2003. Total employment (1987–2003), dependent employment (1980–2003).
- Thomson DataStream: Spread of Mexican sovereign bonds (JPMorgan EMBED) over U.S. Treasury bonds. 1994 q1–2006 q4.

Appendix 2   Equations[6]

A2.1   The structure of NiGEM

The NiGEM model is essentially New Keynesian in its approach, in that agents are presumed to be forward-looking, at least in some markets but nominal rigidities slow the process of adjustment to external events.

It has complete demand and supply sides, and there is an extensive monetary and financial sector. Rational or model-consistent expectations are used throughout the model. As far as possible, the same theoretical structure has been adopted for each of the major industrial countries, except where clear institutional or other factors prevent this. As a result, variations in the properties of each country model reflect genuine differences emerging from estimation and key data ratios, rather than different theoretical approaches. However, we have endeavoured to maintain a similar underlying structure to the standard NiGEM framework, allowing more detailed disaggregation where necessary, so that the overall pattern of behaviour should reflect that of other countries.

Linkages between countries in the NiGEM model take place through trade, through interacting financial markets and through international stocks of assets. Hence a change in, say, U.S. equity prices affects Europe through its effects on U.S. imports, through its effects on interest rates and exchange rates, and also through its effects on the wealth of the European personal sector through equity prices.

We have ensured that the model is theoretically coherent, and this requires that there are no financial 'black holes' to absorb imbalances. All inflows of income must be matched by an outflow of income from another sector or country. The world current account must add up in order that global assets and liabilities match, and the model should be approaching an asset equilibrium by the terminal date. This in turn requires that the stock of government debt does not explode. The world current account is brought into approximate balance by the model. The volume of world exports approximately equals the volume of world imports, but any discrepancy is allocated to exports in proportion to the share of world trade.

The underlying economic structure of the model is relatively standard. Domestic demand, aggregate supply and the external sector are linked together through the wage-price system, income and wealth, the financial sector, the government sector and competitiveness. The supply-side of the economy is centred around a production function that determines factor demands. Wages are determined by a simple bargaining process over the share of labour in total output. Domestic prices are determined as a mark-up over production costs, which are a weighted average of domestic production costs and import prices. The mark-up is based on the elasticity of demand, which is determined as a pro-cyclical function of the business cycle, captured by capacity utilisation. The wage-price system affects competitiveness and income and wealth.

Competitiveness feeds into the external sector, while income and wealth feed into domestic demand through private consumption. The wage-price system also affects total government receipts and expenditure through indirect taxes and transfers to households.

The external sector feeds into domestic demand through the impact of net foreign assets and interest income on household income and wealth, while domestic demand feeds back into the external sector as a determinant of imports and inward FDI. Inward and outward FDI affect the external sector through both exports and imports. The financial sector affects domestic demand through the impact of interest rates on investment and consumption, and feeds into the government sector through interest payments on government debt. The government sector feeds into consumption through the stock of government debt, which affects household wealth, and income tax, which feeds into real disposable income.

In order to undertake effective policy analysis we have to be able to use the assumption that agents can look forward and that expectations are rational. This in turn requires that agents use the implications of the model in their expectation formation. The use of rational expectations for policy analysis requires that the modeller construct a coherent forward base of about 20 years to run off. Forward-looking simulations will not normally solve if the model has not achieved some sort of equilibrium toward the end of a simulation run. This condition is not imposed on the model, but in order to achieve a solution, it is essential that the model being used contains an equilibrium growth path and has the feedback to return to that real equilibrium. Otherwise, the model will not be able to find a solution. The only terminal condition imposed on the model is rate of growth for forward-looking variables. The NiGEM model allows a 30-year time horizon.

For long-run properties, it is essential that certain relationships are homogeneous to ensure that nominal shifts do not have permanent real effects and key ratios such as household savings to income are stable and to ensure there are not black holes in the model. Integration of the main core model with the submodel for trade and a government sector model is essential for the analysis of the impact of external shocks, as well as domestic measures such as tax changes. The long-run structure of the new model is firmly grounded in theory. However, parameters in all key behavioural equations have been econometrically estimated to ensure data consistency and to improve the short-run forecasting properties of the model. We do not recommend re-estimating the entire model each time new data is available. The model should represent the world we think we live in, and if we are correct this should change only when there is clear evidence of a significant structural shift in behaviour. Responding to one-off data revisions and new data which may be outlying is likely to distort projections.

This section draws on Barrell et al. (2004).

Consumption and Personal Income

We assume that consumers consider their current income (RPDI income including non-labour income net of taxes) and their real financial wealth (RNW)[7], and that they adjust toward a long run relationship involving these variables. Adjustment costs are assumed to be quadratic, and behaviour is forward-looking. The resulting equation is:

$$\Delta C_t = \lambda [C_{t-1} - a * RPDI_{t-1} - (1 - a) * RNW_{t-1}] + \delta * \Delta C_{t+1} + \epsilon_t \qquad (3)$$

We assume that wealth is affected by financial markets through equity and bond prices, and hence if these markets 'expect' something in the future then it will be reflected in prices. News that changes expectations will cause wealth to be revalued, and hence will affect behaviour now.

Personal incomes are generated from compensation received by those in employment, by transfers from the government, and from other income which depends upon net domestic and foreign profits received and on government interest payments. Income recipients also pay direct taxes on their incomes. Consumers are assumed to be the ultimate owners of all assets and hence of all income streams. All assets and liabilities are explicitly modelled, and so are associated income streams associated with assets.

Production and labour market

For each country, we have an underlying CES production function which constitutes the theoretical background for the specification of the factor demand equations, forms the basis for unit total costs and provides a measure of capacity utilisation, which then feeds into the price system. A CES production function that embodies labour augmenting technological progress (denoted λ) with constant returns to scale, can be written as:

$$Q = \gamma [s(K)^{-\rho} + (1 - s)(Le^{\lambda t})^{-\rho}]^{-1/\rho} \qquad (4)$$

γ and s are production function scale parameters, and the elasticity of substitution, σ, is given by $1/(1 + \rho)$. Variables K and L denote the net capital stock and labour input measured in terms of employee hours. With long-run constant returns to scale, we obtain log-linear factor demand equations of the form:

$$Ln(L) = [\sigma \ln\{\beta(1 - s)\} - (1 - \sigma) \ln(\gamma)] + \ln(Q) - (1 - \sigma)\lambda t - \sigma \ln(w/p) \quad (5)$$

$$Ln(K) = [\sigma \ln(\beta s) - (1 - \sigma) \ln(\gamma)] + \ln(Q) - \sigma \ln(c/p) \quad (6)$$

The parameters of the production function vary across countries and w, c and p denote respectively labour costs per head, nominal user costs of capital and the price of value added (at factor cost) and β denotes the mark-up. We estimated a long run labour demand curve to retrieve the elasticity of substitution and the technical progress parameters. We calibrated the remaining parameters and utilised the elasticity of substitution in the capital demand equation. These parameters are also used in the construction of an indicator of capacity utilisation that affects the mark-up of prices over unit total costs. The capital stock adjustment equation depends upon the long run equilibrium, and the user cost of capital is influenced by the forward-looking real rate, as well as by taxes and by depreciation. The speed of adjustment to equilibrium in the investment/ capital stock adjustment equations also depends upon the short-term real interest rate, with the effects being similar across countries.

We assume that employers have a right to manage, and hence the bargain in the labour market is over the real wage. In the long run wages rise in line with productivity all else equal. Given the determinants of the trajectory for real wages, if unemployment rises then real wages fall relative to trend, and conversely. There is continual structural change in labour markets and sustainable unemployment changes when policies change, and must continually update our model so that it reflects the economies we are studying, rather than being just a simple description of past data. Both the determinants of equilibrium and the dynamics of adjustment change, and adjustment, especially in Europe is slow.

There is no explicit equation for sustainable employment in the model, but as the wage and price system is complete, the model delivers equilibrium levels of employment and unemployment. An estimate of the NAIRU can be obtained by solving the price equation based on unit total costs for the real wage. Unit total costs depend in turn the user cost of capital and the distribution parameters, and hence the real rate of interest will affect the NAIRU, as will the rate of capacity utilisation. Equilibrium output depends on factor inputs into the production function. The equilibrium supply of labour is the product of on the level of employment given by the NAIRU and trend hours worked, which decline over time

Financial markets

For most purposes, we assume that exchange rates are forward-looking, and 'jump' when there is news. The size of jumps depends on the effects on interest rates that are anticipated for the future, and hence policy rules affect financial markets. We assume that bond and equity markets are also forward-looking, and long-term interest rates reflect short rates that are expected in the future. The long rate is the forward convolution of expected short rates, whilst the equity price is related to the discounted present value of future expected profits.

Forward-looking long rates LR (and long real rates) have to look T periods forward

$$(1 + LR_t) = \Pi_{j=1, T} (1 + SR_{t+j})^{1/T} \tag{7}$$

Forward-looking exchange rates RX have to look one period forward along the arbitrage relation involving domestic and foreign interest rates (SRH and SRF)

$$RX_t = RX_{t+1} (1 + SRH_t) / (1 + SRF_t) \tag{8}$$

Forward-looking equity prices are solved out from the infinite forward recursion and depend only on the expected equity price next period and the discount factor, which in turn depends upon the equity risk premium

$$EQP_t = Profits_1 + EQP_{t+1}discounted \tag{9}$$

We also adjust for the expected real growth of the capital stock and its implications for profits per unit of equity. The equity risk premium also feeds into the physical investment decision.

The price equations are all statically homogenous, but in some cases do not display dynamic homogeneity, as this imposes too strong a restriction on the data to be acceptable to model users.[8] Hence, in some countries, but not the U.K. for instance, the mark-up of prices over costs depends upon the rate of price inflation. However, this is not relevant to the results in this chapter, as we do not change the trend rate of inflation in any of the simulations. There are marked capacity effects in the price system. If output is above capacity, prices rise more rapidly than their determinants (foreign prices, total unit costs, expectations) would suggest, and the reverse is the case if the economy is below capacity. If prices fall relative to baseline because the economy is below capacity, then real financial wealth rises, and competitiveness improves, and both help raise capacity utilisation through higher domestic demand and exports.

External sector

Our trade equations depend upon demand and relative competitiveness effects, and the latter are defined in similar ways across countries. There are a number of competitiveness measures we can construct. For exports we assume that exporters compete against other people who export to the same market (RPX), and demand is given by the import in the markets to which the country has previously exported (S)

$$\Delta X_t = \lambda[X_{t-1} - S_{t-1} + b * RPX_t] + c_1 * \Delta X_{t-1} + c_2 * \Delta S_t + \varepsilon_t \tag{10}$$

Imports depend upon import prices relative to domestic prices (RPM) and on demand (TFE)

$$\Delta M_t = \lambda[M_{t-1} - b_1 * TFE_{t-1} + b_2 * RPM_t] + c_1 * \Delta M_{t-1} + c_2 * \Delta TFE_t + \varepsilon_t \tag{11}$$

Government and GDP

It is important to have sketch models of direct and indirect taxes, and of government spending. We consider the financing of the government deficit (BUD), and we allow either money (M) or bond finance (DEBT).

$$BUD = \Delta M_t + \Delta DEBT_t \tag{12}$$

The debt stock affects interest payments and forms part of private sector wealth. Current fiscal revenues are disaggregated into personal taxes (variable TAX, which includes both personal income tax and social security contributions), corporate taxes (CTAX) and miscellaneous taxes (mainly indirect; MTAX). We also have government consumption and investment (GC and GI), interest payments (GIP) and transfers (TRAN). As GC and GI are in constant prices, we convert them to nominal terms using the private consumption deflator CED and the GDP deflator P, respectively. The budget balance thus reads:

$$BUD = TAX + MTAX + CTAX - TRAN - GIP - Gc * CED - GI * P \tag{13}$$

Government interest payments are modelled as the income on a perpetual inventory, the change in the debt stock each period paying the long interest rate in the issue period until it is replaced[9]. Personal taxes and transfers affect disposable income, as do interest payments[10]. All budget items feed into the economic system through their impact on the budget balance, and thus on the economy's asset stocks.

Policy rules

Fiscal and monetary policy rules are important in 'closing the model' and our rules are discussed at greater length in Barrell and Dury (2000).

Fiscal Policy rules

We assume budget deficits are kept within bounds in the longer term, and taxes rise to do this. This simple feedback rule is important in ensuring the long run stability of the model. Without a solvency rule (or a no-Ponzi games assumption), there is no necessary solution to a forward-looking model. We can describe the simple fiscal rule as

$$Tax_t = Tax_{t-1} + \varphi[GBRT - GBT] + \delta[GDRT - GDR] \qquad (14)$$

Where Tax is the direct tax rate, GBR and GBRT are the government surplus target and actual surplus, GDR and GDRT are the stock of debt to GDP and the target for the stock, φ and δ are the feedback parameters. The former is designed to remove an excess deficit in less than five years, whilst the latter is set to zero in this exercise. Targets have to be set consistently.

Monetary policy rules

We assume that the monetary authorities target something that stabilise the price level or the inflation rate in the long term. The speed of response of the authorities affects the properties of the model. A typical policy for a central bank may be to target some nominal aggregate such as nominal GDP or the money stock, which may rise in line with nominal GDP in the long run. A standard monetary policy rule would be to change the interest rate according to some proportion of the deviation of the targeted variable from its desired path. For example, a proportionate control rule on the nominal GDP or the money stock would be:

$$r_t = \lambda_1(P_t Y_t - P_t^* Y_t^*) \qquad (15)$$

where P = Price level and Y is real output. The star denotes the target variables. However, a nominal target only stabilises inflation in the long run and policy makers are likely to be concerned with keeping inflation at some desired level in the short term. During the 1990s, several moved to a new monetary policy regime of inflation targeting and have announced a formal inflation-targeting framework where decisions are guided by the deviation of inflation from some target level. We might write a similar rule with the money stock replaced with the inflation rate. This would give a simple proportional rule on the inflation rate (we may use either the current or the expected inflation rate – in this paper we use expected rates) $r_t = \gamma_2(\Delta P_{t+j} - \Delta P_{t+j^*})$ where j indicates the lead or lag in the feedback rule.

The ECB uses a combination of these two approaches. A combined policy of nominal aggregate targeting and inflation rate targeting would then give:

$$r_t = \gamma_1(P_t Y_t - P_t^* Y_t^*) + \gamma_2(\Delta P_{t+j} - \Delta P_{t+j^*}) \tag{16}$$

The policy rules on the model use the Consumer Price Index (CPI) inflation rate. We choose the combined rule as our default monetary policy rule because it represents the mixed framework that is used in Europe by the European Central Bank (ECB).

A2.2 General structure of behavioural equations

The key behavioural equations of NiGEM are estimated using cointegration econometric analysis. They are thus made up of two components, the long run relationship and the short-run dynamics around the long run. The long run relationship describes the equilibrium of the system in the absence of any shock and would normally be related to the behaviour of the economic agents of the economy, households, firms (including financial intermediaries) and government. Economic agents react to external shocks by adjusting the supply and demand of labour, goods, or prices, and these adjustments lead the economy toward a new long-run equilibrium. The dynamics of adjustment that pull it toward the equilibrium are the second element of the behavioural equation. The long run relationship is usually expressed as $Y_{t-1} = \alpha - \alpha_1 * X_{t-1} + v_t$, where α and α are parameters to be estimated and v_t is an error term. The behavioural equation is usually expressed as an error correction mechanism (ECM),

$$\Delta Y_t = \alpha + \lambda * [Y_{t-1} - \alpha_1 * X_{t-1}] + \beta_1 * \Delta Y_{t-1} + \beta_2 * \Delta X_t + \varepsilon_t \tag{17}$$

The term in brackets is the long-run relationship, which has been re-written in a way that emphasises the degree of dis-equilibrium from the long-run. This term is often referred to as the 'error' in the error correction mechanism. The remaining terms of the equation form the adjustment around the long run. Y_t and X_t are variables or vectors of variables, Δ is the change operator, λ, a, α_1, β_1 and β_2 are parameters or vectors of parameters and is an error term. The parameter λ is particularly important in the dynamics because it is the major indicator of the speed with which any dis-equilibrium is removed.

A2.3   Equations of the Brazilian and Mexican banking sector in NiGEM

This section presents the financial equations of the Brazilian and Mexican model. The current version of the two blocks is a backward-looking aggregate-demand aggregate-supply model. Expectations are treated implicitly by the inclusion of current and lagged values of the variables. All national accounts variables are in constant prices, whilst personal sector variables are in current prices. This setting was kept for the model of Mexico. However, this was not possible for the Brazilian model. As was mentioned above the Brazilian inflation rate plummeted from 2084 per cent per annum in 1994 to 400 per cent per annum in 1995, and averaged 7 per cent per annum in 2004. Given these wide fluctuations in the past 10 years, we opted for eliminating the effects of price changes in the model. So, national accounts, personal sector and financial variables are deflated in the Brazilian model. For instance, the change in the log of domestic credit to firms, $\Delta lbrlnsdf_t$, should be read as the change in the log of $brlnsdf_t/brced_t$. The exceptions are the spread on Brazilian sovereign bonds, and, naturally, the nominal interest rates. The main implication of this modelling choice is that the inflation rate is not used as an independent variable in the equations of the Brazilian block.

The model uses quarterly data, and the equations are generally estimated for a period between 1984 and 2005. Concerning the estimations, the Error-Correction Model technique has been used to specify the general form of the equations. More details on the estimations of the model equations are available in Barrell and Gottschalk (2006).

Spreads

$$\Delta lbrssprd_t = 4.5443 - 0.68265 * [lbrssprd_{t-1} - 1.9768 * brrr_{t-1}]$$
$$ (3.67) \quad\quad (-3.59) \quad\quad\quad\quad\quad\quad (-2.63)$$

$$+ 16.6614 * \Delta lbrced_{t-1} + 0.86898 * \Delta lbry_{t-1} - 0.36514 \quad\quad (18)$$
$$ (2.52) \quad\quad\quad\quad\quad (1.31) \quad\quad\quad\quad\quad (-1.34)$$

$$* d97q4 + 0.6779 * d98q3 - 0.4978 * d0301$$
$$ (3.29) \quad\quad\quad\quad\quad (-1.51)$$

$R^2 = 0.32$, $\sigma = 0.3$, $DW = 1.69$, $LM(4) = 2.08$. Sample: 1996 q1–2003 q4. rr_t is the real short-term interest rate, $\Delta lbrced_{t-1}$, the consumer expenditure inflation, $\Delta lbry$, real GDP growth rate. The terms in brackets are the t-ratio tests, in this and in all equations below.

$$\Delta lmxssprd_t = 3.8318 - 0.71145 * lmxssprd_{t-1} - 0.03346 * mxr3m_{t-1}$$
$$\underset{(4.38)}{} \quad \underset{(-4.50)}{} \quad \underset{(4.14)}{}$$

$$+ 4.9817 * \Delta lmxced_{t-1} + 0.86146 * \Delta lmxxvol_t - 0.86472 \quad (19)$$
$$\underset{(-1.95)}{} \quad \underset{(0.83)}{} \quad \underset{(3.87)}{}$$

$$* d95q1 + 0.59044 * d98q4$$
$$\underset{(2.95)}{}$$

$R^2 = 0.67$, $\sigma = 0.18$, $DW = 2.29$, $LM(4) = 2.95$. Sample: 1994q1–2003q4.

The nominal short-term interest rate is noted as $r3m_t$ while $\Delta lced_{t-1}$ represents the consumer expenditure inflation, and $\Delta lxvol$, the growth rate of exports.

Credit

Firms

$$\Delta lbrlnsdf_t = 2.0352 - 0.45514 * (\frac{lbrlnsdf_{t-1}}{bry_{t-1}}) - (-0.023547)$$
$$\underset{(3.33)}{} \quad \underset{(-3.58)}{} \quad \underset{(-1.68)}{}$$

$$* brkindex_{t-4} - (-0.0086556) * brsprda_{t-1} \quad\quad (20)$$
$$\underset{(-1.89)}{}$$

The log of the domestic loans to private firms is *lbrlnsdf*, the log of industrial production, *lbrmvol*, the log of import volumes, and *brkindex*, the capital adequacy ratio of Brazilian banks.

$$\Delta lmxlnsdf_t = 1.2387 - 0.14352 * [(\frac{lmxlnsdf_{t-1}}{mxy_{t-1}}) - (-0.12563)$$
$$\underset{(3.8)}{} \quad \underset{(-2.3)}{} \quad \underset{(2.55)}{}$$

$$* mxkindex_{t-1} - (-0.70705) * lmxmvol_{t-1}] + 0.39399 \quad (21)$$
$$\underset{(-2.33)}{} \quad \underset{(1.53)}{}$$

$$* \Delta lmxip_{t-2} - 0.056241 * d99q3$$
$$\underset{(-2.06)}{}$$

lmxlnsdf is the log of the, *lmxip* the log of industrial production, *lmxmvol*, the log of import volumes, *mxkindex*, the capital adequacy ratio of Mexican banks. In equations 4 and 5, we see that in equilibrium domestic credit to firms as a ratio of GDP is mainly geared toward financing imports of intermediate inputs. Industrial production is included in the equation as a measure of economic performance of private firms. Capital adequacy requirements of domestic banks clearly affect domestic credit negatively.

Households

$$\Delta lbrlnsh_t = 1.8796 - 0.45097 * (\frac{lbrlnsh_{t-1}}{bry_{t-1}}) - (-0.000958)$$
$${(3.33)}{(-3.58)}{(-1.68)}$$

$$* brsprda_{t-1} * \Delta lbrnw_{t-1} + (0.030877) * d95q1 \qquad (22)$$

lbrlnsh is the log of the domestic loans to households, *lbrnw* the log of net wealth. The banking spread, *brsprda*, is the difference between the lending and the deposit rate. The inclusion of the banking spread was prompted by the results of a 4-year research programme on banking costs developed by the Central Bank of Brazil. Details of this research can be found in Koyama and Nakane (2002).

$$\Delta lmxlnsh_t = 1.7739 - 0.087395 * [(\frac{lmxlnsh_{t-1}}{mxy_{t-1}}) - (-3.07)$$
$${(5.18)}{(-4.53)}{(-7.06)}$$

$$* mxrpdi_{t-1}] + 0.3673 * \Delta lmxced_{t-1} + 0.18961 \qquad (23)$$
$${(3.02)}{(1.67)}$$

$$* \Delta lmxlnsh_{t-2} - 0.054278 * d95q1$$
$${(3.03)}$$

lmxlnsh is the log of the domestic loans to households, *lmxrpdi* the log of real disposable income, and *lmxced* the log of the consumer expenditure deflator, the change of which measures inflation. Capital adequacy requirements have no impact on personal credit in both countries, as could be expected from the fact that household borrowing as a ratio of GDP was relatively low in the 1990s. Personal income and wealth are significant variables for household credit in both countries.

Domestic credit to government

$$\Delta lbrlnsdg_t = 16.8868 - 0.14977 * [(\frac{lbrlnsdg_{t-1}}{bry_{t-1}}) - (-0.99069)$$
$${(-1.09)}{(-1.86)}{(-0.82)}$$

$$* (brgc_{t-1} + brgi_{t-1}) - (0.3722) * brrr_{t-1} - (0.62871) \qquad (24)$$
$${(-1.75)}{(2.05)}$$

$$* brkindex_{t-1}] - 0.43273 * \Delta brlnsfg_{t-4} - (0.69969)$$
$${(-4.75)}{(1.03)}$$

$$* \Delta brkindex_{t-4}] + 39.9065 * d97q1$$
$${(7.29)}$$

$$\Delta lmxlnsdg_t = -31.5097 - 0.98511 * [(\frac{lmxlnsdg_{t-1}}{mxy_{t-1}}) - (-0.0011491)$$
$$\underset{(-2.43)}{} \quad \underset{(-7.05)}{} \qquad \qquad \qquad \qquad \underset{(-2.67)}{}$$

$$* (mxgc_{t-1} + mxgi_{t-1}) - (0.38632) * mxrr_{t-1}] \qquad (25)$$
$$\underset{(1.57)}{}$$

$$+ 0.42887 * \Delta mxlnsfg_{t-4}$$
$$\underset{(4.14)}{}$$

Foreign loans to government

$$\Delta brlnsfg_t = 1.2245 - 0.12562 * [(\frac{lbrlnsfg_{t-1}}{bry_{t-1}}) - (-0.04) * wdkind_{t-1}]$$
$$\underset{(-1.02)}{} \quad \underset{(-2.07)}{}$$

$$- (-0.018972) * brssprd_{t-1} - 0.56855 * brrr_{t-1} \qquad (26)$$
$$\underset{(-1.44)}{} \qquad \qquad \qquad \underset{(1.33)}{}$$

$$- (9.8335) * d98q4 + (9.1346) * d97q1$$
$$\underset{(-5.27)}{} \qquad \qquad \underset{(5.88)}{}$$

$$\Delta lmxlnsfg_t = 1.7562 - 0.53179 * [(\frac{lmxlnsfg_{t-1}}{mxy_{t-1}}) - (-0.04) * wdkindex_{t-2}]$$
$$\underset{(1.16)}{} \quad \underset{(-2.07)}{}$$

$$- (-0.54504) * \Delta wdkindex_{t-4} + (6.3129) * mxssprd_{t-1} \qquad (27)$$
$$\underset{(-1.44)}{} \qquad \qquad \qquad \underset{(1.33)}{}$$

$$- 0.90844 * \Delta mxlnsfg_{t-2} + (7.3994) * d98q4$$
$$\underset{(-5.07)}{} \qquad \qquad \underset{(1.05)}{}$$

brlnsfg and *lmxlnsfg* are foreign loans to the Brazilian and Mexican governments. This variable is the foreign component of the central government's net borrowing necessities, which we use as a proxy for foreign lending to government. An alternative variable would be the value of the government bonds held by foreigners and foreign loans to government. The former is not available; the latter is published by the Bureau of International Settlements (BIS). As expected, foreign lending to the public sectors of both countries is a negative function of the respective spreads on sovereign bonds *lbrssprd* and *lmxssprd*.

Total loans to firms and total loans to government are defined as simple algebraic sums of foreign and domestic loans.

Cost of capital

Lending rate

$$brcc_t = 32.4997 + 1.8401 * (brkindex_{t-1} - wdkindex_{t-1}) + 0.52661$$
$$\underset{(14.85)}{} \quad \underset{(7.01)}{}$$

$$* brrr_{t-1} + 1.0534 * (brr3m_{t-1} - usr3m_{t-1}) \qquad (28)$$
$$\underset{(6.55)}{}$$

$brcc_t$ is the lending rate, $brkindex_t$ and $wdkindex_t$ as the equations above, and $brdepr_t$ the deposit rate paid by Brazilian banks on domestic demand deposits.

$$mxcc_t = 18.0964 - 0.7007 * [mxcc_{t-2} + 0.8749 * mxdepr_{t-1}]$$
$$\underset{(6.34)}{} \quad \underset{(-2.60)}{} \qquad \underset{(5.92)}{}$$
$$+ 42.8434 * d95q1 \tag{29}$$

where $mxcc_t$ is the cost of borrowing, $mxkindex_t$ the capital adequacy ratio of Mexican banks, and $mxdepr_t$ the deposit rate paid by Mexican banks on domestic demand deposits.

User cost of capital

$$bruser_t = 33.1408 + 3.7363 * (brkindex_{t-1} - wdkindex_{t-1})$$
$$\underset{(4.94)}{} \quad \underset{(4.75)}{}$$
$$+ 0.01974 * \Delta brssprd_t] \tag{30}$$
$$\underset{(1.93)}{}$$

where $bruser_t$ is user cost of capital, $sprdus_t$ the interest rate differential between Brazil and the U.S., $brssprd_t$ is the spread of Brazilian sovereign bonds over U.S. Treasury bonds, and $d95q1$ is a dummy equal to 1 in 1995 q1.

$$mxuser_t = -70.1956 - 0.31654 * [mxuser_{t-1} - (-1.9589) * sprdus_{t-1} - 4.7217$$
$$\underset{(-2.44)}{} \quad \underset{(-1.92)}{} \qquad \underset{(-1.92)}{} \qquad \underset{(1.44)}{}$$
$$* mxkindex_{t-4} - 0.5141 * mxssprd_{t-1}] - 7.4787 * d95q1 \tag{31}$$
$$\underset{(4.94)}{} \qquad \underset{(4.75)}{}$$

where $mxuser_t$ is user cost of capital, $sprdus_t$ the interest rate differential between Mexico and the US, $mxssprd_t$ is the spread of Mexican sovereign bonds over U.S. Treasury bonds, and $d95q1$ is a dummy equal to 1 in 1995 q1.

GDP components

Capital requirements have a direct impact on two components of GDP, private consumption and investment. We assume that private sector investment is a function of GDP, the user cost of capital and loans. For the sake of simplicity, we exclude the emission of debt instruments, such as corporate bonds from the investment equation. The Basel capital requirements can affect investment by reducing the loans to firms, or by increasing the cost of capital.

Investment

$$\Delta lbrpsi_t = 3.1911 - 0.09552 * [(\frac{lbrpsi_{t-1}}{bry_{t-1}}) + 0.47669 * bruser_{t-1}$$
$$\underset{(5.57)}{} \underset{(-5.37)}{}$$

$$-(-0.0098458) * brkindex_{t-1} -(-0.16464) * lbrloansf_{t-1}] \qquad (32)$$
$$\underset{(-1.55)}{} \underset{(-3.83)}{}$$

$$+ 0.22957 * \Delta lbrpsi_{t-2} + 0.048065 * \Delta lbrloansf_t$$
$$\underset{(1.62)}{} \underset{(2.23)}{}$$

$$+ 0.076104 * d00q1$$
$$\underset{(2.23)}{}$$

where *lbrpsi* is the log of the capital stock, and *lbrloansf* are total loans to firms, i.e., the sum of domestic and foreign loans.

$$\Delta lmxpsi_t = -0.40438 - 0.20248 * [(\frac{lmxpsi_{t-1}}{mxy_{t-1}}) + 0.47669 * mxuser_{t-1}$$
$$\underset{(-2.62)}{} \underset{(-2.33)}{}$$

$$-(0.59539) * lmxloansf_{t-1}] + 1.1823 * \Delta lmxmvol_{t-1} \qquad (33)$$
$$\underset{(1.55)}{} \underset{(4.88)}{}$$

$$+ 0.051862 * d95q1$$
$$\underset{(0.64)}{}$$

where *lmxpsi* is the log of the capital stock, and *lmxloansf* are total loans to firms, i.e., the sum of domestic and foreign loans.

Consumption
Consumption depends on real disposable income and the wealth of households. We define real disposable income as the sum of wages, transfers from government, other personal income, less income taxes, deflated by the consumer expenditure deflator. Other personal income is the sum of distributed dividends and net interest payments to households on their investments. Here, we may consider banking deposits and savings accounts as being households' main investments. Although it may be considered simplistic, this actually captures the financial investments of most households in developing countries. Net interest payments are thus given by the interest rates paid to deposits and savings net of the interest applied to loans. Capital requirements can affect households' net interest payments by increasing the interest rate on loans, by reducing the amounts lent to households, or by reducing the interest rates paid to deposits and savings.

$$\Delta lbrc_t = -0.044703 - 0.46632 * [(\frac{lbrc_{t-1}}{lbrpdi_{t-1}}) - (-0.015522)$$
$$\underset{(-2.28)}{} \underset{(-4.88)}{} \underset{(-0.57)}{}$$

$$* (lbrc_{t-1} - lbrnw_{t-1}^R)] + 0.30212 * \Delta lbrdi_{t-3} \qquad (34)$$
$$\underset{(-0.57)}{}$$

lbrpdi$_t$ is the log of real disposable income, and *lbrnw$_t$* is the deflated net financial wealth. Household income is defined as the sum of mixed income (*bri*), compensation (*brcomp*), wages and social payments), government transfers (*brtran*), and other personal income (*bropi*). Those are the sum of dividends paid by firms to households (*brdivd*), net interest payments by households (*brnip*) and rent from land and insurance policy. The last two components of other personal income are aggregated into. The net interest payments are the difference between interest paid by households on their domestic loans and the interest received on their domestic deposits and savings. For the sake of simplicity, we have aggregated demand deposits and savings, and the same interest rate is applied to both. These relationships are identities in the model. As mentioned above, all components of household income have been deflated by the consumer expenditure deflator.

$$\Delta lmxc_t = -0.55172 - 0.21668 * [(\frac{lmxc_{t-1}}{lmxrpdi_{t-1}}) - (-0.0042073)$$
$$ (-1.73) \quad\quad (-1.77) \quad\quad\quad\quad\quad\quad\quad\quad (-1.68)$$

$$* (lmxc_{t-1} - lmxnw_{t-1} - lmxced_{t-1})] + 0.56998 * \Delta lmxrpdi_{t-1} \quad (35)$$
$$\phantom{* (lmxc_{t-1} - lmxnw_{t-1})} (-1.68)$$

lmxrpdi$_t$ is the log of real disposable income, *lmxced$_t$* the log of consumer expenditure deflator, and *lmxnw$_t$* is net financial wealth. As above, household income is defined as the sum of mixed income (*mxi*), compensation (*mxcomp*, wages and social payments), government transfers (*mxtran*), and other personal income (*mxopi*). Those are the sum of dividends paid by firms to households (*mxdivd*), net interest payments by households (*mxnip*) and rent from land and insurance policy. The last two components of other personal income are aggregated into.

$$mxpdi_t = mxi_t + mxcomp_t + mxopi_t - mxtax_t$$
$$mxopi_t = mxdivd_t + mxnip_t + mxopic_t \quad\quad\quad\quad (36)$$
$$mxnpi_t = mxcc_t * mxloansh_t - mxdepr_t * mxdepoh_t$$

$$brpdi_t = bri_t + brcomp_t + bropi_t - brtax_t$$
$$bropi_t = brdivd_t + brnip_t + bropic_t \quad\quad\quad\quad (37)$$
$$brnpi_t = brcc_t * brloansh_t - brdepr_t * brdepoh_t$$

mxdepoh$_t$ is the deposits made by households. The interest rates *mxcc$_t$* and *mxdepr$_t$* are in decimal form rather than in percentage. The net financial wealth of households is by definition the sum of households' financial assets (demand and time deposits, savings, gold) net of the sum of households' financial liabilities (consumer credit and mortgages).

Data on Mexican household financial position are quite difficult to obtain before 1993. We have thus used two proxies. Net wealth (*nw*) was proxied by the monetary aggregate and liabilities were proxied by total domestic credit[11]. The model equation for household net wealth is also an identity. It is the sum of net foreign assets converted into domestic currency (*mxrx* * *mxna*) and household deposits, net of liabilities (*mxliabs*). Analogous definitions apply for equations (19). We have assumed for the sake of simplicity that government consumption and investment follow the change on total loans to government (*brloansg_t*).

$$brgc_t = brgc_{t-1} * \left(\frac{\Delta brloansg_t}{brloansg_{t-1}} \right)$$

$$brgi_t = brgi_{t-1} * \left(\frac{\Delta brloansg_t}{brloansg_{t-1}} \right) \tag{38}$$

$$mxgc_t = mxgc_{t-1} * \left(\frac{\Delta mxloansg_t}{mxloansg_{t-1}} \right)$$

$$mxgi_t = mxgi_{t-1} * \left(\frac{\Delta mxloansg_t}{mxloansg_{t-1}} \right) \tag{39}$$

Finally, the capital requirements of national and international banks are the only exogenous variables in the model.

A2.3   Variables used in NiGEM

The variables used in the Brazilian and Mexican blocks of NiGEM are listed in Tables 2 and 3 for Brazil. The Mexican variables are presented in Tables 4 and 5.

Table 6.A1.1   Variables in NiGEM Brazil model

BRBPT	Balance of payments transfers, US$ Mn
BRCBR	Current balance as % of GDP
BRCBV	Current balance, US$ Mn
BRCED	Consumer expenditure deflator, 1995=100
BREFEX	Effective exchange rate, 2000=100
BREFEX2	Extended Eff exchange rate, 1994=100
BREQPR	Rate of return on foreign liabilities
BRGA	Gross foreign assets, US$ Mn
BRGL	Gross foreign liabilities, US$ Mn

Continued

Table 6.A1.1 Continued

BRGLREV	Gross foreign liabilities revaluation
BRIP	Industrial production, 1995=100
BRIPDC	Interest, profit, dividend Cred, US$ Mn
BRIPDD	Interest, profit, dividend Deb, US$ Mn
BRMVOL	Imports of goods and services, volume, 1994=100
BRNA	Net foreign assets, US$ Mn
BRPMG	Import price of manuf, Peso, 1994=100
BRPXG	Export price of manuf, US$, 1994=100
BRREFEX	Real effective exchange rate, 2000=100
BRROR	Rate of return on foreign assets
BRRPX	Relative export price, 1994=1
BRRULT	Relative trend unit labour costs, 1994=1
BRRX	Exchange rate, units per US$
BRS	Export markets index, 2000=100
BRTECHL	Technological progress variable
BRTECHN	Technological progress variable
BRULT	Unit labour costs, 1994=100
BRXVOL	Exports of goods, volume, 1994=100
BRY	GDP, Pesos Bn, 1995 prices
BRCEDT	Consumer expenditure deflator Target
BREQP	Equity prices, 2000=100
BRINFT	Inflation Expectations target
BRNOM	Nominal GDP, Bn peso
BRNOMT	Nominal GDP Target
BRPY	GDP deflator, 1993=100
BRR3M	3 month interest rates
BRRPM	Real import prices, 2000=1
BRYTREND	GDP trend (potential output)
BRGC	Government consumption, Bn Real, deflated
BRGI	Government investment, Bn Real, deflated
BRC	Private consumption, Bn Real, deflated
BRDS	Stockbuilding, Bn Real, deflated
BRPSI	private sector Investment, Bn Real, deflated
BRXVOL	Exports of goods and services, Bn R$, deflated
BRMVOL	Imports of goods and services, Bn R$, deflated
BRY	GDP Bn R$, deflated
BRCOMP	Total compensation, Bn Real, deflated
BRI	Mixed income of households, BN Real, deflated
BRPDI	Personal disp. income, Bn Real, deflated
BRTAX	Personal taxes, Bn Real, deflated
BRNW	Net wealth, personal sector, Bn Real, deflated
BRLIABS	Net liabilities personal sector, Bn Real
BRTRAN	Transfers to households, Bn Real, deflated
BROPI	Other personal income (total), Bn Real, deflated
BREE	Employees in employment, Thousands
BRE	Total employment, Thousands
BRCC	Cost of credit, annual percentage

Continued

Table 6.A1.1   Continued

BRDEPR	Deposit rate, annual percentage
BRDEPO	Total deposits, Bn R$, deflated
BRDEPOH	Deposits households, Bn R$, deflated
BRK	Capital stock, Total, Real Bn, deflated
BRSPRDA	Spread on banking loan rate, percentage
BRLOANS	Loans to non-finan. private sector, Bn Real, deflated
BRLOANSF	Loans to private firms, Bn Real, deflated
BRLNSFF	Loans to firms, Bn Real, deflated
BRLNSDF	Loans to firms, Bn Real, deflated
BRRR	Real interest rate
BRCCR	Real cost of borrowing
BRUSER	User cost of capital, percent
BRKDEP	Dep. rate of total cap.stock
BRKINDEX	Capital adequacy (Cooke ratio), percent
BRLOANSH	Loans to households, Bn R$, deflated
BRNIP	Net interest payments, Bn Real, deflated
BRDIVD	Dividends paid to households, Bn Real, deflated
BROPIC	Other pers. income, Bn Real, deflated
BRPI	Personal income, Bn Real, deflated

Table 6A2.2   Variables in NiGEM Mexico model

MXBPT	Balance of payments transfers, US$ Mn
MXCBR	Current balance as % of GDP
MXCBV	Current balance, US$ Mn
MXCED	Consumer expenditure deflator, 1995=100
MXEFEX	Effective exchange rate, 2000=100
MXEFEX2	Extended Eff exchange rate, 1994=100
MXEQPR	Rate of return on foreign liabilities
MXGA	Gross foreign assets, US$ Mn
MXGL	Gross foreign liabilities, US$ Mn
MXGLREV	Gross foreign liabilities revaluation
MXIP	Industrial production, 1995=100
MXIPDC	Interest, profit, dividend Cred, US$ Mn
MXIPDD	Interest, profit, dividend Deb, US$ Mn
MXMVOL	Imports of goods and services, volume, 1994=100
MXNA	Net foreign assets, US$ Mn
MXPMG	Import price of manuf, Peso, 1994=100
MXPXG	Export price of manuf, US$, 1994=100
MXREFEX	Real effective exchange rate, 2000=100
MXROR	Rate of return on foreign assets
MXRPX	Relative export price, 1994=1
MXRULT	Relative trend unit labour costs, 1994=1
MXRX	Exchange rate, units per US$
MXS	Export markets index, 2000=100
MXTECHL	Technological progress variable
MXTECHN	Technological progress variable

Continued

Table 6.A2.2 Continued

MXULT	Unit labour costs, 1994=100
MXXVOL	Exports of goods, volume, 1994=100
MXY	GDP, Pesos Bn, 1995 prices
MXCEDT	Consumer expenditure deflator Target
MXEQP	Equity prices, 2000=100
MXINFT	Inflation Expectations target
MXNOM	Nominal GDP, Bn peso
MXNOMT	Nominal GDP Target
MXPY	GDP deflator, 1993=100
MXR3M	3 month interest rates
MXRPM	Real import prices, 2000=1
MXYTREND	GDP trend (potential output)
MXGC	Gov consumption, Bn Pesos, 1995 prices
MXGI	Gov investment, Bn Pesos, 1995 prices
MXC	Private consumption, Bn Pesos, 1995 prices
MXDS	Stock building, Bn Pesos, 1995 prices
MXPSI	Private Sector Investment, Bn Pesos, 1995 price
MXK	Capital Stock, Total, Pesos Bn, 1995 prices
MXEE	Employees in employment, Thousands
MXE	Total employment, Thousands
MXCOMP	Total compensation, Bn Pesos
MXOPI	Other personal income, Bn Pesos
MXOPIC	Other personal income, Bn Pesos
MXNIP	Net interest payments to households, Bn Pesos
MXDIVD	Dividends paid to households, Bn pesos
MXI	Household income, Bn pesos
MXPDI	Personal disposable income, Bn Pesos
MXRPDI	Real pers dispos income, Bn Pesos
MXTAX	Direct Taxes, Bn Pesos
MXNW	Net wealth, personal sector, Bn Pesos
MXLIABS	Gross liabilities personal sector, Bn Pesos
MXTRAN	Transfers, Bn Pesos
MXCC	Cost of Credit, annual percentage
MXDEPR	Deposit Rate, annual percentage
MXCF	Average Cost of Funds, annual percentage rate
MXLOANS	Loans to non-finan. private sector, Bn pesos
MXDEPO	Total deposits in banks, Bn pesos
MXDEPOH	Deposits by households in banks, Bn pesos
MXLNSFF	Foreign loans to firms, Bn pesos
MXLOANSD	Domestic loans to firms, Bn pesos
MXLOANSF	Loans to private firms, Bn pesos
MXKINDEX	Capital adequacy, dom. banks, in percent
MXWDKIND	Capital adequacy, OECD banks (exc. MX), in percent
MXSPRDA	Spread on banking loan rate, percentage
MXRR	Real interest rate, percent
MXCCR	real cost of borrowing
MXUSER	User cost of capital, percent
MXKDEP	Depreciation rate of total cap stock

Notes

National Institute of Economic and Social Research (NIESR), 2 Dean Trench Street, Smith Square London SW1H 3PE, United Kingdom. We have benefited from discussions with Ricardo Gottschalk, Stephany Griffith-Jones and Martin Weale. We are indebted to Cecília Sodré for unpublished data on capital adequacy in Brazil. This work was supported by a grant from the UK Department for International Development (DFID). The usual disclaimer applies.

1. More precisely, the risk weight of public entities may be 0, 10, 20, or 50 % at the discretion of the regulator under Basel I.
2. The Basel Capital Accord applies to European banks with strictly domestic activities, unlike domestically active U.S. banks, which represent the vast majority of the 8000 American banks. The U.S. regulators announced in 2006 that few internationally active banks operating in their country would adopt Basel II (see chapter 1). The rest would comply with the domestic prudential system based on the Cooke ratio and national regulations. See Circular 11620 of the Federal Reserve Bank of New York, available at http://www.ny.frb.org/banking/circulars/11620.html.
3. See, also, Griifth-Jones, Spratt and Segoviano (2003; 2002).
4. In this chapter Mexico is not included in any OECD aggregate.
5. Between 2007 and 2009 interest rates declined even further, to less than 10 % (see Central Bank of Brazil website, www.bcb.gov.br).
6. Only the equations estimated for the banking sector are presented here. The remaining equations of the Brazil and Mexico blocks of NiGEM were not included.
7. In previous versions of the model short term nominal interest rates had an effect on consumption decisions in countries such as the U.K. However, given the degree of financial liberalisation in the economies we study we presume that these effects are now absent as determinants of consumption.
8. Dynamic homogeneity is absent from the French and Germany price systems, but is present in the UK.
9. The perpetual inventory attempts to take account of countries like Italy and Belgium where there are large proportions of short-term public debt.
10. Variable GIP also influences net property income paid abroad, and thus the current account and asset stocks as well.
11. According to the national definition of $M4$, as in the Country Notes of the International Monetary Statistics (IFS-IMF), it comprises bills and coins outside banks, checking and current account ($M1$), other demand and time deposits, federal and private securities held by the private sector and other instruments held by pension funds ($M2$), demand and time deposits of non-residents in domestic banks and government securities held by non-residents ($M3$) and finally deposits of residents and non-residents held in branches abroad of domestic banks.

7
Basel II: Regulatory Gaps, Pro-Cyclicality and Bank Credit Levels to Developing Countries

Stephany Griffith-Jones

7.1 Introduction

As is well known, both Basel I and Basel II were designed by regulators from developed economies to meet the main perceived regulatory challenges they and their largest banks faced. Basel II contains a number of positive features, particularly in the standardised approach. From the perspective of developing countries, for example, the removal of the OECD/non-OECD distinction and the reduction of the excessive incentive toward short-term lending are positive. More generally, Basel II attempts to better align regulatory capital to risk, which – if well done – could help accomplish a desirable objective.

However, a number of major concerns exist about Basel II. These concerns have been severely accentuated as the global crisis broke out. These issues can be grouped into five areas:

1. The first is whether capital based regulation is enough, on its own, to ensure systematic banking stability; a somewhat related, and very important, concern is that regulation has covered a diminishing share of total financial market institutions and activities. A further concern is that key sources of banking vulnerability in developing countries, such as currency mismatches, are not appropriately addressed in Basel II.
2. The second is whether Basel II would increase pro-cyclicality of bank lending, both domestically and from international banks. This would

increase volatility of growth and investment, as well as increase systemic risk in the banking system.

3. A third concern is whether Basel II will reduce bank credit levels to developing economies, both internationally and nationally; this effect could be worse for poorer countries and those with low perceived creditworthiness. There is evidence that this could reduce investment, demand and future growth.

4. The fourth area of concern is whether the introduction of Basel II could discourage particularly lending to SMEs and to other sectors or modalities crucial for growth, employment and investment.

5. A fifth concern is whether the introduction of Basel II could give important competitive advantages to foreign banks. This could not just have negative consequences for lending to SMEs, especially since there is growing evidence that foreign banks 'cherry pick' and lend more to creditworthy large firms. It could also mean that greater concentration of the banking system due to a larger role for foreign banks weakens the ability and power of national regulators to regulate them properly, which could again pose serious problems for banking stability.

Concerns 4 and 5 are addressed elsewhere in this book. In this chapter, we will examine, in some detail, the three first concerns.

Following this introduction, Section 7.2 addresses whether regulating capital has sufficient coverage, and proposes what areas of the financial system, capital and also liquidity regulation should cover. Section 7.3 discusses pro-cyclicality in Basel II and reviews a number of proposals that have been put forward since the onset of the global financial crisis to reduce pro-cyclicality in the financial system. Section 7.4 discusses whether Basel II will reduce bank credit levels to developing countries, and whether the benefits of diversification could be incorporated into Basel II to better reflect banks' portfolio risks. Section 7.5 concludes our investigation.

7.2 The missing gaps and the need for broader regulatory coverage

One of the main causes of the global financial crisis starting in August 2007 is the fact that effective regulation covers a diminishing share of total capital and banking markets. In particular, in the USA and other developed countries, there was a massive shift of savings from banks to capital markets. In 2007, only 25 per cent of the U.S. financial system's assets belonged to commercial banks (d'Arista and Griffith-Jones, 2009a). However, commercial banks were the only part of the financial system that were regulated for capital requirements, and even that regulation was partial, as off-balance sheet mechanisms were unregulated. Investment banks were very lightly regulated, while other financial actors – like hedge funds – were not regulated at all. Off-shore actors are subject to no or very light regulation. As a result of these regulatory gaps, a massive 'shadow financial system' was allowed to emerge, with no or little transparency or regulation.

As it is often the case, it has been true in the 2007–2009 global financial crisis that the parts of the financial system that were not regulated at all, or were regulated too lightly, have generated more problems. Because of regulatory arbitrage, growth of financial activity (and risk) moved to unregulated mechanisms (Structured Investment Vehicles – SIVs), instruments (derivatives) or institutions (hedge funds). However, though unregulated, those parts of the shadow financial system were de facto dependent on systemically important banks via provision of credit, guaranteed liquidity lines or other commitments.

A clear example of when the lack of capital requirements led to excessive growth of unregulated mechanisms is in the case of SIVs. It is very interesting that Spanish regulatory authorities allowed banks to have SIVs, but required Spanish banks to consolidate these special purpose vehicles in their accounting, implying that they had the same capital requirements as their other assets (Cornford, 2008; interview material). This eliminated the incentive for such vehicles to grow in Spain and thus prevented them from becoming a major problem for banks as SIVs were in the United States.

It is positive that Basel II, unlike Basel I, requires banks to set aside capital to support liquidity commitments to those vehicles; however, such commitments have lower capital requirements for short maturities; furthermore, the Basel Committee is reportedly planning to strengthen these capital requirements to reduce regulatory arbitrage incentives (FSF, 2008). However, such measures would only be partial. A more comprehensive solution would be for all vehicles and transactions to be put on banks' balance sheets; then there should be no regulatory arbitrage, as risk-weighted capital requirements would be equivalent for all balance sheet activities; furthermore, transparency could automatically become far more comprehensive for banks.

It is encouraging that the G20 Working Group on Enhancing Sound Regulation and Strengthening Transparency (G20, 2009) has agreed in March 2009 that:

> All systemically important financial institutions, markets, and instruments should be subject to an appropriate degree of regulation and oversight, consistently applied and proportionate to their local and global systemic importance. Consideration has to be given to the potential systemic risk of a cluster of financial institutions that are not systemically important on their own. Non-systemically important financial institutions, markets, and instruments could also be subject to some form of registration requirement or oversight. (G20, 2009, page XI)

The timeline for implementing this will be two years, after the autumn of 2009. The IMF in its document 'Lessons of the Financial Crisis for Future Regulation of Financial Institutions and Markets and for Liquidity Management' takes a similar approach:

> The perimeter of financial sector surveillance needs to be expanded to a wider range of institutions and markets, possibly with differentiated layers to allow institutions to graduate from simple disclosure to higher levels of prudential oversight as their contributions to systemic risk increases. (IMF, 2009, page 4)

While it is welcome that the G20 and the IMF recognise the need for regulating all systemically important institutions, markets, and instruments (which implies significant progress in relation to the past), it seems problematic to ex-ante define 'systemic importance'. For example, would Bear Stern have ex-ante been defined as a systemically important institution? Furthermore, the risk is that market actors will take advantage again of regulatory gaps, and that the less regulated de facto parts of the system will again create systemic risk. In this sense, we prefer the stronger Brazil, Russia, India and China (BRIC) statement of March 14, 2009 which calls for

> all financial activities – especially those of systemic importance – to be subject to adequate regulation and supervision, including institutions that are in the shadow banking system ... and strongly support the suggestion ... to intensify supervision of hedge funds and private pools of capital. (Reuters, 2009, page 2)

Indeed, we believe that the task of defining equivalent regulation on assets for all financial institutions and activities, both for solvency and liquidity, is essential.[1] To be more specific, all entities that invest or lend on behalf of other people – using other people's money and providing some type of leverage – need to have both relevant transparency requirements and need to be regulated, especially as regards their leverage (solvency), but also their liquidity. Within institutions, all their activities need to have equivalent regulation. Therefore, institutions like hedge funds need to be brought into the regulatory domain, as do all off-balance sheet activities of banks.

With regard to the comprehensive regulation of solvency, equivalent regulation of different actors, instruments and activities should especially refer to leverage, as excessive leverage has been such a major source of systemic risk. However, as the longevity of funding is an important variable, it may be desirable to restrict leverage more (and thus require more capital) for assets funded by short-term liabilities. This will not just protect the solvency of financial institutions, but also encourage them to seek more long-term funding.

Persaud (2009) has forcefully argued that tying leverage requirements to maturity of funding ('mark-to-funding') will also encourage diversity of behaviour amongst different actors, thus discouraging herding across different categories of financial actors, and contributing to financial stability. Persaud proposes, in this regard, that, whatever they are called, those financial institutions that have short-term funding – say less than 12–24 months – should follow bank capital adequacy requirements. Those with long-term funding, according to Persaud, could have a different long-term 'solvency' regime, that would take into account their long-term obligations and long-term valuation of their assets. This interesting proposal as well as other ideas on establishing equivalent regulations linked to capacity for bearing different risks deserves further study. It is, however, key that the concept of maintaining equivalent regulation of leverage, for all actors, instruments, and activities, is designed and implemented in a simple way. Simplicity in defining equivalent leverage is crucial, as complexity both makes implementation difficult and may ease regulatory arbitrage. Separate and sufficient minimum liquidity requirements should be an essential part of regulation, an aspect that was neglected in recent years.

As suggested above, maturity mismatches may be addressed by solvency regulation. But prudential regulation also needs to ensure adequate levels of liquidity for financial intermediaries so that they can handle the mismatch between the average maturities of assets and liabilities, which is inherent in the financial system's essential function of transforming maturities, and which generates risks associated with volatility in deposits and/or interest rates. This underscores the fact that liquidity and solvency problems are far more closely interrelated than traditionally assumed, particularly in the face of macroeconomic shocks. Reserve requirements, which are strictly an instrument of monetary policy, provide liquidity in many countries, but their declining importance makes it necessary to find new tools. Moreover, their traditional structure is not geared to the specific objective of ensuring financial intermediaries' liquidity in the face of the inherent maturity mismatches in their portfolios. The best system could be one in which liquidity or reserve requirements are estimated on the basis of the residual maturity of financial institutions' liabilities, thus generating a direct incentive for the financial system to maintain an appropriate liability structure.

Specific steps have already been taken toward more comprehensive regulation. U.S. authorities are addressing regulatory gaps for example in the oversight of entities that originate and fund mortgages, which is clearly welcome. Furthermore, it is very encouraging that the March 2008 U.S. Treasury Blueprint for Financial Regulatory Reform (U.S Treasury, 2008), though flawed in some aspects, put forward the idea that financial regulation should be comprehensive, and include hedge funds and other private pools of capital. Even more clearly, the U.S Treasury March 2009 plea for future regulation was summarised by U.S. Treasury Secretary Tim Geithner: 'All institutions and markets that could pose systemic risk will be subject to strong oversight including appropriate constraints on risk-taking' (Financial Times March 25, 2009).

As pointed out above, there is increasing support by G20 leaders and finance ministers for comprehensive regulation. However, important differences remain about the desirable extent of coverage of regulations.

Furthermore, the extent to which good declarations will be reflected in implementation of strong and effective regulation, which will also help protect financial stability in developing economies, is a matter of serious concern; it will require careful monitoring and constant pressure from those concerned with financial stability. This concern can be illustrated by the ongoing attempt to regulate hedge funds and private equity in the European Union. As pointed out above, there is a great deal of broad support from the G20, the FSF, as well as major governments for comprehensive regulation, including of hedge funds and private equity. Furthermore, an influential and detailed European

Parliament report (EU, 2008) argues that financial regulation should be comprehensive; it especially emphasises the need to regulate hedge funds and makes specific recommendations to limit the leverage of hedge funds to preserve stability of the EU financial system, as well as take other measures to regulate hedge funds and private equity directly. However, at the time of writing (June 2009), the resulting proposed European Commission Directive, though saying it favours regulation of hedge funds and private equity, is de facto extremely weak on direct regulation (it is however quite good at improving transparency); it for example, proposes only to directly regulate, and require capital, from fund managers (which is minimal) and not from the funds themselves. This would mean de facto no direct regulation of hedge funds and private equity leverage, which is a key source of systemic risk. The European Commission Directive also focuses on funds larger than €250 million, which poses the risk of clusters of smaller than €250 million institutions acting in a coordinated way (possibly even having a joint manager) generating systemic risk.

A broad area relevant to developing countries is whether Basel II has appropriately addressed sources of vulnerability most characteristic of developing economies banking systems, such as maturity and especially currency mismatches. For example, is direct and indirect net foreign exchange exposures of banks – a source of so many developing countries' banking crises in the past – appropriately addressed in Basel II? If not, how should they best be incorporated?

Developing countries need to have in place more specific regulations aimed at controlling currency mismatches (including those associated with derivative operations). The strict prohibition of currency mismatches in the portfolios of financial intermediaries is probably the best rule (as discussed in Griffith-Jones and Ocampo, 2009). Authorities should also closely monitor the currency risk of non-financial firms operating in non-tradable sectors, which may eventually become credit risks for banks. Regulations can be used to establish more stringent provisions and/or risk weighting (and therefore higher capital requirements) for these operations, or a strict prohibition on lending in foreign currencies to non-financial firms and households without revenues in those currencies.

7.3   How to counter pro-cyclicality in Basel II

The most important manifestation of market failure in financial markets through the ages is pro-cyclicality. Risk is mainly generated in the booms, even though it becomes apparent in the bust. Therefore, the time for regulators to act – to prevent excessive risk taking – is precisely in the boom. Indeed, one of their key functions is 'to take away the punch-bowl when the party is at its best.' As a consequence, prudential financial regulation has to have at its heart the principle of counter-cyclicality which implies 'leaning against the wind.'

This must happen through simple rules which cannot be easily changed by regulators so they will not become 'captured' by the general over-enthusiasm that characterises booms that have so often lead to undesirable relaxation of regulatory standards.

Under Basel II, bank regulation does exactly the opposite. Particularly in the IRB and A-IRB approaches, Basel II calculates required capital based on the banks own models; this perversely incorporates the inherent pro-cyclicality of bank lending into bank regulation, thus accentuating boom-bust patterns. This interacted with the use of mark-to-market pricing that links asset booms with excessive leverage.

Counter-cyclical regulation implies that the traditional microeconomic focus of prudential regulation and supervision be complemented by a macro-prudential perspective, particularly by introducing explicit counter-cyclical features in prudential regulation and supervision that would compensate for the pro-cyclicality of financial markets. The simplest recommendations are to increase capital and/or provisions for loan losses during booms, and to avoid mark-to-market asset pricing from feeding into leverage, such as counter-cyclical limits on loan-to-value ratios and/or rules to adjust the values of collateral for cyclical asset price variations. The introduction of a specific counter-cyclical perspective in prudential regulation would go a long way to overcome some of the major criticisms of Basel II. It also implies that financial institutions should be urged to adopt risk management practices that take better account of the evolution of risk over the full business cycle and that are not sensitive to short-term variations in asset prices.

As the Bank for International Settlements argued rightly in its Annual Report 2008, the trends toward globalisation, consolidation and securitisation increase the probability of both excessive behaviour in the boom and costs in the bust, thus increasing the dangerous and negative side effects of financial market pro-cyclical behaviour. This adds additional urgency to introduce counter-cyclical regulation. The questions now are not so much about if, but about how and when counter-cyclical regulation is introduced.

7.3.1 Criteria for counter-cyclical regulation

One element that must be central to reform of prudential regulation is counter-cyclical regulation of leverage, or its counterpart, the capital backing of financial institutions including provisions.

Counter-cyclical bank regulation can be easily introduced, either through banks' provisions or through their capital. On the one hand, it is important that counter-cyclical rules are simple, and done in ways that regulators cannot loosen the rule in boom times when they can be captured not just by vested interests, but by the over enthusiasm that characterises booms. On the other hand, some flexibility may be required, especially to add requirements for capital and/or provisions when new more risky activities emerge.

Introducing counter-cyclical bank provisions has already been done for some time in Spain and Portugal, showing that this is a feasible option and is consistent with Basel rules. The Spanish system requires higher provisions when credit grows more than the historical average, linking provisioning to the credit and business cycles (Ocampo and Chiappe, 2001). Under this system, provisions build up during an upswing and can be accumulated in a fund (along with special back-up for non-performing assets). The fund can be drawn down in a slump to cover loan losses. This counters the financial cycle as it both discourages (though does not eliminate) excessive lending in booms and strengthens the banks for bad times. An advantage of using provisions is that their objective is precisely to finance expected losses (through the business cycle in this case) as distinguished from capital, whose aim is to cover for unexpected losses. Introducing counter-cyclical provisions in Spain has been facilitated by the fact that the design of accounting rules is under the authority of the Central Bank of Spain. This helps overcome the issue that accountants in other countries have not readily accepted the concept of expected losses, on which the Spanish system is based; they preferred instead to focus on actual losses, more relevant for short-term investors. However, accounting principles should be designed in ways that balance the short-term needs of investors with those of individual and systemic bank stability.

The Spanish system is, strictly speaking, only cycle-neutral rather than counter-cyclical, as it essentially follows the pro-cyclical behaviour of lending, but that is still a considerable advance. Counter-cyclical rules regarding changes in the credit exposure of financial institutions would also be desirable. Particularly, financial institutions could be asked to increase general or sector-specific provisions when there is an excessive growth of credit relative to a benchmark, a bias in lending toward sectors subject to strong cyclical swings (like for housing or credit cards) and to the growth in foreign currency loans to sectors producing non-traded goods (see above). Indeed, all maturity and currency mismatches on balance sheets as well as in expected income and payment flows should be subject to provisions. This is particularly relevant for developing economies.

An alternative approach for counter-cyclical bank regulation through provisions is via capital. Here, Goodhart and Persaud (2008) have presented a very specific proposal: increasing Basel II capital requirements by a ratio linked to recent growth of total banks' assets. This proposal has received considerable attention. It provides a clear and simple rule for introducing counter-cyclicality into regulation of banks. Another virtue of this proposal is that it could be fairly easily implemented, in that it builds on Basel II. Finally, it has the advantage that it does not face the accounting difficulties outlined above for provisioning.

In this proposal, each bank would have a basic allowance for asset growth, linked to macro-economic variables, such as inflation and the long-run economic growth rate. This allows regulators to better link micro to macro stability. It would measure actual growth of bank assets as a weighted average of annual growth (with higher weights for recent growth).

To emphasise more recent activity, Goodhart and Persaud proposed that exponential weights could be used. Growth above the basic allowance over the past 12 months would have a 50 per cent weight; growth over the preceding year would have a 25 per cent weight and so forth until 100 per cent is approximated. Regulatory capital adequacy requirements could be raised by 0.33 per cent for each 1 per cent growth in bank asset values above the basic allowance. For example, if bank assets grew at a rate of 21 per cent above the growth allowance, minimum capital requirements would rise from 8 per cent to 15 per cent (Goodhart and Persaud, 2008).

Two issues arise. Should the focus just be on the increase in total bank assets, or –as suggested above – should there also be some weighting for excessive growth of bank lending in specific sectors that have grown particularly rapidly (such as recently loans to real estate)? Often crises have arisen due to excessive lending during boom times to particular sectors or group of countries (e.g., emerging economies, or economies in a certain region – for example, in recent times Central and Eastern Europe). However, most systemic bank failures have also been preceded by excessive growth of total bank assets.

7.4   Will Basel II reduce bank credit levels to developing countries?

A third area of concern discussed in this chapter is whether the implementation of Basel II could lead to a reduction of total credit to developing economies, both domestically and internationally – and therefore a reduction in financing of investment, as well as a growth in developing economies. There are different estimates in the literature of what the impact on levels and cost of credit to developing countries would be of introducing Basel II.

Simulations carried out by Barrell and Gottschalk – presented in chapter 6 in this book – estimated that GDP could fall by 3.5 per cent in Brazil and 2.2 per cent in Mexico as a result of a moderate credit crunch by both domestic, and especially by international banks, due to the introduction of Basel II.

It has been argued in several papers (e.g., Griffith-Jones, Segoviano and Spratt, 2004) that part of possible reduced lending and increased cost of international bank lending is due to a bad design of Basel II even in its own terms, as the benefits of international portfolio diversification are not included, which leads to an incorrect estimation of risk and capital requirements of lending to developing economies.

7.4.1   The case for diversification benefits

Historically, results of empirical work show that the degree of correlation between both the real and financial sectors of developed economies is greater than that which exists between developed and developing economies. This hypothesis was tested in Griffith-Jones, Spratt and Segoviano (2003; 2002) for different correlations, first with specific regard to international bank lending and profitability and, secondly, in a more general but supportive sense. All of the findings offered significant support for the validity of this position – that emerging markets hold a relatively low correlation with mature markets. The fact that every statistical test performed, regardless of variable, time-period or frequency, has pointed in the same direction – and all are clearly statistically significant on a variety of tests – offered robust and unequivocal support for the benefits of diversification.

7.4.2   How would these diversification effects be manifested in a bank's portfolio?

On the basis on this evidence, a case could be made that an internationally diversified loan portfolio, with a range of developed and developing country borrowers, would have a lower level of risk – in terms of the overall portfolio – than one which focused primarily on developed country lending. In order to test this hypothesis in the specific context of a bank's loan portfolio, a simulation exercise in Griffith-Jones, Spratt and Segoviano (2003) was undertaken to assess the potential unexpected loss resulting from a portfolio diversified within developed countries, and one diversified across developed and developing regions.

The results were that the unexpected losses simulated for the portfolio focused on developed country borrowers were, on average, almost twenty-three per cent higher than for the portfolio diversified across developed and developing countries. The simulated loan portfolios offered more direct evidence that the benefits of international diversification produce a more efficient risk/return trade-off for banks at the portfolio level. Given that capital requirements are intended to deal with unexpected loss, the fact that the level of unexpected loss in the simulations just reported was lower for a diversified than for an undiversified portfolio, suggested that – in order to accurately reflect the actual risks that banks may face – Basel II should take account of this effect, which as stated earlier is not the case in its current form.

The global financial crisis of 2007–2009, which started in the U.S. and other developed countries, spread with fury and reached the emerging economies and low-income countries across different parts of the world. Developing country currencies and stock markets plummeted, as there was a generalised 'flight to safety'. These events could call into question the diversification benefits, due to increasing synchronsation of the economic cycle of developed and developing economies, caused by their financial and trade links.

However, we believe that, first, although the crisis has been indeed deep among developed countries and spread around the world, developing country's economic downturn has till now been relatively less pronounced; moreover, it is possible that the latter's recovery will be faster, probably led by China. Standard Chartered, an international bank with strong presence in many developing countries, has stood far better the financial crisis than its counterparts, indicating that the diversification benefits proposition may indeed be valid, even under such exceptional circumstances.

One piece of empirical research (Griffith-Jones, Segoviano and Spratt, 2004) shows that introducing the benefits of international diversification would not only imply more accurate measurement of risk, thus appropriately reducing the excessive increase in cost and reduction of lending, it would also diminish pro-cyclicality in capital requirements which would diminish lending volatility and systemic risk.

The empirical research used data from Moody's, available for the USA from 1982 to 2003. This was supplemented with data for Mexico from 1995 to 2000, which enabled US to compare two very different types of markets. In this exercise, the paper compared the implied capital requirements for our `typical' bank under three regulatory regimes: first the standardised approach in Basel II; second, the Foundations IRB approach (that is, assuming a constant Loss Given Default, since we do not have good time series for average LED); and third, a Full Credit Risk Method (IRMA) which incorporates the benefits of international diversification.

Our findings confirm the fears of increased pro-cyclicality under Basel II, and its reduction by introducing benefits of diversification. When the variance of annual capital requirements is considered, it is noted that the variance of the RIB Approach represents an enormous increase compared to the standardised approach. This happens because under the IRB approach capital requirements reflect changes in risk in a way that the more rigid standardised approach does not. This is the case for both the USA and Mexican data.

Another similarity between the two countries is that the variance of the IRB approach is also significantly higher than that for the full credit risk model approach. That is, capital requirements in both countries are considerably more variable using the IRB approach than the ICRM approach. Again, this is reflective of the latter taking into account the benefits of international diversification. Clearly, the operation of the normal business cycle will cause actual risks to change over time. However, it is also clear that these moves are not perfectly correlated in different market sectors or in different parts of individual countries: a U.S. bank whose loan portfolio was entirely comprised of high-tech companies before the collapse of the dotcom bubble would have been in a far riskier position than one with a diversified loan base across industrial sectors.

Just as this is the case within a country, it is even more so between countries, where the drivers of the economy are not the same and business cycles are thus not as synchronised. As an example, during the global financial crisis the U.S. economy has slowed down sharply, while the Chinese economy has slowed down too, but much less so.

7.5   Conclusions

This chapter has discussed in some detail the potential impact of Basel II on capital requirements, costs and levels of lending, pro-cyclicality and regulatory gaps.

The chapter first makes the point that the global financial crisis has exposed a number of regulatory gaps, and suggests what areas should be covered by capital regulation and liquidity regulation as well. Second, the chapter discusses the inherent pro-cyclicality in financial markets, highlights the fact that Basel II in its current form perversely reinforces markets' pro-cyclical behaviour, and then reviews a number of proposals on counter-cyclical regulation that have emerged since the onset of the global financial crisis. The discussion makes it clear that counter-cyclical bank regulation is easy to introduce, can be consistent with Basel II as the Spanish experience demonstrates, and that it is also important that rules are simple and done in ways regulators do not loosen it in times of boom. Moreover, counter-cyclical financial regulation is an increasingly important complement in the modern economy to complement monetary policy. Currently, counter-cyclicality is insufficiently used, both in financial regulation and monetary policy, though more widely accepted in fiscal policy, especially in developed economies.

Finally, the chapter raises the important issue that Basel II may affect the levels and costs of capital flows to developing countries, and raises the question of whether the benefits of diversification should be incorporated in the calculus of risk for the purpose of determining capital under Basel II. The chapter shows that introducing benefits of international diversification will not only lead to a more accurate measurement of risk. It will also reduce the pro-cyclicality of capital requirements through time, which will allow the smoothing of bank lending – and therefore some smoothing of economic cycles in both developed and developing countries. It will also strengthen the stability of the banks, especially the large international ones, which is clearly a key economic objective. However, other measures to make Basel II countercyclical are essential, as discussed above.

Given the limitations and problems of Basel II, there is an urgent need for developing countries to make policy proposals for modifying the new capital accord and its implementation within their jurisdictions, to make it more supportive of financial and macro-economic stability.

Notes

This chapter draws on three forthcoming papers: Griffith-Jones and Ocampo, with Patt (2009, forthcoming), D'Arista and Griffith-Jones (2009a, forthcoming) and D'Arista and Griffith-Jones (2009b, forthcoming). It also draws on previous papers the author has written with Stephen Spratt and Miguel Segoviano, and previous work done with Ricardo Gottschalk.

1. The technical aspects of how to calculate equivalent liquidity (e.g., reserves) and solvency (e.g., capital) requirements across different institutions and activities requires further study, both by institutions like the BIS and FSF, by national regulators, from both developed and developing countries and by academies.

8
Basel II and Development Finance: Establishing Regional Guarantee Funds to Ease Access to Credit for SMEs

Pietro Calice

8.1 Introduction

This chapter focuses on the problem of access to credit faced by small and medium enterprises (SMEs) in developing countries and puts forward a policy proposal that addresses that issue. There is an emerging consensus in the international community on the fundamental role that domestic private sector development can have in helping developing countries accelerate economic growth and reduce poverty. SMEs represent the large majority of all enterprises operating in the developing world and contribute dramatically to their employment and output. Yet, they historically lack access to bank financing.

The new Basel capital accord, dubbed Basel II, which will be implemented in most developing countries in the coming years, is likely to result into more rationed and costly credit for SMEs. However, Basel II recognises a strengthened role to credit guarantee schemes (CGSs), provided that they meet minimum legal criteria and credit quality standards. This will allow lenders to save regulatory capital against SME loans, offsetting the bias against SME lending. However, the bulk of current CGSs operating in developing countries will not bring any regulatory benefit to banks lending to SMEs. This is especially due to their low credit quality. Thus, there is a case for reforming the CGS industry in developing countries. This chapter suggests the introduction of Regional Guarantee Funds (RGFs). These would be guarantee funds set up under the umbrella of existing regional development banks, and would provide loan guarantees to banks and counter-guarantees to other CGSs. The RGFs would be designed and operated in a way to achieve the highest credit rating so as to maximise the incentives for lenders provided by Basel II. They would also rationalise official development assistance, making it more effective and efficient.

This chapter has seven sections. Following this introduction, Section 8.2 highlights the positive role domestic private sector development can play in supporting economic growth and job creation in developing countries. Section 8.3 discusses how Basel II may affect credit to the SMEs negatively, and mitigation techniques such as credit guarantee schemes it has, which can be used to offset this undesirable outcome. Section 8.4 then discusses different modalities of credit guarantee schemes in developing countries, and Section 8.5 explains that notwithstanding their widespread existence in developing countries, most of these guarantees will not be recognised as a credit mitigation technique by Basel II, due to the fact that they do not have a sufficiently high external rating or equivalent probability of default. Section 8.6 then proposes the establishment of RGFs, which would support SME financing in developing countries by providing guarantees to financial institutions and counter-guarantees to existing guarantee schemes that at present are not compliant with Basel II. Section 8.7 offers concluding remarks.

8.2 The policy context: Focus on domestic private sector development

A general consensus has emerged around the key role that the private sector, in particular the domestic private sector, can have in poverty reduction and economic development.[1] Within the private sector, it is the local SMEs that are responsible for most of employment and economic activity in the developing world, though most of these enterprises prosper in the informal economy. While their importance varies across economies, SMEs represent the large majority of the private sector and make a significant contribution to GDP and employment in every country.[2]

The presence of SMEs also correlates with several economic and social variables. Though evidence of a direct causal relationship remains limited in most cases, there are many acknowledged benefits of SMEs in contributing to economic and social progress. SMEs contribute in a significant way to the overall productivity of the economy and to innovation while being an important part of value chains. SMEs provide job opportunities for low-skilled workers and women. They may contribute to make income distribution more equitable and mitigate regional disparities.[3] As Hallberg notes, 'SMEs are the emerging private sector in poor countries, and thus form the base for private sector-led growth'.[4]

A vibrant SME sector can bring great benefits to developing countries. In order to make use of their potential, SMEs need to be provided with an enabling environment. This requires a stable macroeconomic environment, physical and social infrastructure and the rule of law. But even with strong macroeconomic and institutional foundations, additional factors are essential for private entrepreneurship. Chief among these is access to formal external finance. If access to capital is constrained, profitable ventures cannot be undertaken and economic activity can stagnate. Yet, financial constraints for SMEs remain paramount in developing countries as well as in advanced economies.[5]

Higher financing obstacles do not necessarily imply that SMEs are constrained in their growth as they could find alternative ways to overcome these obstacles. However, available evidence suggests that this is actually the case.[6] This suggests that there might be a causal relationship between access to external finance and the viability of SMEs. Such a possibility is also consistent with the recent literature on financial development and economic growth.[7]

8.3   The role of the regulatory regime for banking and guarantees

In most countries, commercial banks represent the main source of external finance for SMEs. It is therefore essential that the banking system be prepared to provide credit to the SME sector. However, there are a number of rigidities that may bias the banking system against lending to SMEs. Among these rigidities is the regulatory framework for banking intermediation.

The new international bank capital framework agreed by the Basel Committee on Banking Supervision (BCBS) in June 2004, known as Basel II, has substantially revised supervisory regulations of capital adequacy of banks. While thought for and worked out by G10 regulators and private financial institutions, Basel II will be gradually implemented in most developing countries in the coming years (see Chapter 5 in this book).

While retaining some of the features of Basel I, including the 8 per cent minimum capital ratio, the new framework renews profoundly the way bank capital requirements are calculated, seeking to arrive at more risk-sensitive capital measurements. This will introduce a bias against higher-risk borrowers, like SMEs (see previous chapters in this book). Aware of this, Basel II provides for a more favourable regulatory treatment for SME loans. In spite of that, there is some preliminary evidence that the new regulation is likely to translate into more rationed and costly credit for SMEs in developing economies.[8]

These negative implications for SME financing might be offset by the regulatory recognition of credit risk mitigation techniques. While Basel I paid very limited attention to the whole subject of risk mitigation, the new capital accord recognises a strengthened role to risk mitigating instruments, in particular to credit guarantee schemes (CGSs).[9] These are mechanisms that reduce the losses that banks may incur in case of default of SME borrowers.

Basel II qualifies as eligible guarantors a relatively large number of subjects, including national governments and central banks; regional and/or local governments; Multilateral Development Banks (MDBs); certain international organisations; banks; and, other entities which meet stipulated credit requirements, in particular a credit rating of at least A-minus or equivalent probability of default. The guarantee must be an explicit, documented, irrevocable and unconditional obligation of the guarantor; it must be effective in any relevant jurisdiction; and, it must be issued as a first-liability. Basel II assigns a risk-mitigating role also to counter-guarantees, provided that these are denominated in the domestic currency and the underlying exposure is funded in the same currency.

This will allow banks to reduce regulatory capital on their SME loan portfolios. The proportion of the exposure covered by the guarantee will be assigned the risk-weight (probability of default) applicable to the guarantor. Any uncovered part of the exposure will remain subject to the risk-weight (probability of default) of the borrower. As a general rule, the higher is the credit quality of the guarantor, the greater will be the regulatory capital relief for the lending bank, and then the higher its incentive to cooperate with a CGS.

8.4 CGSs in developing countries

CGSs have represented a policy instrument for easing access to credit for SMEs in developing countries for the past thirty years. The questionable track record of the early CGSs has justified some criticism about their effectiveness.[10] The shortcomings of the early guarantee schemes have led to an overhaul of many design features concerning organisational and operational issues. Lenders have been increasingly involved in the ownership and management of the schemes. Incentives for moral hazard of both borrowers and lenders have been minimised. Relations between banks and guarantors have been improved. All these revisions have enhanced the efficacy and efficiency of CGSs.[11]

A CGS that aligns incentives among the government, the lenders and the borrowers can be an effective policy instrument to ease access to credit for SMEs in developing countries. CGSs can also play an important counter-cyclical role. If properly designed and implemented, CGSs may fulfil the conditions of a market-oriented poverty reduction strategy, assisting the integration of SMEs into the formal financial markets and creating the conditions for enhanced economic growth and job creation.

There are more than 2,250 CGSs operated in almost 100 countries.[12] Linguistic problems as well as the presence of a diverse landscape of institutions along with different operational mechanisms make a systematic categorisation of CGSs a difficult exercise. However, by referring to the operator of the scheme it is possible to identify four broad categories of CGSs: mutual guarantee associations, public guarantee schemes, international schemes and corporate guarantee schemes. All of them receive public support.[13]

Mutual guarantee associations are private collective entities established by potential borrowers or their representative organisations. They commit to granting a collective guarantee to loans provided by banks to their members, who in turn are shareholders and directly or indirectly contribute to the management of the scheme.

Public guarantee schemes are funded, owned and supported by a local, regional or national authority, and are run by either an administrative unit of the government (guarantee programs) or by a legally separate entity (guarantee funds). They represent the majority of the schemes operated worldwide.

International schemes have come into existence as a form of multilateral or bilateral development cooperation. There are four types of organisations that have developed CGSs: global multilateral agencies; regional multilateral organisations; bilateral donors; and international NGOs.

Corporate guarantee schemes have been set up more recently in many countries to encourage the participation of the private sector. Many schemes are now managed and operated by commercial banks, chambers of commerce or by the firms themselves.

8.5   Basel II poses significant challenges to existing CGSs

The new Basel capital accord opens up dramatically new prospects for existing guarantee schemes. Most of them will not be compliant with the tight requirements set by Basel II, and will not allow lenders to save regulatory capital on SME loans.

Mutual guarantee associations, largely represented in Latin America, will not be recognised as a credit risk mitigation technique under the new capital accord, unless they have an external rating of A-minus or equivalent probability of default. This seems very unlikely given their limited size, the composition and concentration of their guarantee portfolio, the quality of their risk management systems and controls, and their organisational structure. In theory, mutual guarantee schemes could stand higher chances under the most advanced methodology for calculating capital requirements (the A-IRB approach), where there are no limitations to the quality of eligible guarantors. However, it seems unlikely that they will achieve a credit quality assessment such as to engender a significant capital relief for the lending banks. Moreover, it remains to be seen whether the guarantee issued by mutual schemes complies with the tight legal requirements set by Basel II.

A possible option available to mutual guarantee schemes would be to graduate to a financial institution status. This would mean being granted a banking license by the regulator and being subject to supervision. Though there are some examples of mutual schemes which have acquired the status of financial institution, the high costs involved and the possible danger of sending false signals to the rest of the financial system militate against this idea. In addition, for the same reasons highlighted above, these potential financial institutions would not achieve a credit standing such as to allow lending banks to save capital against SME loan exposures.

The limitations that affect mutual guarantee associations apply equally to guarantee schemes operated by NGOs and to corporate schemes. It is highly unlikely that they will achieve a minimum credit rating of A-minus or corresponding probability of default, so their attractiveness for lending banks will be very limited.

Different problems affect public guarantee schemes, which account for the bulk of CGSs operated worldwide. Under the simpler methodology (Standardised Approach) only, Basel II recognises a special treatment to a bank's exposure to the sovereign or central bank where the bank is incorporated, provided that the exposure is denominated in the local currency and funded in the same currency. In this case, the exposure may attract a zero percent risk-weight. Supervisors may extend the same favourable treatment to claims guaranteed (counter-guaranteed) by a sovereign or a central bank, where the guarantee is denominated and funded in the domestic currency.

However, it is unclear whether developing countries will apply this provision. There is a long list of developing countries that already apply capital charges to lending to their own sovereign.[14] Moreover, foreign banks are highly unlikely to be permitted by their home supervisors to assign a zero percent risk-weight to their exposures to developing countries' governments and, by implication, to the guarantees issued by them. This diminishes the attractiveness of guarantee schemes provided by national authorities. Under the Internal Ratings-Based Approach, guarantees issued by developing countries' governments and central banks will attract a coefficient corresponding to their probability of default, which is in general relatively high, so jeopardising the effectiveness of many public guarantee schemes.

It is a quite different matter with international schemes operated by multilateral or bilateral donors. As long as the guarantee issued by these actors meets the legal terms required by the new capital accord, the portion of the loan covered by it will carry a zero percent risk-weight, thus resulting in the largest capital relief for lending banks. This is because either multilateral organisations qualify explicitly for the most favourable treatment under Basel II or bilateral donors are in the highest credit rating category.

However, their impact on SME access to credit will likely be limited. First, the new regime for guarantees affects only CGSs operated by MDBs and other international organisations. These bodies are assigned a zero percent risk-weight for the purpose of bank capital requirements. This represents only a marginal improvement compared with Basel I, where they are risk-weighted 20 per cent. However, the majority of bilateral donors will keep carrying a zero percent risk-weight as in the 1988 capital accord. Second, international schemes represent only a thin minority of CGSs operated globally. According to the latest global census available, international schemes account for 6 per cent and 3 per cent of total capital and guarantees outstanding in the world, respectively.[15] Finally, it is true that these international schemes could provide counter-guarantees to national guarantors, who would benefit from their higher credit standing; however, the excessive fragmentation of existing multilateral and bilateral schemes would reduce considerably the efficacy of this option.

8.6   Establishing regional guarantee funds

All this suggests that there is a case for reforming the current organisational and operational structure of CGSs. Otherwise, the benefits of the new regulatory recognition of credit risk mitigation techniques risk to be wasted, with very bad consequences for the survival and growth of many SMEs around the developing world.

Revising the legal and regulatory framework, in particular implementing the new Basel capital accord, is first and foremost the responsibility of developing countries' national authorities. The international community can and must help, providing technical as well as financial assistance, especially in light of the enormous complexity of the new regulation.

But the international community can and must help also in revising the CGS industry to make it compliant with Basel II, so as to exploit the potential of mobilising financial resources for the SME sector. The case for providing that help is compelling: the international community has committed itself to eradicate poverty worldwide, and a vibrant SME sector can make a vast contribution to the achievement of the MDGs, provided that it can finance its operations and growth. These concerns have found strong support in the Monterrey Consensus, where it is explicitly stated that '[g]uarantee schemes...should be developed for easing the access of small and medium-sized enterprises to local financing'.[16]

The international community can help by providing development assistance to help design and implement the improvements that CGSs need. These efforts can be complemented by financial support. Bilateral and multilateral agencies already provide substantial support to SME credit needs, through both guarantee schemes and dedicated lines of credit to financial institutions. For example, IFC's commitments to SMEs have tripled between 2001 and 2006, reaching US$1.6 billion.[17] A significant amount of development assistance is also directed to the SME sector in the form of business development services.

However, there is a growing recognition that while scaling up aid and other development resources is fundamental for achieving the MDGs, aid effectiveness must increase significantly as well. To this end, by adopting the Paris Declaration on Aid Effectiveness and the Accra Agenda for Action, the international community has committed itself to coordinate donor activities to avoid duplications and minimise transaction costs, emphasising programme-based aid modalities in conjunction with developing countries' strategies and policies.

The international community can draw on a growing body of experience in designing and implementing CGSs around the world. The following proposal is inspired by the long-standing experience of the European Union (EU) in supporting the development of the SME sector, including its access to bank credit. The most important platform for SME projects from the EU budget is the European Investment Fund (EIF). The EIF is a specialised supranational body established in 1994 to support SME financing in the EU and EU candidate countries through guarantee and counter-guarantee operations, venture capital and advisory services. It is owned by the European Investment Bank (64 per cent), the European Commission (27 per cent) and a number of private financial institutions (9 per cent). It is rated AAA by all the major international rating agencies and has been granted the status of MDB by the BCBS, so its risk-weighting is zero per cent for the purpose of bank capital requirements under Basel II. At the end of 2008, it had a risk capital of €3.9 billion and a guarantee portfolio totalling €12.3 billion.[18]

Our proposal for reforming the CGS industry in developing countries is modelled on the EIF. It addresses the challenges posed by Basel II while fitting very well with all the commitments undertaken by the international community outlined above. It suggests the introduction of Regional Guarantee Funds (RGFs), which would support SME financing in developing countries by providing guarantees to accredited financial institutions and counter-guarantees to existing public, mutual and corporate guarantee schemes. Guarantees and counter-guarantees would be compliant with the legal requirements of Basel II. The scheme would be designed and operated in a way to achieve a AAA credit rating or equivalent probability of default so as to attract a zero percent risk-weight for the purpose of bank capital requirements. In this way, it would maximise the incentive for banks to lend to SMEs, freeing up as much regulatory capital as possible without in principle jeopardising the soundness of the banking system. It would also rationalise aid activities, increase the efficiency in the way public money is used and minimise transaction costs.

Consistently with the experience of the EIF, the RGFs would be set up as a legally separate entity under the umbrella of existing regional development banks, i.e., the African Development Bank (AfDB), the Asian Development Bank (ADB) and the Inter-American Development Bank (IADB). The majority of the RGF's capital would be owned by the relevant regional development bank along with multilateral and bilateral donors. This is fundamental to achieve the highest credit rating from rating agencies. Indeed, the most important rating factor when assessing a supranational body is the support provided by its members.[19] All regional development banks and multilateral organisations are rated

AAA, while bilateral donors are generally rated AA-minus or higher,[20] and this would allow the RGF to get a AAA rating.

The RGFs would be participated also by accredited commercial financial institutions operating in the region, both domestic and foreign-owned, and ideally by national and sub-regional development finance institutions. The financial participation of privately-owned financial institutions and the corresponding influence in the decision-making process would be in accordance to the principle of risk sharing. It would also minimise the risk of excessive politicisation of the RGF. The presence of state-owned institutions would ensure that developing countries may contribute to coordinate development actions and retain a degree of leadership over their development policies and strategies, in accordance to the Paris Declaration on Aid Effectiveness and the Accra Agenda for Action. They would also act as the branch network of the RGF. However, the participation of SME representative structures would be difficult to achieve, given the high degree of fragmentation and the low level of unionisation in many countries.

Turning to operational features, the RGFs would distribute the risk among all the participants so as to avoid the danger of moral hazard. The guarantee coverage would be in the range of 50–80 per cent, and could be made dependent on the target group. SMEs would also provide some collateral to their lending banks. The coverage of counter-guarantee could be set at a lower level. The delivery mechanism would be based on the portfolio approach. That is, accredited lenders will be entitled to attach guarantees to loans within an eligible category without prior consultation of the guarantor. This would leave accredited and member commercial banks the functions of screening and monitoring borrowers so as to encourage the learning process, particularly at domestic financial institutions. To this end, the RGFs would also provide technical assistance to lending banks as well as to SMEs. The target group would be selected based on the policy objectives of regional member countries. In addition to established SMEs, it would be advisable to set up windows targeting specific segments, such as young and female entrepreneurs, transition borrowers, SMEs that access formal credit for the first time, and start-ups. To address the specific needs of the latter, the RGFs could also provide risk capital. The RGFs would guarantee investment capital. The leverage of guarantees and counter-guarantees would be set at a level consistent with the capitalisation of the RGF and the desired risk profile; yet, it would be advisable to keep it between three and five times, especially in the early years of operation. The RGFs would be explicitly required to conduct their operations so as to generate appropriate returns on their resources. This market-oriented management would ensure that the RGFs achieve self-sustainability while maintaining a financial profile in line with the rating category. The ANA rating could also permit the RGFs to borrow on the international capital markets at very low costs. Finally, the RGFs would be monitored based on some additional criteria that are easily measurable. Figure 8.1 offers an overview of the RGF structure.

In addition to contributing to mobilise financial resources for SMEs, the proposed policy has other key advantages. First, it rationalises multilateral and bilateral aid directed to support SME access to credit. Second, the mechanism maximises efficiency through the leverage of the RGF. Efficiency will be maximised also through the proper design

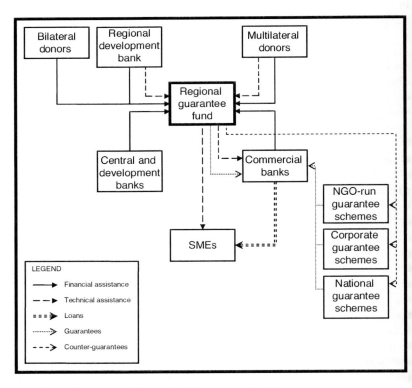

Figure 8.1   Overview of the regional guarantee fund
Source: Author's elaboration.

and implementation of the scheme. Third, the policy minimises costs. Relatively high expenses related to the establishment of new bodies and to the coordination among different actors can be offset by the RGF's sharing of liquidity management with the relevant regional development bank. Transaction costs associated with aid delivery will be reduced through diminished fragmentation. Finally, as a complementary role, the RGFs could help develop and deepen regional local currency bond markets by investing their liquidity in sovereign bonds in the region.[21]

In order to implement the proposed mechanism, multilateral financial institutions could take the lead by sponsoring conferences and workshops to discuss the proposal and provide a research framework for assembling information on current practices with CGSs. This could be followed by expert group meetings where the findings would be discussed and a timetable for execution recommended.

8.7   Concluding remarks

This chapter has proposed the establishment of RGFs to provide guarantees to banks and counter-guarantees to other CGSs in developing countries to support their SMEs and thereby economic growth and job creation.

However, expectations of the positive contribution that such a mechanism could make must not be exaggerated. Guarantee schemes in general are not panacea for solving the problem of access to credit by SMEs. The problem is usually a large and complex one, requiring a number of coherent and interrelated policy initiatives at the macro, meso and micro level. Without an overall enabling environment, SMEs cannot prosper, even if financing is made available. A stable and predictable macroeconomic environment is of fundamental importance, as it is an environment that supports entrepreneurship. Therefore, it is important that governments in developing countries, with the help of the international community, pursue sound economic policies, invest in physical and social infrastructure and enact a legal, tax and regulatory framework that provides a level playing field for economic actors. Complementary to these initiatives are also incentives to induce SMEs to join the formal sector. Finally, it is essential that efforts continue in developing the size and the infrastructure of the financial sector while increasing its reach and its competitiveness. Eventually, CGSs can only work in a sound, stable and efficient financial system.

Notes

1. See Commission for Africa (2005), UN Millennium Project (2005), Commission on the Private Sector and Development (2004), and World Bank (2004).
2. See, for example, Fan, Criscuolo and Ilieva-Hamel (2005).
3. See Altenburg, Eckardt and Van Rompaey (2006), Biggs (2002) and Hallberg (2001) for a review of the literature.
4. Hallberg (2001: 5).
5. See Beck and Demirgüç-Kunt (2006) for a review of the literature.
6. See, for example, Ayyagari, Demirguc-Kunt and Maksimovic (2006) and Beck, Demirguc-Kunt and Maksimovic (2002).
7. See Beck, Levine and Loayza (2000) and Levine, Loayza and Beck (2000).
8. See BCBS (2006).
9. In line with most authors, this chapter uses the term CGS to designate guarantee systems in general, regardless of their peculiar characteristics.
10. See, for example, Vogel and Adams (1997).
11. See Green (2003) and Doran and Levitsky (1997) for a review of best practices with CGSs.
12. Pombo and Herrero (2001).
13. See Green (2003).
14. Powell (2004: 17, footnote 25).
15. See Pombo and Herrero (2001).
16. United Nations (2002: para. 17).
17. See www.ifc.org.
18. See www.eif.org.
19. Support is measured through callable capital, i.e., subscribed but uncalled, by members, and greater emphasis is given on the share of callable capital subscribed by highly-rated members (Standard & Poor's, 2006). Other important rating factors include asset quality, capitalisation and risk management.
20. See, for example, www.standardandpoors.com and www.moodys.com.
21. On 19 May 2007, the G8 released an action plan for developing local bond markets in developing economies.

9
The Basel Capital Frameworks: Bringing Development Finance to the Agenda

Ricardo Gottschalk

Since Basel II was approved in June 2004, banking regulators around the world have laid out plans on how to implement the new capital accord in their own jurisdictions. This process has not been limited to developed countries. Most developing countries have expressed intention of implementing Basel II, and many of them have announced how they intend to do it.

However, most of the discussion that has accompanied preparation efforts to implement Basel II has focused on its technical issues. Little time and efforts have been dedicated to address issues that go beyond the technical aspects of Basel II.

The main purpose of this book has been to draw attention to a missed dimension in Basel discussions, which are Basel's implications for development finance. The view expressed in this book is that this is a vital dimension for developing countries, which are still in a stage of development that requires a financial system that supports economic progress and social inclusion. These are development goals that, for their achievement, require a regulatory framework for the financial system that is aligned with them. Moreover, because these goals are of concern not only of government officials, but also of actors that support private sector development, the SMEs or of those linked to micro-finance institutions to support the small businesses, the poor and the most vulnerable, the book argues that these actors should be aware of Basel impacts on their areas of interest and become actively involved in Basel II discussions.

In addition, the book raises the issue of capacity implementation facing different categories of developing countries. Low-income countries in particular face massive capacity implementation challenges, but this has not been much discussed. As a result, these countries lack support from the international community on dealing with Basel II.

Both development finance and capacity implementation are issues the book addresses in its various chapters. Much of the information is based on interviews with different developing country stakeholders from different countries around the world. The book brings their views on Basel issues. Until now, these views have not been much heard as the debate has been dominated by those who have driven the Basel process. That is, developed countries and their representatives.

Starting with development finance, the book raises the concerns that Basel II may lead to banking concentration and to loan portfolio concentration, too. The possibility that Basel II may lead to banking concentration is associated with the fact that, under the new capital accord, whilst larger banks will be permitted to adopt their own risk assessment models to determine capital requirements, smaller banks will not. As a result, larger banks may require less capital than the smaller banks, giving them a competitive advantage. Looking at the implementation of Basel I in Brazil during the late 1990s, the book shows that capital requirements can indeed be an important contributory factor to banking concentration. Concerns regarding banks' portfolio concentration also stem from the use by banks of their internal risk models to calculate risk for capital requirements. The use of risk measurement techniques to determine the amount of capital to be allocated for different types of assets is likely to result in both more expensive and rationed credit to borrowers perceived as of higher risk, and more and cheaper credit to borrowers perceived as of lower risk. This can cause a concentration in banks' loan portfolio away from small borrowers and toward the larger companies.

Bank portfolio concentration could also lead to a division of labour between larger and smaller banks, with the former directing their lending to large corporations and the latter to the smaller companies lacking access to credit from the larger banks. This division of labour could, in turn, weaken the stability of the banking system, as banks would have less diversified portfolios.

While the book argues that concentration of banks and their portfolios are issues that have not received sufficient attention in Basel discussions, a possible link between Basel rules and financial innovation has been virtually absent in any discussions at all. This book identifies three possible channels whereby Basel rules could curb at least the sort of financial innovation that matters in this book, which is not that which contributed to the financial crisis, but the one which relates to pro-poor product development, engendered by smaller banks geared to the bottom end of the markets. The first channel is less innovation due to banking concentration. The argument is that while larger banks due to their competitive advantage tend to grab for themselves the most profitable segments of the market, smaller banks tend to lend to smaller business and expand activities toward those segments that had been left out of the banking systems. Banking concentration in reducing the number of smaller banks would eliminate the parts of the banking system that are keen to innovate to be able to reach new, unexplored markets. The second channel would be through higher capital ratios, which could inhibit an increase in operational costs to support an expansion strategy in the form of expanding access to financial services, penetrating new market areas, creating new physical forms of territorial presence, developing new forms of risk assessment that get around data information constraints, and developing new market products for the poor. Finally, Basel II in particular may also hinder innovation through regulation specifically targeted at idiosyncratic activities, which are those activities considered bank specific. For example, the requirement for additional capital under Pillar 2 for activities that are bank specific may have the unintended consequence of penalising innovative forms of bank services to the poor.

A further issue the book discusses is the pro-cyclicality in Basel II, which would happen due to its system of risk weights, which can vary during the economic cycle. Although pro-cyclicality is not directly related to development finance, it can accentuate the ups and downs of the cycle, through creating phases of excessive credit expansion followed by phases of credit crunch. The result is increased macroeconomic volatility, which in turn can have negative effects on long-term growth.

Turning to implementation capacity issues, the book shows that this is a major concern for developing countries. Their regulators are confronted with questions such as: how to build capacity to validate and monitor sophisticated models, how to build long and reliable data base to run the models, how to reduce asymmetries of information, and how to enforce national regulation on foreign banks when the former is in conflict with their own interests and with regulation from their home countries? Although there are no easy answers to these questions, developing country actors identify the urgent need to invest in capacity building, both among regulators and bankers, and increase communication and collaboration between developed country regulators and their developing country counterparts.

As pointed out, the book discusses all these issues for different categories of developing countries, from emerging market countries such as Brazil to low-income countries in sub-Saharan Africa. It transpires that possible impacts from Basel II will vary depending on how it is implemented and how it interacts with each country's pre-existing financial structure. Among emerging market economies, the book finds that while Brazil's and India's regulators have been more cautious in how to implement the new capital accord in their countries, South Africa's regulators have given more freedom as to how banks can go about Basel II rules. This, in turn, opens space for possible undesirable developments. At the same time, South Africa can be singled out as the country where its regulators have undertaken the initiative to create banking regulation which supports access to finance, even though this initiative has yet to be fully implemented and thus is still untested. In regard to low-income countries, a key concern that the book discusses refers to their low capacity power to impose their own Basel regulations on foreign banks, and the risk they face that these banks may decide not to comply with their regulation but with that of their home countries.

Since 1999–2000, when discussions on the initial proposals for new capital rules started, a number of ideas have emerged on how to mitigate their possible negative impacts on credit patterns and pro-cyclicality. For example, a menu of options exist on how to reduce the pro-cyclicality of bank credit, which developing countries in particular should worry about, due to the fact that economic volatility in these countries are higher than in the OECD countries. Of course, there are some technical challenges associated with each proposal, which require careful examination. Nonetheless, the options, discussed in the book exist and are feasible, as the Spanish experience with counter-cyclical regulation demonstrates. What really seems to be missing is lack of political initiative. Hopefully, the expectations created by the global financial crisis are that progress will be made on that front.

In what follows, we refer to a few possible measures for adoption, including those put forward and discussed in international academic and policy circles, which could address the issues raised in this book.

- To address inequity arising from the use of the IRB approach by the large banks and the standardised approach by the remaining banks, an equalising factor could be applied over the banks adopting the IRB approach, so as to level up their capital requirements. That would address inequity issues, and could have the additional benefit of discouraging banks from changing their portfolios away from smaller borrowers, typically the ones deemed as riskier. That would be moreover consistent with the Basel Committee's primary intention to address relative rather than absolute risk. The increasing interest in the leverage ratio following the global financial crisis to address excessive leverage and over-expansion of banks could to some extent also help address the inequity issue.

• To address portfolio concentration, in addition to the application of a factor as proposed above, regulators could work on a formula to smooth the risk curve for SMEs, as the Basel Committee has done in the past between the Consultative Papers CP2 and CP3. This could be done in a number of ways, but would be to the country's regulators to choose which method might be the most appropriate one; the decision could be based on technical studies to assess the impacts of alternative measures on credit to the SMEs.

• To deal with pro-cyclicality, this book discusses a number of interesting proposals, including measures to link capital requirements to the growth of total banks' assets, and the use of models that 'look through the cycle', as opposed to the most utilised models that look at one point of the cycle. A further measure would be to reward portfolio diversification. The reason for the latter is that, in addition to reducing risk for a given level of return (which is why diversified portfolios are desirable in the first place), portfolio diversification could contribute to reduced credit pro-cyclicality, as argued in this book. This is because a negative event would affect only that part of a bank's portfolio that share similar characteristics and therefore is vulnerable to the same types of shocks, not the entire portfolio.

Calice in this book also proposes the creation of Regional Guarantee Funds, to be set up within existing regional development banks to provide guarantees to banks and counter-guarantees to credit guarantee schemes not eligible for risk mitigation under Basel II. This would provide these banks and institutions an incentive to lend to the SMEs, as under Basel II such regional guarantees would reduce the capital needs when lending to the perceived riskier segments of the market.

9.1 Development of a Monitoring Framework?

In light of the concerns about possible impacts of Basel implementation in developing countries raised in the book, what follows is a proposal on the establishment of a properly resourced monitoring system for selected financial indicators that could be tracked to monitor potential undesirable developments arising from Basel II implementation. Of concern are those developments that can have negative consequences for financial sector development that support developmental goals, especially financial inclusion. As discussed throughout the book, these developments are banking concentration, number of banks' agencies and their geographic distribution, banks' portfolio concentration, cost of credit, pro-cyclicality of bank credit, and credit to the poorer segments of the market.

It should be noted that these developments may take place irrespective of Basel II implementation. Therefore, if for example, portfolio concentration trends are detected following Basel II implementation, it is important that further research is conducted to pinpoint the key factors driving these trends, and to isolate possible Basel II effects from other effects. Table 9.1 below presents a set of possible indicators that could be tracked for each possible development in the banking system.

Some of the indicators in Table 9.1 would have to require long time-series data, going back to the pre-Basel II implementation period. Also, due consideration would have to be given to what frequency data to use – for example, if high frequency data are available and chosen, variations due to seasonal factors would have to be fully accounted for.

Finally, these indicators would have to be categorised by different types of banks – for example, larger and smaller banks; banks adopting the more complex approaches versus banks adopting the standardised approaches, or even banks still under Basel I rules. It is very important that the information on these various indicators is not just gathered but analysed in a timely fashion and actions are undertaken if undesirable trends emerge. For effective monitoring, it would be advisable that each country adopting Basel II establish an appropriately resourced government-based monitoring system. In addition, there should be a dissemination strategy in place regarding monitoring work and information gathered, and an open access to the latter. The purpose is to have a system in place that is effective in alerting regulators, policy makers and other stakeholders committed to development finance, to the need for action when problems arise to avoid undesirable outcomes for financial sector development and financial inclusion.

The measures proposed thus far address the three issues this paper has highlighted as key ones. In addition to these, a number of other issues constitute a major challenge for regulatory authorities, especially from developing countries.

Table 9.1 Possible developments from Basel II and monitoring indicators

Possible developments	Monitoring Indicators
Banking concentration	• Herfindahl Index • Assets held by largest five banks as proportion of total assets • Banks' absolute capital scaled by banks' capital ratio
Number of bank agencies (points of presence) and geographic distribution	• Number of agencies by bank • Number of agencies in low-population density to total number of agencies, by banks • Number of agencies in low-income areas to total number of points of presence.
Banks' portfolio concentration	• Corporate lending: lending to top segment to total lending ratio • Corporate lending: lending to bottom segment to total lending ratio
Cost of credit	• Lending rates/ratio of lending to deposit interest rates for different categories of borrowers.
Pro-cyclicality of bank credit	• Bank lending to the private sector to total assets ratio • Loan growth against some benchmark
Credit to the poorer segments	• Corporate lending: loan to poorer segments to total loan growth • Retail lending: loan to poorer segments total loan growth

Source: Author's own elaboration.

For example, will regulators have the capacity to validate models and monitor them adequately within the proposed time frame? Is the timetable proposed by developing country regulators long enough? Should regulators not need more time to be able to adequately validate and monitor risk assessment systems adopted by banks, especially those that will opt for the most advanced models? Should the proposal for adopting internal models for measuring operational risk not be eliminated, given the sheer complexity of measuring operational risk and the difficulties regulators would face to monitor their use? And in the case it is adopted, could a factor not be equally employed to avoid that some banks end up with lower capital requirements for operational risk than others? Also, it would be important that the regulatory authorities could take account of the fact that the risk management practices should be effective, but not excessively intrusive to the point of inhibiting lending activities and programmes that have a social purpose.

This book thus shows that implementation of Basel rules poses a number of challenges to national banking regulators. But what lessons can we learn from the country experiences with Basel rules this book discusses?

The Brazil case (and to some extent the India case as well) shows that the Basel rules are not neutral, and this should be borne in mind when a country is considering adopting such rules. In this regard, it is important that measures being considered for adoption are carefully examined, and that their implications for development finance are identified and properly addressed. But the Brazil case also shows that, had the country not had its development finance architecture in place, the impacts of Basel I on development finance would have been far bigger. For example, although Basel I did affect credit in Brazil, there is no evidence that the credit to the SMEs, to rural producers or to the urban poor was negatively affected, at least in a major way. A main reason for this outcome is that credit patterns during the period under Basel I have been influenced by directed credit policy, which in a number of cases were intended to protect the less favoured segments.

From this, the lesson we can draw for other developing countries is that institutions that support development finance are key and should therefore be preserved, as there is nothing indicating that an entirely market based banking system will serve the financing needs of the small businesses and the poor. This is even more so under Basel I and especially Basel II, as the latter has a clear bias against perceived higher risk borrowers, which usually are the small businesses and the poor. But many poor countries do not even have development finance institutions, in a number of cases because they have reformed their banking systems and in the process dismantled such institutions.

The lack of such institutions makes prudence toward the adoption of Basel rules even more necessary for these countries. One should not forget that capital markets in poor countries are still very small and that the banking sector is still the major source of finance to the economy. Of course, one may contend that micro-finance in poor countries managed by foreign NGOs and other organisations have had an important role in providing resources to the small businesses and the poor. However, mainstream finance should also be able to reach these segments, and to finance projects (large or otherwise) that can benefit them indirectly as well. It is thus important that the system is regulated in ways that it can serve both the economy and the neediest as well.

More broadly, it is important that a continued effort is made to build capacity and especially negotiation capacity so that countries are able to implement Basel II at their own pace and in accordance with their own policy goals, interests and needs. Finally, it should be noted that the ongoing financial crisis in developed countries is affecting developing countries negatively through different channels. However, on the positive side, the crisis opens space for alternative approaches. It thus should be seen by developing countries as an opportunity to challenge the fundaments of Basel II, and to feel confident to propose non-marginal modifications within their own jurisdictions and at the regional level as well, so that their regulatory frameworks for the banking system are more supportive of pro-development financial systems.

Bibliography

Alternburg, T., U. Eckardt, and F. Van Rompaey (2006) Productivity Enhancement and Equitable Development: Challenges for SME Development. Vienna: UNIDO.

Ayyagari, M., A. Demirgüç-Kunt, and V. Maksimovic (2006) 'How important are financing constraints? The role of finance in the business environment', World Bank Policy Research Working Paper, 3820.

Banerjee and Duflo (2005), 'What do banks (not) do?' Economic and Political Weekly September.

Barajas, A., R. Chami, and T. Cosimano (2005): 'Did the Basel Accord cause a credit slowdown in Latin America?' IMF Working Paper WP/05/38, International Monetary Fund.

Barrell, R., and A. Pina (2004): 'How important are automatic stabilisers in Europe? Stochastic simulation assessment,' Economic Modelling, 21, pp. 1–35.

Barrell, R., and K. Dury (2000): 'Choosing the regime: Macroeconomic effects of U.K. entry into EMU,' Discussion Paper 168, National Institute of Economic and Social Research (NIESR).

Barrell, R., B. Becker, J. Byrne, S. Gottschalk, I. Hurst, and D. van Welsum (2004): 'Macroeconomic policy in Europe: experiments with monetary responses and fiscal impulses,' Economic Modelling, 21, pp. 877–931.

Barrell, R., D. Holland, A. Choy, and S. Gottschalk (2002): 'Enhancing the Hong Kong model,' National Institute of Economic and Social Research, mimeo.

Barrell, R., J. Byrne, and K. Dury (2003): 'The implications of diversity in consumption behaviour for the choice of monetary rules in Europe,' Economic Modelling, 20, 227–435.

Barth, J., G. Caprio, and R. Levine (2001): 'Bank regulation and supervision: What works best,' World Bank Policy Research Working Paper 2725, World Bank.

Basel (1998) International Convergence of Capital Measurement and Capital Standards (July 1988, updated to April 1998), Basel Committee on Banking Supervision, Basel, April.

Basel (2004) 'Implementation of Basel II: Practical Considerations', Basel Committee on Banking Supervision, July.

Basel (2006) 'International Convergence of Capital Measurement and Capital Standards: A Revised Framework – Comprehensive Version', Bank for International Settlements, June.

Basel (2006) 'Results of the fifth quantitative impact study (QIS 5)', Bank for International Settlements, June.

Basel Committee on Banking Supervision. (1996): 'Amendment to the capital accord to incorporate market risks.'

Basel Committee on Banking Supervision. (1997): 'Core principles for effective banking supervision,' Basel Committee on Banking Supervision.

Basel Committee on Banking Supervision. (2004): 'International convergence of capital measurements and capital standards: A revised framework,' Basel Committee on Banking Supervision.

Beck, T., and A. Demirgüç-Kunt (2006) 'Small and medium-size enterprises: Access to finance as a growth constraint', *Journal of Banking and Finance*, 30, pp. 2931–2943.

Beck, T., A. Demirgüç-Kunt and V. Maksimovic (2002) 'Financial and legal constraints to firm growth: does size matter?' World Bank Policy Research Working Paper, 2784.

Beck, T., R. Levine, and N. Loayza (2000) 'Finance and the sources of growth', *Journal of Financial Economics*, 58, 1–2, pp. 261–300.

Benito, A., J. Whitley, and G. Young (2001): 'Analysing corporate and household sector balance sheets,' *Financial Stability Review*, December, pp. 160–174.

Berger, A., and Udell, G. (1994) 'Did Risk-based capital allocate bank credit and cause a "credit crunch" in the United States?' *Journal of Money, Credit and Banking*, Vol. 26, No 3, Part 2: Federal Credit Allocation: Theory, Evidence, and History, August, pp. 585–628.

Bernanke, B.S. (1983): 'Non-monetary effects of the financial crisis in the propagation in the Great Depression,' *American Economic Review*, 73, pp. 257–276.

Biggs, T. (2002) 'Is small beautiful and worthy of subsidy? Literature Review', IFC Mimeo.

Borio, C., Furfine, C., and Lowe, P. (2003) 'Procyclicality of the financial system and financial stability: issues and policy options', BIS Papers No 1.

Buser, S., Chen, A., and Kane, E. (1981) 'Federal deposit insurance, regulatory policy, and optimal bank capital', *Journal of Finance* 35, pp 863–882.

Byrne, J., and E. P. Davis (2003): Financial Structure, An Investigation of Sectoral Balance Sheets in the G7. Cambridge University Press.

Caprio, G., and P. Honohan (1999): 'Beyond capital ideals: Restoring banking stability,' World Bank Policy Research Working Paper 2235, World Bank.

Carneiro, F., Vivan, G., e Krause, K. (2004) 'Novo Acordo da Basiléia: Estudo de Caso para o Contexto Brasileiro', Resenha BM& F, no 63, São Paulo.

Catalan, M., and E. Ganapolski (2005): 'Cyclical implications of changing capital requirements in a macroeconomic framework,' IMF Working Paper WP/05/168, International Monetary Fund.

Central Bank of Brazil (1994) 'Resolution 2099' of 17/09/1994.

Central Bank of Brazil (1997a) 'Resolution 2399/1997'.

Central Bank of Brazil (1997b) 'Circular no. 2784/1997'.

Central Bank of Brazil (2004) 'Brazil Central Bank's Communication No 12.746' of 8/12/2004.

Central Bank of Brazil (2007) 'Brazil Central Bank's Communication No 16.137' of 27/09/2007.

Commission for Africa (2005) 'Our Common Interest', Report of the Commission for Africa, March 11, 2005.

Commission on the Private Sector and Development (2004) 'Unleashing Entrepreneurship: Making Business Work for the Poor'. New York: UNDP.

Cornford, A. (2008) 'An Agenda for Financial System Reform'. SUNS-South-North Development Monitor, 6511, July 7.

Credit Suisse First Boston (1997): 'CreditRisk+,' Credit Suisse First Boston, http://www.csfb.com/institutional/research/credit risk.shtml.

D'Arista, J., and Griffith-Jones, S. (2009a, forthcoming) 'Agenda and Criteria for Financial Regulatory Reform', G24 Discussion Papers, forthcoming.

D'Arista, J., and Griffith-Jones, S. (2009b, forthcoming) 'Agenda and Criteria for Financial Regulatory Reform' in Griffith-Jones, S., Ocampo, J. A. and Stiglitz, J. (eds.) Time for a Visible Hand: Lessons from the 2008 World Financial Crisis. New York: Oxford University Press, forthcoming.

Daoud, D. (2003): 'Quelle réglementation du capital bancaire pour les pays en développement?' Revue d'Economie Financière, 73, pp. 311323.

de Juan, A. (1996): 'The roots of banking crisis: Microeconomic issues, supervision and regulation,' in Banking crisis in Latin America, ed. by R. Hausmann, and L. Rojas-Suarez. Inter-American Development Bank.

de la Torre, A. (2002): 'Reforming development banks: A Framework.' PowerPoint presentation given at the World Bank Staff Workshop on Reforming Public Sector Banks, 10 December, Washington, DC.

Doran, A., and J. Levitsky (1997) 'Credit Guarantee Schemes for Small Business Lending: A Global Perspective. Volume I: Main Report'. London: Graham Bannock and Partners Ltd.

Ediz, T., Michael, I., and Perraudin, W. (1998) 'Bank Capital Dynamics and Regulatory Policy', Bank of England, mimeo.

Eichengreen, B., and A. Mody (1998): 'What explains changing spreads on emerging market debt: fundamentals or market sentiment?' Working Paper 6408, NBER.

EU (2008) European Parliament, Committee on Economic and Monetary Affairs. (2008, April 18). Draft Report with Recommendations to the Commission on Hedge Funds and Private Equity. Brussels, Belgium.

Fan, Q., A. Criscuolo, and I. Ilieva-Hamel (2005) 'Whither SME Policies?' Development Outreach, World Bank Institute, March 2005.

Financial Stability Forum. (2008). Report of the Financial Stability Forum on Enhancing Market and Institutional Resilience, Basel Switzerland.

Financial Stability Institute (2004) 'Implementation of the new capital adequacy framework in non-Basel Committee member countries: Summary of responses to the Basel II implementation assistance Questionnaire', July.

Financial Stability Institute (2008) '2008 FSI Survey on the Implementation of the new capital adequacy framework in non-Basel Committee member countries: Summary of responses to the Basel II implementation survey', Bank for International Settlements, August.

Financial Times (2009), March 25th.

Genesis Analytics (2004) 'A policy lens to view financial regulation', prepared for FinMark Trust, December.

Ghosh Soumya Kanti, 'Who let the dogs out,' Financial Express, April 9, 2008.

Ghosh Soumya Kanti, 'Basel Bonanza for Indian Banks' Economic Times, May 26, 2008.

Ghosh Soumya Kanti, 'Estimating LGD for Indian Markets' Economic & Political Weekly, July 19, 2008.

Ghosh Soumya Kanti, 'Rational Exuberance' Economic Times, September 22, 2008.

G20 (2009) 'Enhancing Regulation and Strengthening Transparency'. G20 Working Group on Enhancing Sound Regulation and Strengthening Transparency (Working Group 1). Final Report, March 25th.

Global Risk Regulator (2006), November edition, www.globalriskregulator.com.

Goodhart, C., and Persaud, A. (2008). 'A proposal for how to avoid the next crash'. Financial Times, January 31st, p. 9.

Goodhart, C., and Segoviano, M. (2005) 'Basel and Procyclicality: A Comparison of the Standardised and IRB Approaches to an Improved Credit Risk Method', LSE, London, unpublished.

Gottschalk, R., and Griffith-Jones, S. (2003) 'Capital Account Liberalisation in Tanzania', final report prepared for the Bank of Tanzania, May.

Gottschalk, R., and Sodre, C. (2007) 'Implementation of Basel Rules in Brazil: What are the Implications for Development Finance?' IDS Working Paper 273, December.

Green, A. (2003) 'Credit Guarantee Schemes for Small Enterprises: An Effective Instrument to Promote Private Sector-Led Growth?' SME Technical Working Paper Series, 10. Vienna: UNIDO.

Griffith-Jones, S. (2003) 'How to Prevent the New Basel Capital Accord Harming Developing Countries', paper presented at the IMF-World Bank Annual Meetings at Dubai, September.

Griffith-Jones, S., and Ocampo, J. A., with Patt, E-A (2009, forthcoming) 'Global Governance for Financial Stability and Development', UNDP Paper Series: Development Dimensions of Global Economic Governance.

Griffith-Jones, S., S. Spratt, and M. Segoviano (2002): 'The onward march of Basel II: Can the interests of developing countries be protected?' Institute of Development Studies mimeo, http://www.ids.ac.uk/ids/global/Finance/ifpubs.htlm.

Griffith-Jones, S., S. Spratt, and M. Segoviano (2003): 'Basel II and developing countries: Diversification and portfolio effects,' Discussion Paper 437, LSE Financial Market Group, 34.

Griffith-Jones, S., Segoviano, M., and Spratt, S. (2004) 'CAD 3 and Developing Countries: The Potential Impact of Diversification Effects on International Lending Patterns and Pro-cyclicality', IDS, unpublished.

Griffth-Jones, S., and Ocampo, J.A. (2009) 'The Financial Crisis and its Impact on Developing Countries', UNDP Working Paper No 53, April.

Hallberg, K. (2001) 'A Market-Oriented Strategy for Small and Medium-Scale Enterprises', IFC Discussion Paper, 48.

Hoggarth, G., A. Logan, and L. Zicchino (2005): 'Macro stress tests of U.K. banks,' in Investigating the relationship between the financial and real economy, vol. BIS Papers Number 22, pp. 392–408.

Hussain, M. E., and Hassan, M. K. (2005) 'Basel Capital Requirements and Bank Credit Risk Taking in Developing Countries', Department of Finance, LeBow College of Business, Philadelphia, unpublished.

IADB (2005) 'Unlocking Credit: The Quest for Deep and Stable Banking Lending', Economic and Social Progress in Latin America and The Caribbean', 2005 Report, Banco Inter-Americano de Desenvolvimento, 281 paginas, Washington DC.

IMF (2009) 'Lessons of the Financial Crisis for Future Regulation of Financial Institutions and Markets and for Liquidity Management', Monetary and Capital Markets Department, February 4th.

International Monetary Fund and World Bank (2002): 'Implementation of Basel core principles for effective banking supervision: Experiences, influences and perspectives,' mimeo.

International Monetary Statistics (2004): 'Country Notes,' International Monetary Fund.

Jackson, P., et al. (1999): 'Capital requirements and bank behaviour: The impact of the Basel Accord,' Working Papers 1, Basel Committee on Banking Supervision.

Kim, D., and Santomero, A. (1988) 'Risk in banking and capital regulation', *Journal of Finance*, 43, pp. 1219–1233.

Kjersti, A. (2005): 'The Basel II IRB approach for credit portfolios: A survey,' Note SAMBA/33/05, Norsk Regnesentral.

Koehn, M., and Santomero, A. (1980) 'Regulation of bank capital and portfolio risk', *Journal of Finance*, 35, pp. 1235–44.

Koyama, S., and M. Nakane (2002): 'O spread bancário segundo fatores de persistência e conjuntura,' Notas Técnicas 18, Banco Central do Brasil.

Levine, R., N. Loayza, and T. Beck (2000) 'Financial intermediation and growth: Causality and causes', *Journal of Monetary Economics*, 46, 1, pp. 31–77.

Montgomery, H. (2005) 'The effect of the Basel Accord on bank portfolios in Japan', *The Japanese and International Economies*, 19, pp. 24–36.

Moody's Investor Services (2003): 'Sovereign bonds default, rating transitions and recoveries (1985–2002),' Moody's Special Comment – Global Credit Research, http://www.iiiglobal.org/topics/sovereign/Sovereign Bond Defaults Levey.pdf.

Ocampo, J.A., and Chiappe, M.L. (2001). Counter-Cyclical Prudential and Capital Account Regulation in Developing Countries. Paper prepared for Swedish EGDI.

Orgler, Y., and Taggart, R. (1983) 'Implications of corporate capital structure theory for banking institutions, *Journal of Money, Credit, and Banking* 15, pp. 212–221.

Peek, J., and Rosengreen, E. (1995) 'The capital crunch: Neither a borrower nor a lender be', *Journal of Money, Credit and Banking*, Vol. 27, No. 3, Aug, pp. 625–638.

Persaud, A. (2009) 'Mark to What?' The Financial Express, 13th March. www.financialexpress.com

Podpiera, R. (2004): 'Does compliance with Basel Core Principles bring any measurable benefits?' IMF Working Paper WP/04/204, International Monetary Fund.

Pombo, P., and A. Herrero (2001) 'Los Sistemas de Garantias para la Micro y la PyME en una Economia Globalizada'. DP Editorial.

Porteous, D. (2004) 'The Regulator's Dilemma, Report prepared for FinMark Trust, July.

Powell, A. (2004) Basel II and Developing Countries: Sailing through a Sea of Standards', World Bank Policy Research Working Paper, 3387.

Powell, A. (2004): 'Basel II and developing countries: Sailing through a sea of standards,' World Bank Policy Research Working Paper 3387, World Bank.

RBI (2004).

RBI (2008).

RBI, Report on Currency and Finance, various issues.

RBI, Basic Statistical Returns of Scheduled Commercial Banks in India, various issues.

RBI, Core Principles of Effective Banking Supervision: The Indian Position. October 1999.

RBI, Report on Trends & Progress of Banking in India, various issues.

Reuters (2009) 'Full Text of BRIC countries joint communiqué, March 14th, four pages.

Rojas-Suarez, L. (2003): 'Comment on panel: Basel II and emerging markets,' in The Future of Banking Regulation, http://www.lse.ac.uk/fmg/

Salviano Junior, C. (2004): 'Bancos estaduais: dos problemas crônicos ao Proes,' Banco Central do Brasil.

SARB (2006) 'Annual Report 2006, Bank Supervision Department, South African Reserve Bank.

Saunders, A., Strock, E., and Travlos, N. (1990) 'Ownership structure, deregulation, and bank risk taking', *Journal of Finance*, 45, 643–654.

Sen Sunanda, and Ghosh Soumya Kanti 'Missing link in the loan waiver scheme'. *Mainstream*, V.46(No.23), 2008(24.5.2008): pp. 8–10.

Sen Sunanda, and Ghosh Soumya, 'Basel Norms, Indian Banking Sector and Credit to SMEs and Poor' *Economic and Political Weekly*, 19th March 2005.

Shrieves, R., and Dahl, D. (1992) 'The relationship between risk and capital in commercial banks', *Journal of Banking and Finance* 16, pp. 439–457.

Soares, R.P. (2002) 'Evolução do Crédito de 1994 a 1999: Uma Explicação', Planejamento e Políticas Públicas, n. 25, Jun/Dez., pp. 43–87.

South African Reserve Bank (2007) 'Co-operative Banks Act, No 40.

Spratt, S. (2008) Development Finance: Debates, Dogmas and New Directions, Routledge, London.

Standard and Poor's (2006) 'Criteria for Multilateral Lending Institutions'. Available at www.standardandpoors.com

Stiglitz, J., and Weiss, A. (1981) 'Credit Rationing in Markets with Imperfect Information', *The American Economic Review*, Vol. 71, No. 3, June, pp. 393–410.

Sen Sunanda, Global Finance at Risk: On Stagnation and Instability in the Real Sector. Palgrave Macmillan 2003 and OUP (paperback) 2004.

Troster, R. L. (2004) 'Concentracao Bancária', Febraban, unpublished.

UN Millennium Project (2005) 'Investing in Development: A Practical Plan to Achieve the Millennium Development Goals'. New York.

United Nations (2002) 'Report of the International Conference on Financing for Development', Monterrey, Mexico, 18–22 March 2002.

U.S. Treasury Department (2008). Blueprint for Financial Regulatory Reform. Washington, DC: U.S. Treasury Department, March.

Van Roy, P. (2005) 'The impact of the 1988 Basel Accord on banks' capital ratios and credit risk-taking: an international study', European Centre for Advanced Research in Economics and Statistics (ECARES), Université Libre de Bruxelles, mimeo.

Vogel, R.C., and D.W. Adams (1997) 'Costs and Benefits of Loan Guarantee Programs', *The Financier – Analyses of Capital and Money Market Transactions*, 4, 1 & 2, pp. 22–29.

Weder, B., and M. Wedow (2002): 'Will Basel II affect international capital flows to emerging markets,' OECD Development Centre Technical Papers 199, OECD.

World Bank (2004) 'World Development Report 2005: A Better Investment Climate for Everyone'. Washington, DC and New York: World Bank and Oxford University Press.

World Bank (2006) 'Making Finance Work for Africa', Preliminary Draft, May.

Index